To

A Square – Ajit and Anjali Tendulkar
For spotting, nurturing and preserving

India's Kohinoor

SACH

GAUTAM BHATTACHARYA

FOREWORD BY
MAHENDRA SINGH DHONI

VIKAS®

S A C H

Skill . Attitude . Commitment . Honesty

This book is titled *SACH* not because the Kumbles and the Gangulys address him thus. This word carries a double meaning. *SACH* means reality and truth in Hindi. Sachin Ramesh Tendulkar is not a midsummer night's dream. He is not a myth. Or a fairy tale. He does exist in flesh and blood in our times. That, in short, is Sach ...

VIKAS® PUBLISHING HOUSE PVT LTD
E-28, Sector-8, Noida-201301
Phone: 0120-4078900 • Fax: 0120-4078999
Registered Office: 576, Masjid Road, Jangpura, New Delhi-110 014
E-mail: *helpline@vikaspublishing.com*
Website: *www.vikaspublishing.com*

ISBN: 978-81-259-4565-9

Creative Designer: Sneha Pamneja
Editorial Coordinator: Veena Baswani
© Photographs: Pradeep Mandhani,
Mid Day- Mumbai, Utpol Sorkkar

Published 2011

CONTENTS

The Star Cast and the Crew

People who were kind enough to be interviewed were all very important parts of this attempted discovery on Sachin. Their inputs were so varied and multi-dimensional, that at times, the author was left wondering as to how he knew so little about the man even after covering him for twenty-two long years. Thus, the interviewees formed the real Starcast. All 83 of them!

CAST

Dilip Kumar, Dev Anand, Sunil Gavaskar, Kapil Dev, Asha Bhosle, Gary Kirsten, Jagmohan Dalmiya, Sourav Ganguly, Mahendra Singh Dhoni, Rahul Dravid, Anil Kumble, Virender Sehwag, Ajit Wadekar, Tiger Pataudi, Sharmila Tagore, VVS Laxman, Mithun Chakraborty, Dilip Vengsarkar, Ravi Shastri, Mahesh Bhatt, Ameen Sayani, Zaheer Khan, Javagal Srinath, T N Seshan, General Shankar Roy Chowdhury, Professor Dr Subhas Bhende, Sushmita Sen, Sanjay Narang, Atul Kasbekar, Vidya Balan, Salim Khan, Jagjit Singh, Shantanu Moitra, Dr Devi Shetty, Dr Sukumar Mukherjee, Chetan Bhagat, Pritish Nandy, Ramachandra Guha, Vinita Kamte, Rituparno Ghosh, Prakash Padukone, Sania Mirza, Saina Nehwal, Justice Edwin King, Abdul Qadir, Krishnamachari Srikanth, Mohinder Amarnath, Laxman Sivaramakrishnan, Harbhajan Singh, Vinod Kambli, Yograj Singh, Rohan Gavaskar, Peter Roebuck, Vinay Naidu, Madhav Apte, Joginder Sharma, Malcolm Conn, Scyld Berry, David Frith, Ajit Agarkar, Ratnakar Shetty, Suresh Raina, Pappu Sanzgiri, Makrand Waingankar, Prashant Shetty, Hemant Kekre, Marcus Couto, Sudhir Gautam, Enid Larwood, Ramesh Mane, Sanjay Raut, Akshay Sawai, Jawyant Lele, Atul Ranade, Mangesh Adhatrao, Sharad Rao, Kiran Mokashi, Gursharan Singh, Ramesh Pardhe, Viv Richards, Imran Khan, Greg Chappell and Sachin Tendulkar.

Recollections used from earlier interviews with the departed

Harold Larwood

Keith Miller

Bill O'Reilly

Sir Don Bradman

Crew

Arindam Chaudhuri

Anjan Chatterjee

Pappu Sanzgiri

Mohan Das Menon

Makrand Waingankar

Saira Banu

Sudip Ghosh

Abhijit Majumder

Abhijit Sarkar

Indrani Halder

Anirudhdha Roy Chowdhury

Koustav Roy

Ranjan Bandopadhyay

Satyam Roy Chowdhury

Pradeep Mandhani

Samar Pal

Anand Bhoasle

Kathakali Jana

Indira Basu

Rajan Nair

Upala Kar

Ram Kamal Mukherjee

Jaidip Mukherjee

Bimal Das

Dr Kunal Sarkar

Diptangshu Mandal

Soumitra Mitra

Raya Bhattacharya

|||||||||||||||||||||||||||||||||||||||||||||||||||||||||||||||||||||||||||||||||||||||||||||||||||||||||

Special Thanks

|||||||||||||||||||||||||||||||||||||||||||||||||||||||||||||||||||||||||||||||||||||||||||||||||||||||||

Sachin Tendulkar
M S Dhoni
and
Mr Aveek Sarkar
For sending me for the last twenty-two years to all parts
of India and around the world on Tendulkar coverage

Photo credits

|||||||||||||||||||||||||||||||||||||||||||||||||||||||||||||||||||||||||||||||||||||||||||||||||||||||||

Pradeep Mandhani
Mid Day- Mumbai
Utpol Sorkkar

FOREWORD

→ **Mahendra Singh Dhoni**

I never thought or dreamt that I would ever get to meet Sachin Tendulkar in flesh and blood. He was, of course, my hero, as he is for millions and millions of budding cricketers. The only time I had come face to face with him was in Pune in early 2000. East Zone was playing West and my hero hit a big hundred. I was in the reserves of the West Zone. During the drinks break, I went out on the ground with a bottle of water for my team, as was customary. Suddenly Sachin came in front and asked for a drink of water. That was my first face-to-face meeting with him, if that can be called a first meeting!

A proper introduction took place when I went to Dhaka with the Indian team. We didn't fly together and were only introduced at the team dinner. As the seniormost, he welcomed me. I didn't know what to say and what not to say!

I still have this habit of not watching a full fifty-overs match. I just can't get myself to do it. But I have always watched an Indian match whenever Sachin batted. I distinctly remember switching off the TV set when in the World Cup Finals in South Africa, after attempting a huge run chase, Sachin got out. And of course I watched his Centurion knock in the same World Cup, where he and Sehwag tore into the Pakistan attack.

There are plenty of things to learn from Sachin. To start with ... his humility ... how he carries himself ... the effort he puts in on the field even after playing for twenty-two years ... the way he slogs at the practice sessions ... how he works on his technique and also builds on his strengths .... My mantra for youngsters is very simple – just look at Sachin and learn!

The other day a journalist asked me if Sachin would be the same if he had started playing today, armed with just three seasons of IPL money. I replied, 'Absolutely. He would be the same. God made him to play cricket.'

The amount of experience he brings in is unbelievable. If you have played four hundred ODIs, it means you have seen the change in this format. At one time, 260 seemed a safe target. Now even 315 is not considered a very safe one. Sachin knows how cruel the sport can get. He prepares for it. It is a pleasure to have him on your side as you can always exercise options. If you are stuck in a match, with Sachin around, there is always an option that if Plan A doesn't work, you can try Plan B or even Plan C.

He is like a mentor to all of us. I call him the God of cricket. Along with Rahul, VVS, Kumble and Sourav, he has contributed hugely towards building a happy, winning team.

I remember so many of Sachin's knocks that it is difficult to pick out the best. I rank his Gwalior 200 and the Chennai fourth innings knock very highly. And, of course, the Sharjah sandstorm knock.

He can grace the Indian dressing room for as long as he wants to play. Despite being a senior his fitness levels are exemplary. He fulfills

I often think if cricket is Ram, then Sachin is Hanuman – Ram's biggest disciple.

everything that you would require from a team player. Additionally, he brings in a wealth of experience. So it is only PLUS – PLUS with him in the dressing room.

One of his big qualities is that he guides the other cricketers batting with him. He helps them to analyze the match situation and keeps on guiding them. Every innings from him is actually worth a double innings. At times, it seems he knows what kind of ball the bowler is going to bowl. He is always a step ahead of the bowler.

Whenever I have played against him as the captain of the opposing team, I never plan my strategy in detail. I just decide it on the ground. There is no use planning too much for him. He is too smart for all that and if you restrict yourself to a fixed plan, chances are that you will be stuck with it and he will go away happily with yet another hundred!

The only reason that I didn't request him to be a part of India's T-20 World Cup campaign was because I thought we needed to respect his decision. He could easily walk into our T-20 team or, for that matter, into India's greatest ever T-20 side.

It is for him to decide how he wants to plan his exit. I just want him to be happy when he does it. It could be two years from now or five years or fifteen years. Let it be. For the massive contribution he has made to Indian and international cricket, he deserves a fairytale ending – a triple hundred and the World Cup winner's medal!

Why do I call him the God of cricket? Because he can do everything on a cricketing field – bat with the left hand ... bowl seam up ... flipper ... googly ... off spin ... quicker ones ... throw with the left hand – everything. I have not seen him wicket keeping. Maybe he knows even that. And, of course, he can bat a little bit!!!

My years with the Indian cricket team have taught me something that is very simple – *there is nothing beyond Sachin Tendulkar on a cricketing field.*

Most people who admire Sachin only see the successful part of him – scoring runs, collecting trophies, smiling in endorsements like a happy, satisfied and successful man. I wish they had an opportunity to see the other side too. They would see how diligently he works behind the scenes, with how much care and intensity he prepares himself each day even after twenty-two years. No wonder we call him the God of cricket. I often think that if cricket is Ram, then Sachin is Hanuman, Ram's biggest disciple.

A lot of us in the team marvel at the manner in which he has handled the monumental expectations he carries as baggage. Come to think of it, every time he goes out to bat, an entire nation goes with him to the crease.

To counter the pressure, he keeps it very simple. He doesn't think about the outcome at all. He keeps himself immersed in the process and sets himself very small targets – maybe ten runs at a time. Then it is much easier.

If I was asked what would be the favourite story about Sachin that I would relate to my grandson 20-30 years from now, there is, of course, the experience of being at the other end of the wicket when he completed his 5oth test hundred in South Africa. But side-stepping that, I would talk about his humility. You don't learn only technique from him. You learn humility as well. I will say he is as close to the idea of a perfect man that I have ever seen, not just in one role. In various roles – as a husband, a dutiful father, a loving senior on and off the field, a responsible member of society – in everything.

I am extremely glad that Gautam Bhattacharya, one of the most senior journalists on the circuit, is doing this book on Sachin. He has been covering cricket for a long time and I have seen him on most of my overseas tours. From the outset I have had sufficient confidence in him and despite contrasting cricketing arguments at times, the trust has never been betrayed.

I do not have the habit of giving exclusive interviews. Usually I restrict myself to press conferences. Even outside I speak to a select few in the media. The types I am comfortable with are those who won't betray my trust. They point out my flaws in a constructive way when they feel necessary, and do not take advantage of one day's sudden heat-of-the-moment remark.

Gautamda most certainly belongs to this special select category. I have noticed so often that whenever he asks a question at a press conference, it is always of a serious cricketing nature. I am fed up of journalists who try to create a controversy at the slightest pretext. He is not that type thankfully and enjoys my respect.

I will say this to him. Gautamda, you have worked long enough. More than 20 years. By the time I retire you should be winding up as well. Let us go together.

But then, you can always write the odd book – like this very well-deserved one on Sachin !

Best wishes

Mahendra Singh Dhoni

AUTHORSPEAK

First things first.

This is a biography of the subject.
FALSE

This can, at best, be described as a profile shot of the subject.
TRUE

This is a travelogue of Sachin Ramesh Tendulkar's 22-year-old journey in international cricket.
FALSE

This covers glimpses of his journey and the attempts to travel out of the box.
TRUE

This is all about the success story of unarguably India's greatest ever sporting hero.
FALSE

This is all about the Indian sporting genius who, despite rising from a middle-class milieu, earnestly chased his dreams and in the process, became a global symbol of excellence.
TRUE

If Hollywood was ever to make a movie on cricket, it need not go beyond Tendulkar. As he is the closest to the cricketing version of the movie *Slumdog Millionaire*. The beginnings, of course, were not that humble for him. He grew up in a middle-class family. But the subsequent relentless struggle and the unpolluted international fame he has acquired through a cricket bat is simply unparalled.

SACH is all about modern India's greatest living icon who, incidentally, pursues cricket.

For someone with such an awesome record and impact, you would expect tonnes of cricketing literature to be available on him. Heaps of books! Yet there are only five or six.

And there are still people, and that includes some of the interviewees, who expressed their apprehension about this project. A well-known journalist even told me that I would be better off writing a book on 'Uncensored Ganguly'! Other high-profile interviewees expressed concern. One of them said, 'So, yet another book on Tendla!' Another said: 'Unless Sachin comes out openly against the match fixers, there is no story to be chased.' In other words – unless that happens, a book on him does not deserve to be written.

Strange as it may seem, if you walk into any big store to buy cricket cassettes, you will get Tendulkar aplenty. But attempt your luck at the leading bookstores across the country – chances are that you won't find any. Despite Sachin having had one of the best runs in his career – from Ahmedabad to Delhi, from Kolkata to Bengaluru – I hardly found any new book on him. Exasperated, I had to finally call a Sachin biographer in Mumbai. Just to get some clarity on where the old books on him would be available.

There is a method in this apparent madness. Make no mistake. Writing about Tendulkar is almost as difficult as bowling against him!

Tell me, what would you write about someone whose life has been so well documented since the age of sixteen? Every record that he makes, everything he says at a press conference or elsewhere, attracts so much attention that people remember almost everything. What else are you going to tell them? It is not as if there are reporters designated in India to cover only Tendulkar. The entire media talks about him whenever it gets an opportunity. He opens his Twitter account and immediately there are close to one million followers. That he is so closely watched makes life difficult for people who write about him. The public already knows so much. What fresh insights are you going to offer?

Bradman was very big in Australia. But compared to the Sachin hysteria, Bradman doesn't stand favourably. And it is not just the crazy audience or the ever-hungry media. Cricketers who have played alongside and are still playing react the same way. They come across as Sachin devotees rather than colleagues. There is a deep sense of awe which gets further ingrained with every passing second.

I have no suitable words to thank Mahendra Singh Dhoni enough for the Foreword that he gave. But for me, the real Foreword was the sincerity that he showed while talking about Tendulkar. It had to be seen to be believed! The usually reclusive Dhoni avoids one-on-one media interviews like the plague. Yet he spoke with so much fondness that afternoon after completing a product shoot in Kolkata that I finally suggested reproducing what he had said as a Foreword. Dhoni instantly agreed. But not satisfied with his efforts, he asked for another editorial session. And the Foreword that you see – every line, every expression, even the humour – are all the words of the Indian Captain. He would not take a chance with this. After all, he has talked about Sachin who he thinks is the 'God of cricket'.

The night I interviewed Rahul Dravid in South Africa, he was hardly in a state to talk. Victim of a food-poisoning attack, he had been put on a drip earlier in the day. His room was in complete shambles. He could not even find the remote. For someone whose room was always as spick and span as his defence, that night was an exception. Yet he didn't cancel his appointment to talk about Sachin. For me this was a revelation of sorts.

SACH

And Anil Kumble – I approached without any appointment. Yet he spoke with lots of feelings about the Champion he had shared the dressing room with for more than two decades. Sehwag spoke, not like Sehwag the cricketer, but like a cricket-crazy enthusiast who, after winning a contest, had earned the right to go out and open the innings with his hero. Sourav Ganguly, his former batting partener and a friend for life, was, of course, as accomodating as always.

And then there was the mighty Dilip Kumar! I don't think he has made any significant statement or public appearance for the past five-six years. Yet Tendulkar was such a subject that even the legendary Dilip Kumar was prepared to break his silence.

Dev Anand, you will discover later as you go through the book, has indirectly played an important role in Sachin's life. I had to speak to him at any cost! But had serious doubts whether the evergreen hero, now 87, would find time. Reports suggested that he was occupied with the post-production work of his new movie. But Dev Anand took out time and spoke to me three times!

When T N Seshan talked about Sachin, he hardly seemed the tough, uncompromising man that he was known to be. The manner in which Seshan stoutly defended Sachin's stand on not getting involved in the match-fixing issue as a reformer, I felt as if a doting grandfather was endorsing the actions of his loving grandson. Of all the people I met and spoke to, only Ameen Sayani stated that he had never seen Sachin bat. But he had seen him bowl and take a wicket on telly once years ago. In his inimitable 'Geetmala' presentation style, Ameen Sayani wrote back saying, 'Seeing him on telly – a silent prayer went up from my heart: God, please take special care of this kid. But I need not have prayed. Sachin was destined for success anyway.' Mind you, this from someone who, following a crowd disturbance at the Brabourne Stadium in the 1950s was so disillusioned that he switched off from cricket for ever.

The beauty of Tendulkar is that the world opens up windows for him. And, as a writer, all I had to do was just stand near the windows to get fresh insights, fresh perspectives from people who may not have spoken about him earlier. Or spoken only about cricketing aspects. Even the Indian team members and the coach, Gary Kirsten, shared intimate details they may not have divulged before. While talking to all of my 83 interviewees, including

Tendulkar, I realized that the earlier debate on Sachin being awarded the Bharat Ratna was completely unnecessary. That, at the end of the day, an award was only an award! It could well be the country's highest civilian award. But so what? Tendulkar was now part of Indian folklore!

The subject of this book did the utmost for someone who had first interviewed him some 22 summers ago. Despite being so incredibly consumed by one of the busiest cricket seasons, Sachin agreed to give me time. I did tell him about my fear that since his image was so huge, however hard you tried, you ended up getting a side profile or you would fail altogether, and that it was impossible to handle the expectation of a book on him. Sachin laughed and said nothing. And I must say here that the intimidating nature of the job was made somewhat easier as he was sympathetic to my needs.

However, I could not break through the defence of the Tendulkar family. They are intensely private people and the thing least important on their agenda is the public spotlight. The ever-reclusive Ajit Tendulkar did, of course, call up personally to wish me luck with the project. He said, 'Our sentiments are with you on this project.' For me that was touching. I did talk to some of the neighbours at Sahitya Sahawash, the original Tendulkar residence. Dr Subhas Bhende was one of them. The ex-professor at Kirti College and Ramesh Tendulkar's former colleague spoke remarkably well. He said he could not wait to lay his hands on the book. I spoke to him last December. By the time the book was in the post-production stage in early January, I was informed he had passed away. I am now completely clueless as to how to send him the book that I had promised to send as early as possible. Could it be that the erudite Dr Bhende will organize it himself 'up there' and share the same with one Ramesh Tendulkar!

The extensive research that this book involved took two gruelling months of travel and a series of non-stop interviews. Whether the book finds favour with the readers or not is in the hands of destiny. I can only state that at least 97 per cent of the material has been procured first hand, a lot of which, you have probably not read before. In hotel-room service lingo – it has been cooked afresh. Here I must thank two brilliant professionals for their unstinted support. The Delhi-based, well-known photographer Pradeep Mandhani who has contributed most of the pictures that have been used. And cricket statistician par excellence Mohan Das Menon. In my opinion, both have batted extremely well for this project.

That Vikas, a fairly conservative publishing house, decided to join the adventure, was more than a welcome surprise. It was not going to be the usual 'cricket-cricket' book on Tendulkar that you would expect from a cricket writer. The take was completely different and involved a ready risk of rejection. And it still does. Yet, led by the die-hard, cricket-afficianado publisher Piyush Chawla, they showed sufficient interest in the project. Veena Baswani, the Editor-in-Chief, deserves special compliments for staying up day and night for completion of the same. Designer Sneha Pamneja was not too much into cricket. But after this book, I shall have to check and find out.

As my mornings and afternoons were spent in interviewing and compilation, the only time to write was through the night. I would usually begin at midnight after office hours and continue up to 3.30 am. The next morning would be spent again in contacting someone … taking notes … handling the quotes. Trust me, it was not bad. It was terrible! There was hardly any family life. Hardly any proper communication. For a project that was finalized as late as mid-October 2010, we had to get off the ground by December. I can only say that without my wife Raya and daughter Lahoma's sacrifice, this book would never have seen the light of day. They never lost patience and bore the torturous lifestyle inflicted upon them with a smile.

Armed with the experience of writing on Sachin at completely odd hours, I would now recommend the same exercise to my colleagues and fellow cricket writers. Attempt writing on Tendulkar at three in the morning. You will find the experience surreal. His exploits are cast in such a fairy-tale mould that the complete darkness outside the house and the serenity add a special flavour. I have always been mesmerized by this magic and never found a parallel anywhere. Sachin evokes so many different emotions and situations that you may have rarely experienced before. And the beauty is that none of this is fiction.

AGE 16: His first day with the bat in test cricket. Wasim Akram on a lively, green wicket sends down possibly the fastest ever spells an Asian fast bowler has ever delivered. Sitting at the Karachi press box, you shiver and get worried about the teenager's safety. That itself is a new emotion as you have never seen a sixteen-year-old make his debut earlier.

AGE 16: He is hit on the nose by a Waqar Younis delivery. Bleeds. Gets up. He hits the next ball for four. When he returns later to the pavilion, the entire press box, including some very senior journalists, get up to accord him a standing ovation. New experience. In my twenty-six years of cricket reporting, have never encountered any such thing again.

AGE 19: The old English doorman at the Old Trafford ground in Manchester cries. He has just seen Tendulkar complete his first ever test hundred and save India. He is crying as it has evoked memories of his all-time favourite cricketer Dennis Compton. New experience. Till date, have not seen a doorman cry again.

AGE 26: After having lost his father, comes back for a World Cup match. Gets a hundred and then turns his gaze skywards in search of his father. The entire Bristol Press Box by now is full of moist eyes. Completely new experience. New emotion.

AGE 29: Sends Pakistan packing at Centurion with such a superb display that the country starts celebrating Diwali in March. And he, the creator, sitting in his hotel room, switches off the lights. All by himself, closely watches Australia, the likely opponents in the Final, play live on TV. New experience. Never seen anyone detach himself after demolishing Pakistan!

AGE 34: Sits alone in his hotel room in Port of Spain sporting a face that is bewildered, following the World Cup devastation. India has just crashed out of the tournament at a very early stage. He could not save them this time after having scored a duck. So wearing that Number Ten jersey, he has spent the last twenty-four hours all by himself. Has eaten only one sandwich. New experience. Never seen commitment like this before.

These and many more are only my personal inputs. Journalists who have seen him closely and travelled with him surely have their very own stories. Hopefully, by the time Sachin scores his 60th test hundred, at least 60 books should be available on him at the book stores.

For we will never see anyone like him again. Nor will the future generation in all probability see such a once-in-a-century phenomenon. I consider it a social responsibility to share the Sachin memories and pass them on.

Why shouldn't we celebrate our good fortune? We have been privileged. We should flaunt it. After all, we have a Tendulkar! Happy reading!

Gautam Bhattacharya
10 January 2011
Kolkata

LIFE ON A SPEEDING TRAIN →

25 YEARS

40

QUESTIONS

SACHIN TENDULKAR HAS NEVER EVER ANSWERED

PERIOD SPAN → 1986-2011

➜ 1986

1. You had started practising under Achrekar full time and the special relationship with a cricket bat had already begun. Can you describe the relationship?

The bat is the most important instrument in my life. The instrument that has changed my life for ever ...

2. Sivaji Park by now had become the most important destination in your life. Does the special significance of the place touch a cord even today?

I can never forget Sivaji Park! Even today when I pass through Sivaji Park, I can just sense it. May be I am busy in doing something else. Talking to someone inside the car or listening to music. Yet without even looking outside, I would be able to tell we are crossing Sivaji Park. Such is the strong connect ...

|||||||| Achrekar, the guiding light

||||||||||||||||||||||||||||||||||||||||||||||||||||||||||||||||||||||||||||||||||

➔ 1987

3. Sachin Tendulkar got rejected. He was sent as a promising quickie to Dennis Lille's MRF camp. But was sent packing along with the other failed candidates. A list that also included an youngster from Bengal called Sourav Ganguly ... How hard was it to face the rejection — an unique incident in your entire cricketing career?

|||||||| Early 'rejection' came in the form of Dennis Lille

I was okay with it. In any case I was not aspiring to become a fast bowler. I thought of myself as a fast bowling all-rounder. That is precisely the reason I had carried my batting kit to Chennai. I didn't get an opportunity to bat. I did bowl for one or two sessions. As for Sourav, I don't remember meeting him there. Later on at the national camp, I caught up with him.

4. You were one of the ball boys in the Reliance Cup Semi-Final at Wankhede and watched Gavaskar's last innings in international cricket. What are the memories you have of that match?

I don't think I was there for the Semi-Final. I may have been outside Mumbai. But I was there for the group league match against Zimbabwe. I was standing right there in front of the Indian dressing room. Then Mr Gavaskar invited me inside. I was introduced to all the players. I was too much in awe. But what a feeling it was ...

→ 1988

5. This year saw you creating the World Record partnership with Kambli. This also marked a year when you decided to use an helmet as a part of your protective gear. Obviously it was not possible to visualize at that stage that one day, when cricket romantics sit down to decide on the World's greatest ever batsman, they might say: 'Oh, Don and Viv, his two closest opponents, never required an helmet.' What would you think of such an observation?

I think it is only sensible to use protective gear if you have it in circulation. Twenty years from now there will be some other protective gear which I can't imagine today. The fact of the matter is that in the past, such protective equipment didn't exist. You can only use what you have today, isn't it?

6. Not many people would perhaps know that the first time the mighty Tendulkar rubbed shoulders with the big boys on the field, he represented Pakistan. This was in a festival match at the CCI as a substitute fielder. Apparently the then Pakistani captain Imran Khan kept you too deep. So you couldn't complete a catch and back home, in the local train, constantly grumbled about the captain's field placements. True?

Absolutely true (Laughs). I went in as a substitute. Imran was the Pakistan Captain. No words were exchanged with him. But yes, I may've got the catch if I was kept slightly ahead Laughs)...

||||||| Facing page: An unforgettable childhood memory

→ 1989

7. Your inaugural series with the Indian Cricket Team to Pakistan took place this year. At the Sialkot Test you were struck on the nose by a nasty Waqar Younis bouncer. That particular night while nursing your nose, what did you think of the strange new world you were now a part of?

I still remember that particular night. We had a dinner invitation. The entire team went, barring me. I had tremendous pain at night. But never for a minute was I thinking negative. I had to keep on applying ice. My head felt heavy. This was not my first injury. The school ground where we played – the wicket there was never rolled properly. We used to look after the turf and obviously it remained uneven. Even there I got struck.

IIIIIIII Thrown to the wolves – he handles them well

Once on the tooth. Once on the nose. Waqar's pace, of course, was something different. But as I said, it didn't alter my line of thinking. That night I told myself: this is what international cricket is all about. You have to adapt and adjust.

||||||| With Waqar – both made their debut in Karachi Test Match

8. Apart from getting hit by a Waqar delivery and recovering so fast, there was another magic moment on that tour. You hitting Abdul Qadir for four sixes and breaking a dressing-room windowpane. It almost became cricketing folklore as to how Qadir had teased you and what you said in reply. Subsequently when you met Qadir, was that discussed again?

No (laughs). None of us raised it. Actually what happened was that, in the previous over, I had hit Mushtaq. So Qadir suddenly walked up to me and said, 'Is bachche ko kyun mar rahe ho? Humko markey dikhao.' ('Why are you hitting this child? Try hitting me.')To which I replied, 'Aap to great bowler hain. Aapko kaise maroon! (You are a great bowler. How can I hit you!) Then the sixes happened and the dressing-room windowpane broke. Strangely, when I visited the ground after fifteen long years again, the stadium looked different. I couldn't remember how the dressing room had looked in those days. The Peshawar ground looked somewhat smaller.

→ 1990

9. You scored your first test hundred in England and earned a lot of praise from the British press. Do you remember anything of that? Quite a few top-class sportsmen have had problems with the British press. What do you think of them? Were they ever unkind towards you?

I don't think I ever had problems with them. Not that I read much. Half the time I might just see the picture and not read anything at all. On match days, as a routine I don't read anything at all. I feel that whatever there is in the match report is just somebody else's opinion. Why read that and put extra pressure on myself? If I have to ask someone, I can always go up to that person and talk.

Talking about that Manchester innings – sitting back today – I only remember that particular knock. Not who had said what. Because even then, I wasn't reading papers. My first ever press conference took place post that hundred. Before that I mostly spoke to journalists on a one-on-one basis. This was the first time I spoke to all of them at a formal conference.

And particularly about the British press – I have never had any reasons to complain. For that matter – against any other media. As I told you, I hardly read the reports ...

→ **1991**

10. You had already achieved superstardom and the Walkman became a constant companion. Was it a careful ploy to keep unwanted attention at bay?

The Walkman was there from 1988. I have always been very fond of music. Music helped me to keep my mind on the game. Which was so necessary.

11. Your fan base also started growing around this time. Over the years it only increased in geometric progressions. Today, if you were to pick one special fan, who would that be?

As for the fans – there have been so many. But one guy I can mention who travels with us all over the world. He has the map of India drawn on his head. The whole body painted with the tri-colour and my name written over it. His name is Sudhir. Comes from Bihar ....

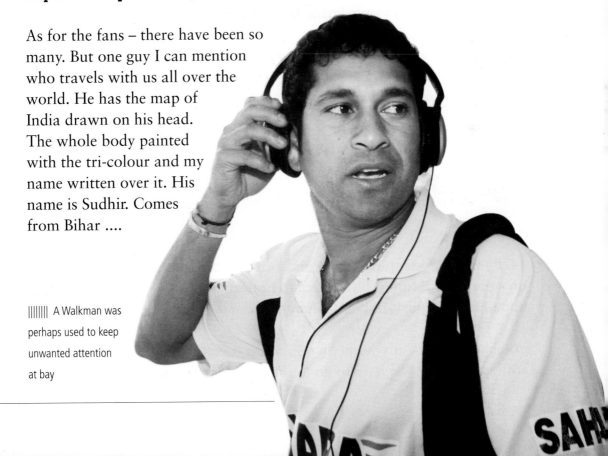

|||||| A Walkman was perhaps used to keep unwanted attention at bay

→ 1992

12. Don Bradman was alive and you were performing in his country. Did it motivate you all the more?

Not really. In any case I wanted to do well in Australia. Wanted to go there and do something special. The track in Perth was hard and quick. I really watched the ball very, very closely as, otherwise, you wouldn't have scored on that kind of surface. Again the track at Sydney was as usual – a surface which assisted spinners. I managed to get hundreds on two completely different surfaces. After that I felt I was ready to play anywhere.

13. What are the similarities in your batting style with Sir Don? Experts opine that remarkable balance could be one.

Unfortunately whatever little footage I have seen of his is very limited. On the basis of that you can hardly say anything. But balance is the key for scoring runs consistently. And then, while watching the ball, the head has to be steady ...

→ 1993

14. By now it was quite apparent that you are not just blessed with an exceptional talent but you also had a strong body to support the same. How important is it for youngsters to build a strong body?

You have to work at your body to make it strong. A good body comes with hard work. You have to go to the gym. Have to work hard on the field. The most important time to work on your body is the five-year period when you are between sixteen to twenty. That is the time to really work hard and push your body. To make sure you are now strong enough to sustain yourself for another fifteen years ...

15. By now you must have been subjected to a bit of sledging. Did you ever sledge personally?

I have never sledged per se merely for the sake of sledging. I did that only once as a part of team strategy. This was at the Kenya Champions Trophy. We were playing Australia. The match was played under overcast conditions. The wicket was also very damp. I had told Sourav beforehand that I would do something to upset Mcgrath's rhythm. So, in the very first over, I stepped out to him. The first thing I said to him was: 'Today I will hit you out of the ground.' He got really angry and started spraying the

||||||| Dressing room camaraderie

ball around. This was exactly what we wanted. As on that surface, he may have been very dangerous. We did win that match ultimately and I felt very happy. My sledging did work for the team.

My own experience of sledging came very early on my first tour to Australia. I remember having blocked a delivery and the ball landed near my foot. I tried picking it up when Allan Border shouted from gully, 'Don't touch the ball.' So I stopped immediately.

 **1994** ||||||||||||||||||||||||||||||||||||||||||||||||||||||||

16. The team had gone to Sharjah after a long gap of many years. You played Wasim and Waqar after a while at the international level. Did you notice any difference in their attitude towards you?

Nothing major. By such time, they were far more experienced. I would say both had become complete bowlers. Waqar had made his debut along with me in the Karachi Test. By then, he had also grown in stature. I, however, made no special preparations for the duo. By such time I had become quite confident of tackling any type of bowling on any given surface.

17. You also started growing a stubble for important matches. The practice has continued even today. How does a stubble help in enhancing performance?

Oh, no! (Laughs)It is just normal. Nothing to do with performance. (Laughs)

|||||||| An unusual moment – but then, an unusual achievement too!

1995 |||||||||||||||||||||||||||||||||||||||||||||||||||||||||||||||||

18. By now, Brian Lara had become your closest competition on this planet. Did you look on him as a benchmark for improving your personal standards?

Not exactly. I wasn't following his career minutely to get inspired. I was motivated enough on my own. Didn't want to overcharge myself. But I would certainly watch Brian on TV. He is one of my favourite all-time players. Contrary to what people thought there was no rivalry between us. As a matter of fact we clicked right from the time we met.

|||||||| Marriage only made him stronger and more focussed

We first met in Canada in 1990. We were playing for Rest of the World against Imran's Pakistan. They had the two Ws. And I remember doing a 160-170 run partnership with Brian. Thoroughly enjoyed the experience of batting with him. Watching him from the other end was simply great.

→ 1996

19. You batted brilliantly throughout the World Cup, yet we lost miserably in the Semi-Final. A teammate-cum-childhood friend of yours cried openly at the Eden Gardens. Till date we have never been told how you reacted privately on that night!

The 1996 defeat was shattering. We were playing with high hopes. Quite confident that we would go on to play Australia in the finals at Lahore. As for the defeat, I couldn't sleep that night.

||||||||| With Kambli, a partnership that went on for quite long till ...

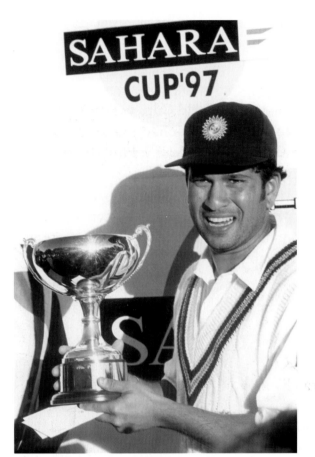

I did watch the Final at Lahore on TV and kept on thinking that we ought to have been there that day. The loss left me devastated.

20. This was also the year in which Bob Woolmer started using the laptop on a world stage for the minutest cricketing preparations. Don't you think the role of the computer in cricket has been slightly overemphasised? Your performance is the biggest indicator that skill can march well ahead of the laptop!

||||||| The picture says it all!

The computer does play an important role in today's cricket. You forget so many things. With the computer you can store them. For me the biggest advantage is you can study the opposition. The computer helps and provides you with that vital two to three per cent difference. As far as I am concerned it is not overrated.

→ **1997**

21. You were leading the Indian team of which Rahul and Sourav had become an integral part. Laxman made his debut in the same year. And Kumble, of course, was already there. You were later called the 'Magnificient Five'. Can you talk about them?

From the manner in which Rahul and Sourav had batted in their debut test match, it was quite evident that they were there to stay. Rahul's forte was excellent technique and he loved to occupy the crease for long hours. Rahul concentrated extremely well – I mean, still concentrates very well. Sourav was somebody who figured out his game well enough. He knew which bowler to hit and which one to defend. Sourav liked scoring runs in boundaries. He was a boundary hitter. Laxman depended on hand-eye coordination. He was the most wristy player.

And Kumble, of course, is the greatest bowler that I have ever played with. Apart from being a champion match-winning bowler, his greatness lay in the fact that he would bowl the last delivery of the day with the same amount of fire irrespective of his performance during the day.

|||||| With Sir Gary at his den in Barbados

→ 1998

22. This, of course, was a magical year. Sharjah master class happened and so did the battle with Warne. If you tell young players to relive the Sachin Spirit of '98, what would you tell them?

I wouldn't know. Just played my normal game. I had prepared myself well and went along with that. Meticulous preparation is important in any form of cricket. Whenever I am playing, I give myself the best opportunity to succeed by preparing properly. You have to study the opponent bowlers and prepare accordingly.

My form was good during that season and, may be, it was a bit of coincidence that I always performed against the Australians, be it with the bat or ball. In the Kochi One-dayer, I won the Man of the Match with five wickets. Then later, in the Champions Trophy, I scored again against them. As for facing Warne, I had told my team in the Chennai dressing room that one of us had to get a big hundred. If that happened, the game would be set for a victory. My plan did work on that day.

→ 1999

23. This was a year in which you tragically lost your father. Yet it was extraordinary the manner in which you conquered the tragedy by getting a hundred in the very first match. This was repeated a few years later too when you lost a very close friend of yours, Mark Mascarenhas. Recently, before the Colombo Final, Raj Singh died and again your batting didn't show any signs of the devastation.

SACH

How do you find it possible to keep your mind away from personal tragedies and watch the ball as closely as ever?

I can't answer this honestly. It is very hard to explain. Something happens inside the ground. The body and mind take charge.

It is very tough and you have to possibly experience it to understand. You have to be very, very tough and brave to handle such situations. In my case I do get affected. When my father died and I returned home, the family members, including my mother, asked me to go back and play for the country. They said, 'Father would have loved that ...'

 **2000** IIIIIIIIIIIIIIIIIIIIIIIIIIIIIIIIIIIIIIIIIIIIIIIIIIIIIIIIIIII

24. The ugly face of match-fixing surfaced and the country was stunned. Sachin Tendulkar, however, remained a tower of resilience. He showcased integrity as always. Looking back, don't you feel proud of your role during this period?

I was just doing what every Indian was supposed to do. I was just doing my duty and didn't think it was any different from what I had done in the past. I was just following the same routine. Around the time I received a certificate from the Income Tax department for paying my taxes honestly. This gave me a lot of satisfaction and I was just hoping my father had been alive to see it ...

25. Nasser Hussain employed the New Leg Theory against you which was very negative. They called him the 'New Jardine' for that. It is well documented that Bradman never forgave Jardine for employing Bodyline. Do you also have a similar kind of feeling for Nasser? And another query? How would you have countered Bodyline if it was bowled against you?

Difficult for me to say how I would have tackled Bodyline. You need to be there and at times find a quick solution on the field. As for Nasser, I didn't mind at all. It was their strategy. They were trying to keep the runs down and the set of planning was different. Flintoff came round the wicket and Ashley from another end. My relations with Nasser never got affected (laughs). And I think he was a very good captain.

26. Mike Denness stunned the cricketing world by suspending you for ball tampering. This was a completely unreal situation with India reacting strongly and Denness sticking to his decision. Looking back what do you feel today?

You know I was completely shocked and shattered when he said the charge against me was for ball tampering. I tried telling him what the truth was. That I was just cleaning grass. I was not picking the seam. At no stage did I do that. If someone is trying to remove grass from the ball, how can you levy ball-tampering charges against him? But the match referee would hear none of it. Since then, whenever I clean the ball, I keep the umpires posted. But despite the incident, I was so happy for the trust and faith that the entire country expressed in me. At times it has been written that a nation walked with me every time I went out to bat. Here there was no bat. Yet they showed such faith in my integrity that I was touched. Till date I can't forget that.

 You can't get more perfect than that!

→ 2002

27. By this time, Sehwag had also started opening with you, though not so frequently. With Ganguly, of course, you formed the most devastating opening combination in one-day cricket. Can you tell us how different were they as opening partners?

Different, I would say. Sehwag keeps his mind as much free and uncomplicated as possible. He trusts his instincts and reacts very fast. Of course, he goes there with a solid game-plan but in-between the deliveries he relaxes. I have seen him even sing (Laughs). Sourav, in contrast, is intense. As a batsman his approach is very calculated. He evaluates the opponents well before going out to bat. Sourav, as I said earlier in the book, loves getting his runs in boundaries. At times, in tense situations, I have walked across to him and spoken a few words in Bengali just to make him feel a little relaxed.

 **2003**

||||||| The unbeatable combination – Sachin and Sehwag

28. In the 2003 World Cup you were simply awesome. Yet, in the series prior to that in New Zealand, you looked woefully out of touch. They say, before leaving for South Africa, you remained engrossed in a serious cricketing discussion with your brother Ajit.

Apparently you discussed your plan of operations in South Africa with him. A simile can be drawn with Bradman, who had discussed his plans with a friend just before he took on Bodyline for the first time.

Legend also has it that while you were going out to bat at Centurion against Pakistan, Sehwag asked you, 'Kya karna hai?' ('What do we have to do?') You told him, 'Kya karna hai. Marna hai.' ('What do we have to do? Beat them.') And then you went and played that murderous knock.

As for the meeting with Ajit, I did discuss a few things. But it was nothing extensive. To be honest with you I didn't change my game much in South Africa. I did work quite hard for the World Cup as I wanted to do something special. I felt I was in the zone during this period. In New Zealand, I wasn't opening the innings. But here we had a team meeting – Sourav, I and John. And it was decided that I would open.

In the first match against Holland, I took some time to adjust. I gave myself enough chance to build up a momentum. Against Pakistan – when we were chasing their big total, we knew the Pakistanis would try to charge in the very first spell. So we had to attack them

 At the Down Under, where he is more than a king

straightaway. But it wasn't that the manner we went against them was pre-planned in any way. Just happened ...

➡ 2004

29. It was mostly after the World Cup and post the double hundred at Sydney, that compliments flew fast and thick. Some kept on calling you the World's greatest batsman. Others said, 'Sachin resembles everything that is pure and honest in cricket. And some went to the extent of saying, 'I have seen God. He bats for India at number 4.' Looking back, which one would you call the closest to your heart?

None of these. Sir Don's statement that this fellow bats very much like me. That was real special.

30. One of those rare controversial incidents in your life. Possibly the only time in your entire career that in a crowded press conference you expressed open disgust with the team management for declaring when you were six runs away from your double hundred. Today how would you review the incident? Would you regret it now?

I don't regret it. I had nothing to hide. Look, it's not that I went to the press conference and began by saying, 'I am greatly offended' or anything of that sort. I was specifically asked a question whether I was disappointed at not having got the double hundred? I would have been lying if I had said that I was not disappointed. Of course I was disappointed. And I admitted it. Come on, you don't expect me to lie. Do you? Anyway all that is behind us now.

 **2005** ||||||||||||||||||||||||||||||||||||||||||||||||||||||||||||||||||||||||||||||||||

31. Greg Chappell's e-mail to the Board was splashed in the papers. Dada lost his captaincy despite a series win against Zimbabwe. Sitting in faraway Mumbai, what were you thinking?

Honestly, I wasn't thinking about all that. I was more concerned about my own rehabilitation. I was working on my tennis elbow. For me, getting the injury sorted out was the top priority. In any case, sitting so far away, I knew very little. People who were part of that dressing room would have known better.

|||||| Two of his biggest competitors – Ponting and Lara

➔2006

32. Life with Chappell began in full earnest. This was supposed to be a difficult period as stories emerged of dissension between seniors and juniors. At times, you appeared impatient and openly expressed your disgust with people moving behind the sight screen. This is something we have never seen you do before. Some attributed it to your state of mind.

It was frustrating to see people move up and down behind the sight screen. I only hoped that people who were doing it understood this was a one-ball game. As for the other part of the question, I didn't pay attention to what the others were saying. I knew my personal level of relationship with the juniors. That is why I found no reason to react.

33. Chappell also started advocating his new cricketing philosophy that tremendous emphasis should be placed on fitness. And that big names would not matter unless they were physically fit. As a senior, did you feel you were subjecting yourself to a new challenge?

I didn't find the challenge any bigger in 2006. If someone comes and says you need to be fit to play international cricket, after my having spent seventeen years on the circuit, I would find the remark irrelevant.

 **2007**

34. Another turbulent year! The World Cup campaign was a disaster. The batting order was reshuffled. Chappell blamed the seniors. You counter-attacked him in print, which was sensational. Your house was attacked following our first round exit.

My house was never attacked. That was wrong information. Though the reaction was pretty emotional all over the country as we played miserably. That is possibly the worst ever defeat in my cricketing career. I agree, it was a very difficult phase.

As for counter-attacking in print, I only spoke out when somebody questioned my commitment. Someone has been playing for eighteen long years. People have seen for themselves all these years. And to get questioned by someone who had completed just fifteen months! I thought, there was a difference between the two. Wasn't there?

→2008

35. Happy days were here again. You almost began a new phase in your life. You were back to your old, attacking self. Two of your teammates retired this season. Anil and Sourav.

I was determined to show that there was enough cricket still left in me. Since our World Cup campaign was a disaster, it made me more motivated to work harder. The only way to remove the disappointment was to go and sweat.

As for the colleagues who retired, one felt sad. But then one realized, this was an inevitable part of life ...

36. A huge disaster in the form of 26/11 happened. Where were you during the Taj attack?

We were playing at Cuttack. At night came to know about the attack. Of course, first you call home and enquire about the safety of your near and dear ones. Then keep glued to TV to try and find out what exactly is going on. What was happening to the nation was difficult to digest. I felt very sad and couldn't come to terms with it. I was almost numb and didn't know what had hit me. It took a while to get myself back on track. That must surely rank as one of the most disappointing days of my life.

→ 2009

37. Around this period you said something that was very interesting. In an uncharacteristic manner you snapped back: 'I had stones thrown at me and I turned them into milestones.' What were you referring to?

I meant that people who make statements against your style of play, don't know your mind. Neither do they know the condition of your body. It is just their opinion. For all you know it need not be right. If you basically know yourself pretty well, it doesn't matter what people say. You know what you are capable of. If you remain confident of yourself, outside opinion won't matter. You would just go out and continue to do things your way. I have always concentrated on my game and remained focussed. I have used disappointment as a reason to go out and work harder.

Tried to bring in positives out of negatives. I always found ways and means for myself to work harder. When the going was good, in any case, I pushed myself all the more. Then I didn't require a reason.

→ 2010

38. You continued to excel and did full justice to the tag - 'God of cricket'. It was sheer magic as you routinely went past landmarks and created your own mountain. Did you derive inspiration from other legendary performers to get energized at times? When you watch Mr Bachchan playing the child in *Paa* or Lata Mangeshkar sing to the tune of 'Aaja re ...', do you derive additional energy?

I get energized even by the heroic deeds of cricketers. One is learning every day. Each day your mind remains open to new things. There is no harm in accepting that you don't know enough and that you need to learn new things.

I get inspired by different sources. Inspired seeing the passion in some of the greats. Dev Anand – I admire his energy. In his youth, apparently my father looked like him from certain angles. Then the Mangeshkar sisters. Lataji and Ashaji. Recently I was part of an audience where Asha Bhosle was singing. At the age of seventy-five, she has so much energy and passion left for her work that you immediately say, 'Wow!' These are the people who enjoy every moment of their creative lives. They don't want short-cuts. And, of course, Mr Bachchan. May be because these people are all from Mumbai, I meet them more than others. *Agneepath* is one of my favourite films. One particular

|||||||| With two of his idols: (top) Amitabh Bachchan and (bottom) Asha Bhosle

dialogue from that movie still gives me goose bumps — 'Main Vijay Dinanath Chauhan ...' When I participated in KBC ('Kaun Banega Crorepati') to raise money for the Latur Earthquake Fund, the first thing I said was, 'Mr Bachchan, please say that for me again.' He smilingly obliged.

Apart from them, A R Rahman is also someone I admire. Music has been my passion and I love listening to his style of music. Like the rest of India, I felt very proud when *Jai Ho* won the Oscars. I remember sending him a text from New Zealand where the team was playing then.

39. Even though retirement is a few years away, at some time or the other, Sachin Tendulkar is expected to sit in the TV commentary box. If you do so, what would be your style? Will it be pro-player? Or if necessary, will you be hard on the players?

I will go for positive commentary. I don't believe in criticizing players harshly. You have to understand that no one ever steps on to the field to make a mistake. Why do you have to talk about the mistakes they have made? Why not about the good things that they have done? As a commentator, I would love to explain to the viewers the mind game that is going out in the middle. I would love to prepare them in advance for what might happen next. As to what the bowler must be thinking. Or what the batsman is planning to do.

 **2011** ||||||||||||||||||||||||||||||||||||||||||||||||||||||||||||||||||||||

40. At times are there fears that sooner or later your special ability to bring smiles to billions of Indians will come to an end? That an entire nation won't walk with you any more? That you might feel like a retired major who may not be able to lift his gun, while the nearest bank gets looted?

I am not thinking of that at all. To me everything that has happened in my life has been God's gift. I believe in destiny. Things happened as God wanted them to happen. Whatever has to happen will happen. As long as the team is getting the best out of me, I shall continue. I don't want a situation in the future where I will sit down and moan, that I should have tried harder. So I give my best and leave the rest to God.

THE PERFECT DIAMOND → **60 Quotes**

1. Sachin represents the right virtues of mankind and is a symbol of excellence. In every part of society there are bad and good elements. For every terrorist that brings out the bad and evil, there is a Tendulkar to balance and represent the good.

>> VINITA KAMTE, wife of late ASHOK KAMTE, the brave police officer who laid down his life on 26/11

2. God sends some people to this earth with lots of care and with his own script. Nothing can destroy them. Nothing can affect them. They are *God's Apna admi* ... Dilipsaab, Didi, Amitabh and Sachin ...

>> ASHA BHOSLE

3. He may not chew gum. But he has composure and reflects an attitude that exudes the intent he comes with. The intent to dominate ...

>> SIR VIVIAN RICHARDS

4. I at least knew clearly that I had no backers and would have to do everything on my own. But Sachin remained in a confused state of mind. He didn't know whether the coach was for or against him. His performance, not surprisingly, had suffered big time in that Greg Chappell phase.

>> SOURAV GANGULY

5. Even someone as brilliant as a Shane Warne or a Steven Waugh has polarised public opinion in Australia. A lot of people felt the team was getting too aggressive and arrogant. There was a lack of humility despite being the world beaters. And when the same people looked at Tendulkar they said, 'Wow a champion, yet a good sport!' Tendulkar has never polarised public opinion in Australia.

>> MALCOLM CONN,
Australian cricket writer

6. Never ever loses his temper inside the dressing room. I am yet to see Sachin throwing his bat around even when given out wrongly. May be he will have an extra bowl of ice cream. And that is when you realize he is pretty upset.

>> ZAHEER KHAN

7. People only talk about his genius. They don't get to see the backroom. I do. And I only see intense preparation, hours and hours of practice, sweat, hard work. Leaving nothing – absolutely nothing to chance.

>> GARY KIRSTEN

8. We are privileged to be living in an era when India is carving out a position of self-respect in the world. Who else exemplifies this better than Sachin himself ...

>> DR DEVI SHETTY

9. The most fascinating part of the persona is that 'Don't-show-off' attitude. Very inspiring to watch Sachin on TV. He and Roger Federer are two of my favourite sportsmen.

>> SAINA NEHWAL

10. Sachin's critics! Kuch to log kahenge ... Logon ka kam hai kahena ... Choro bekar ki bato se ...

>> HARBHAJAN SINGH

11. I will put him in the Satyajit Ray class – which for me is the ultimate! Though Ray also had huge leadership abilities.

>> SHARMILA TAGORE

12. The finest innings ever played by an Indian? I would go for Gavaskar's 96 at Bengaluru. But if you ask me in totality – I would say Sachin has been the greatest. Not only has he been a role model on the field, but even off the field, his dedication, determination and his sense of fair play has been exemplary.

>> TIGER PATAUDI

13. My favourite Sachin story is not of an outstanding innings or his exploits with the bat. But the fact that despite attaining such heights he never deviated from his middle-class values. One day the children will surely ask me and I will tell them in detail about this great quality of his.

>> RAHUL DRAVID

14. At times I wondered if cricket was the game all of us played, then Sachin surely pursues some other sport.

>> RAVI SHASTRI

15. There is an inner drive in Sachin to continuously better his excellence. You can't cultivate this in people. And when he finally reaches the landmark, he very rightly pays homage to the unknown source which is called energy.

>> DEV ANAND

16. My personal directorial acumen says there is an actor in Sourav Ganguly. Not so much in Sachin. I don't think he will ever act in my movie or vice versa. But then Tendulkar doesn't need to act. I find him real icon-like. Very steady and reassuring. There is a bit of Rajiv Gandhi in him! Innocence with an element of poise and tranquility thrown in.

>> RITUPARNO GHOSH

17. Please tell him not to wear that helmet. Don never wore one.

>> HAROLD LARWOOD

18. Tendulkar's footwork is the best in the business. He never gets caught in two minds. That helps his shot selection. He is always in the right position.

>> SHANE WARNE

19. You are my grandson's age. Let me tell you, please don't play ladies' cricket (One-dayers). You are in the same orbit with Don. He never played this pyjama stuff.

>> BILL O'REILLY

20. I want Sachin to stand as tall as a Mahatma Gandhi ... Why should Lara be compared to him ... No one else should he allow in this special orbit...

>> KAPIL DEV

21. With the bat Sachin is the Angry Young Man of Indian cricket. He can only be compared to Dilip Kumar ... And in personal life so humble that I can only think of one parallel from the film industry — Mohammad Rafi.

>> SALIM KHAN

22. You can easily sense the intense preparedness especially when he is facing a Shane Warne or a Shoaib Akhtar. He radiates electrifying energy with a gracefulness that is God's gift to him.

>> DILIP KUMAR

23. I love to see Tendulkar bat. I love to see so many of them bat. But if it comes down to a question of pay and watch, I would say I shall only pay to see Tendulkar bat.

>> BRIAN LARA

24. Sachin is timeless. In the years to come he will always be the reference point for excellence ... For me the essence of Tendulkar is the song – 'Behti hawa sa tha woh ... Udti patang sa tha who ... Kahan gaya, use dhoondo.'

>> SHANTANU MOITRA

25. I think Douglas Jardine might have encouraged some of his fielders to sledge Sachin. Somehow he seems to have got away with it for many years. Opponents have been too respectful perhaps.

>> SCYLD BERRY,
Editor, *Wisden*

26. For me, Bradman class belongs to two Indian batsmen: Sunil Gavaskar and Sachin Tendulkar. If Sunil is the Raj Kapoor of Indian cricket, Sachin surely is Amitabh Bachchan ...

>> AJIT WADEKAR

27. India without Sachin Tendulkar is akin to the 1948 Australians without Don Bradman. Still good but without the cream and with the cream gone, the opposition will always walk a little taller.

>> BARRY RICHARDS

28. Bradman felt he was looking at a mirror image of himself when he watched the little Indian. Their techniques were very much the same, except for their grip on the bat. Their compactness and shot production were also close. They both liked to attack and take control of bowlers. Like Bradman, Tendulkar has everything.

>> RONALD PERRY,
author of *Bradman's Best*

29. I want him to play till he is 45. God has sent him here with a specific purpose. To bat as long as he can.

>> RAMACHANDRA GUHA,
cricket historian

30. Tendulkar is much more across the party line. India in his times has a nuclear bomb, is aspiring to become a member in the UN Security Council. He is an expression of happy, liberated India.

>> PETER ROEBUCK

31. Sachin is definitely a Ryan-(or Rancho in *Three Idiots*) type character who did his own thing and yet excelled in it. He stands for excellence in general. Anyone or any organisation seeking excellence would be inspired by him.

>> CHETAN BHAGAT

32. Sachin is exceptional. He can only be compared to Lata Mangeshkar. If I were to sing for him I would dedicate my favourite song to him: 'Yeh daulat bhi le lo, yeh shauharat bhi le lo. Woh kagaj ki kasti o barish ka pani ...'

>> JAGJIT SINGH

33. Myself and Sachin in one team would be good. I presume we will combine well. Like me, he also can't stand mediocrity. And, of course, his face can be used by the Election Commission as a symbol.

>> T N SESHAN

34. The relationship between cricket and Sachin is that of Ram and Hanuman. Sachin is the biggest disciple of cricket as much as Hanuman was of Ram.

>> MAHENDRA SINGH DHONI

35. Kambli, if he was raised in the Sahitya Sahabash, would definitely have been a better Kambli. But he never would have become a Sachin. Sachin is God's gift.

>> PROFESSOR SUBHASH BHENDE,
Sachin's neighbour

36. If I were to pick one Hindi movie that represents Tendulkar, it will be *Mughal-e-Azam*. Majestic, classical, impeccable.

>> DILIP VENGSARKAR

37. No Bollywood biggie would be able to write a script for him. That's for sure. Why? God can't be described in a screenplay ...

>> MITHUN CHAKRABORTY

38. There are some special players who light up a cricket ground. They make it much more beautiful than it actually is. And when they leave, the same grounds suddenly look so empty, so colourless. It happened with Sunil Gavaskar. It happened with Viv Richards. It happened with Imran Khan. I am afraid once Sachin retires, cricket grounds all over the world will similarly look deserted.

>> ABDUL QADIR

39. Now we, the ex-trainees under him, realize why Achrekar Sir got the Dronacharya. He had spotted the Arjuna so very correctly in a crowd.

>> MANGESH ADHATRAO,
Sachin's senior trainee at the Achrekar School

40. The story of myself and Sachin has always been the story of the staircase and the elevator. But I must admit, he worked extremely hard inside that elevator. At times he had to use the staircase because of injuries. But to his credit, he quickly recovered.

>> VINOD KAMBLI

41. Before he played for India, Sachin was sharing a room with our Mumbai coach J. Kamath for one of our away Ranji matches. Midway through the night, he got up and started taking singles, while speaking in Marathi, 'Come, come.' He also started knocking. The coach was so stunned he couldn't sleep well for the rest of the night.

>> KIRAN MOKASHI

42. I have batted with Sachin on a few occasions and always felt a little uncomfortable. The very thought that Tendulkar is with you at the other end is enough to make you feel nervous. And then the scary thought: what happens if I run him out. The crowd will kill me!

>> AJIT AGARKAR

43. To Arjun, I will say, when you grow up, you try to be the best that you can be. You don't get bogged down by people's expectations that you are Sachin Tendulkar's son and must play in a certain way.

>> ROHAN GAVASKAR

44. Gilchrist in one test match missed two catches, appeared half a yard slower and then immediately decided to quit. Sachin is like that. I can bet my life that he will not overstay his welcome. He is the sort who is capable of doing a brutally frank self-analysis.

>> ATUL KASBEKAR

45. I get extremely moved every time Sachin gets a hundred and then looks skywards. He acknowledges the fact that an unknown source may have ushered him into this world. He himself doesn't know the source but thanks the process. So in his greatest moment of triumph the man surrenders completely to the force up there.

>> MAHESH BHATT

46. Even in the restaurant business which supposedly is outside his territory, Sachin is very clear about what he wants. Never general but very specific. He has this thought process of not taking short cuts and doing things strictly by the book.

>> SANJAY NARANG,
Tendulkar's business partner in his restaurant project

47. He doesn't only have control over his mind but also the body which is amazing. During the double hundred he scored in Sydney, I was with him at the other end. Sachin didn't play the cover drive even once as he was getting out playing that shot earlier in the series. I told myself: Wow!

>> VVS LAXMAN

48. He must have been a king in his previous birth. In the dressing room and outside, we see a lot of king-like qualities in him.

>> RAMESH MANE,
masseur, Indian Cricket Team

49. My favourite Tendulkar story is that in his very first series itself I could identify the top talent. I lost no time in going up to him and reminding him: 'Boy, one day you will become the biggest star in World Cricket. Then don't forget your first ever captain, one Krishnamachari Srikanth.' Even today I remind him of that.

>> KRISHNAMACHARI SRIKANTH

50. I have very limited knowledge of cricket. Even less about the cricketers. But as a performer, Sachin inspires me hugely. Aamir Khan from films and Sachin from cricket – they are my favourites. In between people said so many things about Sachin. What did he do? Said nothing. His bat spoke for him. So graceful. I want to be like that.

>> VIDYA BALAN

51. Exceptional talent. He has 2/3 strokes for every delivery! That armed with discipline all the way.

>> ANIL KUMBLE

52. From observing Sachin Tendulkar minutely you not only learn how to become a better and successful cricketer. But also learn how to be a good human being. How to greet a groundsman or a tea boy with as much warmth as you do a big man. We youngsters in the team look up to him as a living educational institution.

>> SURESH RAINA

53. Looking at Tendulkar in a wider spectrum, I feel there can be little doubt that he is the nearest thing the world has seen to Don Bradman since the supreme Australian put his bat away.

>> DAVID FRITH,
Former Editor, *Wisden Cricket Monthly*

54. Have seen quite a few sportspersons all over the world. What is unique about Sachin is that he has performed magnificiently for more than two decades despite the enormous pressure of being under the scanner of millions of countrymen who expect so much out of him.

>> SANIA MIRZA

55. The triple hundred will happen. Don't worry. He is not retiring tomorrow. In any case I want him to play till the time I retire.

>> VIRENDER SEHWAG

56. Sachin's appetite does amaze me. I was mentally finished with cricket the day I retired. Not for a moment did I want to come back. They are playing so much cricket now. Still to retain that boy-like enthusiasm for cricket after having played for twenty-two long years is mind-blowing.

>> SUNIL GAVASKAR

57. There are few players I will pay money to go and watch. But the Little Master is a batsman for whom I would happily part with my cash at the turnstiles. When Tendulkar is in full flow, it is a privilege to watch him.

>> IAN BOTHAM

58. Medical science can't explain Sachin's genius. From the outside it appears that he is ruled by a creative ego. The type that prefers determination, struggle and fight to reach the top. The type that hates taking short cuts.

>> DR SUKUMAR MUKHERJEE

59. Sachin's genius is also backed by very strong family ethics. When he was beginning to get famous, his late father had advised him: 'Even if you get a very lucrative offer, don't ever advertise for cigarettes or alcohol.' What is remarkable is that till today, he adheres to this. Sachin still doesn't do such ads and refuses offers which run into crores and crores.

>> ATUL RANADE,
childhood friend

60. I won't jump out of the window and say: Hey, Sachin is next to Bradman. In my World Eleven, Sachin will be there. But I may not put him at Number 4. At the same time, I must admit, Sachin has handled greater expectations than Bradman over a longer period of time.

>> GREG CHAPPELL

If wishes were horses ...

If he was sent on a Kashmir peace delegation ...

Had he played without a helmet ...

Had he preceeded Gavaskar ...

Had Jardine employed Bodyline against him ...

Had he played the four West Indian fast bowlers ...

HAD JARDINE EMPLOYED BODYLINE AGAINST HIM ...
||||||||||||||||||||||||||||||||||||||||||||||||||||||||||||||||||||||||||||

a) Run scoring would have been very difficult. With that sort of line of attack and the field placing that was permitted then. If you can keep five to six fielders on the leg and bowl continuously fast on the ribs, it is almost impossible to get a good score. Even someone as brilliant as Sachin would have struggled.

>> **Javagal Srinath**

b) Hasn't he faced Bodyline in his career? Didn't Wasim Akram and the fearsome Pakistanis try to give him some pounding in his maiden series? In Perth on his first ever Australian tour, didn't they come hard at the teenager. He, of course, now has more protection than Bradman ever had. But then Tendulkar is such a sharp cricket brain armed with enormous talent that he would've found a solution to Bodyline.

>> **Peter Roebuck**

c) Had he been facing Larwood and Voce and since we are entering the realms of fantasy, I would speculate that helmeted and well padded, Sachin might have averaged 50.

>> **David Frith**

HAD HE FACED THE BALL OF THE CENTURY ...
||||||||||||||||||||||||||||||||||||||||||||||||||||||||||||||||||||||||||||

a) He would have paddle-swept the delivery for a boundary.

>> **Harbajhan Singh**

b) Difficult to say. He may have got out. He may have defended. Don't forget Warne too, was a great bowler.

>> **Anil Kumble**

c) It would have gone for a boundary. He would have swept Warne. Sachin is so good on his legs.

>> **Virender Sehwag**

HAD HE MADE HIS TEST DEBUT TODAY ARMED WITH THREE SEASONS OF IPL MONEY ...
||||||||||||||||||||||||||||||||||||||||||||||||||||||||||||

a) He wouldn't have changed one bit. The man has got character. If a man has character, circumstances do not necessarily change him.

>> **T N Seshan**

b) Don't worry. He would be the same. God made him to play cricket.

>> **Mahendra Singh Dhoni**

c) Oh! Even if he had begun today, early fame and money wouldn't have distracted him. Tendulkar, as I have known him, would have remained the same. His roots are very strong. Always remember that.

>> **Ratnakar Shetty,**
Senior Indian Cricket Board official

HAD HE PLAYED WITHOUT AN HELMET ...
||||||||||||||||||||||

a) Why should anyone think along this line! Cricketers of my generation grew up with helmets. If you have technology available, the modern generation will obviously use that. Some day you might even suggest using the pad-gloves from the 1930s as Bradman had to play with them.

>> **Rahul Dravid**

b) I don't think a helmet helps to the extent people would like to believe. On the contrary, with a helmet you are a fraction of second late. This always plays at the back of your mind that even if you get hit, you will be saved. Since we started wearing helmets, more and more people have been getting hit on the head.

>> **Dilip Vengsarkar**

c) I see nothing wrong in that. Bradman told me if a helmet had been available during his playing years, he would have worn it.

>> **David Frith**

HAD HE PRECEEDED GAVASKAR ...
||||||||||||||||||||||||||||||||||||||||||||||||||||||||||||||||

a) Roles would have got completely reversed. Gavaskar would have been more flamboyant. Sachin would have been defensive. They are both products of the Maharastrian Brahminical milieu which decided on the cultural mindset.

>> **Pritish Nandy**

b) Then Gavaskar would have played like Sachin. Sachin would have played like Gavaskar. Sachin today carries no baggage. His liberated India has a nuclear bomb. Is trying to become a member of the UN Security Council. Gavaskar was a post-colonial warrior. He had a point to prove that Indians were not scared of anything – be it brown, blue, black, white. His was a generation which was tormented and troubled by history and that shaped Gavaskar's cricket.

>> **Peter Roebuck**

c) I think if I was born in 1973 I would have played differently. I was brought up in an India which was troubled. Which had not seen a billionaire. I was brought up in a cricketing environment which suggested if you lift the ball above six inches from the ground, it would be sacrilege. I was part of a generation which had the prime minister of the country appealing to its citizens to forego one meal a day due to a severe crisis of foodgrains ...

>> **Sunil Gavaskar**

HAD HE PLAYED THE FOUR WEST INDIAN FAST BOWLERS ...

a) You required guts and a solid technique to score against them. Sachin has both. And don't forget it was not as if you were facing four of them together. You only played one bowler at a time.

>> **Mohinder Amarnath**

b) I don't think he would have found it difficult. He would have tuned himself accordingly. Don't forget he is your finest ever player.

>> **Kapil Dev**

c) The four fast bowlers would have tested him for sure. But Sachin would have survived well. As he has a temperament to match his technique. And then he also has the special ability to change gears.

>> **Ravi Shastri**

IF HE WAS SENT ON A KASHMIR PEACE DELEGATION …

||||||||||||||||||||||||||||||||||||||||||||||||||||||||||||||||||||||||||||||

a) Oh! Politics is a different game altogether. There are too many layers. Too many variables and surprises. Far too many to handle.

>> **Sunil Gavaskar**

b) On a goodwill mission to Pakistan he will receive a hero's welcome. But Kashmir, I am afraid, is different. Kashmir is far too complicated an issue. A geopolitical matter where Tendulkar's personal charisma is unlikely to help.

>> **General Shankar Roy Chowdhury**

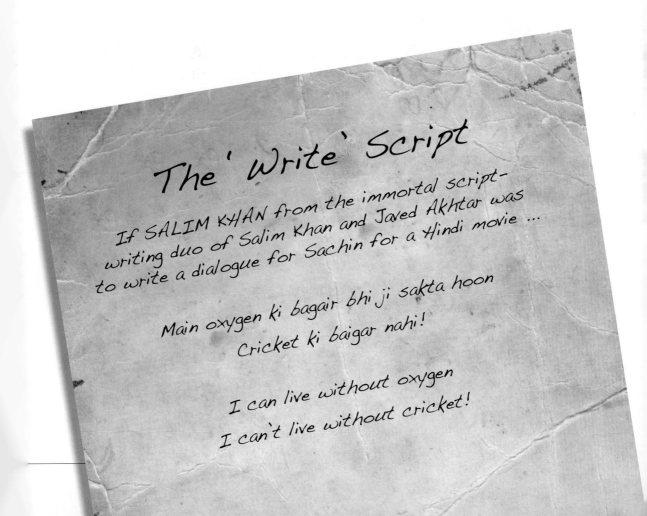

The 'Write' Script

If SALIM KHAN from the immortal script-writing duo of Salim Khan and Javed Akhtar was to write a dialogue for Sachin for a Hindi movie …

Main oxygen ki bagair bhi ji sakta hoon
Cricket ki baigar nahi!

I can live without oxygen
I can't live without cricket!

||||||||||||||||||||||||||||||||||||||||||||||||||||||||||||||||||||||||||||||||||||||||||||||||||||||||||

CHAPTER 1

MERE PAAS SACHIN HAI!

||||||||||||||||||||||||||||||||||||||||||||||||||||||||||||||||||||||||||||||||||||||||||||||||||||||||||

Poor Joginder Sharma! He had absolutely no clue that someone could play such a cruel joke on him. Joginder was driving down to Chandigarh when the Twitter joke was narrated to him over the phone. The former Indian cricketer whose claim to fame was the fateful last over in the T-20 World Cup Final, got completely flabbergasted. He decided to park the car somewhere. Made two immediate return calls to Kolkata. To a person, with whom he was having a conversation for the first time in life. But he had to make those calls. This was something serious and required urgent attention!

Well, the joke that he was subjected to, goes like this:

JOGINDER: 'Mere paas T20 World Cup winners medal hai, IPL Champion ka certificate hai, Champions League winner Trophy hai.
Sachin, tumhare paas kya hai?'

Now it is Sachin Tendulkar's turn to answer and his matter-of-fact reply is:
'Mere paas cricket hai ...'

Joginder initially seemed rattled with the joke. But recovered fast enough to clear the initial lump in his throat. 'Aap likhiye ga yeh script galat hai. This script is faulty. Joginder Sharma may have won a few medals. But what is that in front of someone who has won cricket itself. Usne cricket ko jit liya.'

|||||||| Shoaib claps; Sachin rejoices

Obviously the Twitter joke is a straight take from the Amitabh Bachchan blockbuster of the 1970s – *Deewaar*. The famous confrontation scene between the brothers where the affluent law-breaker son, a prodigal at that, mocks at his middle-class, law-abiding police officer brother, 'Brother, I have got everything: bungalow, money, bank balance … everything … what have you got?'

And then the brother takes the wind out of his sails with one simple sentence – 'Mere paas Ma hai.' ('I have got Mother.') In the Indian ethos, a mother is as important as the motherland. And both are considered superior to heaven. In Indian cricketing parlance, Sachin is the Universal Mother – spotless, sitting on a pedestal and considered to have supernatural healing powers through his cricket.

Mahendra Singh Dhoni and Zaheer Khan – two heavyweight cricketers of the Indian team, openly maintain: SACHIN IS THE GOD OF CRICKET. Incidentally, both weigh their words carefully and are never given to hyperbole.

Ajit Agarkar, one of Sachin's closest friends, openly admits that every time he is in a partnership with Sachin, he gets scared. Notwithstanding the fact that he has a Lord's hundred to his credit, Agarkar gets butterflies in his stomach wondering – while running singles, what would happen if he runs his partner out! Of course he can gauge what would happen. 'The crowd would simply kill me,' he says with fear after spending more than ten years in international cricket.

Virender Sehwag, easily the most sensational player of the cricketing world in the last ten years, almost worships Tendulkar.

Once while batting during an Indo-Pak Test, the Delhi batsman got into an argument with Shoaib Akthar. Shoaib was hurling bouncers at him and Sehwag was letting them go. Towards the end of the over, Shoaib made a taunting remark, 'Can't you hook?' To which Sehwag replied, 'If you have guts, why don't you dare to tease the non-striker? Is it because he is your father that you don't attempt any such thing with him?'

This retort met with a fiery fast bowler's traditional response. An angry Shoaib immediately sent down a bouncer at the non-striker's throat in the very next over. The non-striker in question was obviously Sachin Tendulkar. He gladly accepted the bait by hooking the delivery for a six.

In Indian cricketing parlance, Sachin is the Universal Mother – spotless, sitting on a pedestal and considered to have supernatural healing powers through his cricket.

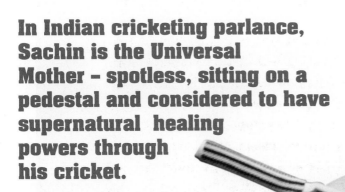

|||||| Autograph signing session

At the end of the over, Sehwag confronted Shoaib, 'Now you know why a father always remains a father. And why a son always remains a son.'

While giving an interview for this book Sehwag was asked, which particular shot of Sachin would he like to have in his armoury. If you, fellow readers, thought he would say 'Sachin's trademark straight drive', you are way off the mark. With all sincerity Sehwag said that he wanted to possess all of Sachin's shots. And then added, 'I want him to play upto the day I play my last.' He was certainly not playing to the gallery or play-acting! In Sehwag and so many others, Sachin evokes such natural reactions. In fact, not just the big stars, even the juniors can't get enough of him. He is their universal *Sachinpaaji*.

And when the masseur of the Indian team, Ramesh Mane, says, 'Sachin must have been a king in his previous birth. He has distinctive king-like qualities,' you don't look at him twice because you realize where he is coming from. Last year a Bengali book of mine released on Tendulkar immediately found its way into the Indian team's dressing room library. Some inspirational books apparently move with the team wherever it goes. Now, in the post-Ganguly phase, none of the members have been able to read this book. It's in Bengali. But there are pictures inside of their dearest Sachinpaaji and then – the cover.

That alone is enough for inspiration!

Merely proclaiming that the cricketer Tendulkar is a phenomenon, a once-in-a-century happening, is so dull. Been said to death. Today the reality is that the man *himself* has become an outstanding phenomenon. Not just through his cricketing deeds as a superstar but because of what he is as a person and a life-saving device! Sachin is a fragrance that has seeped into the very soul of India, allowing it to sleep peacefully, happy in the confidence that he will not let them down.

Forget cricketers. They are from the same profession and are expected to show respect to the Market Leader. It's about people from other walks of life – those who are non-cricketers! Chetan Bhagat, whose best-selling book *Five Point Someone* inspired the Aamir Khan-starrer *Three Idiots* on celluloid is *bowled over* by him despite not being a cricket lover. In an e-mail interview, Chetan Bhagat stated: 'Sachin is definitely a Rancho-type character who did his own thing and yet

|||||||| At the Wagah border

excelled in it.' The author opines, 'Sachin can jolly well give a lecture to the IIT students on sustaining effort, focus and most important, humility.'

Dr Devi Shetty, one of the busiest heart surgeons in the country reflects, 'Sachin's identity as a symbol of humanity and achievements makes us relate to him as everything that is good in the "Indian" character.'

Sushmita Sen, former Miss Universe, goes ga-ga everytime you mention Tendulkar to her. 'Somehow his very presence adds a tinge of nationalism. You start seeing an Indian flag and begin to get goose bumps.'

Salim Khan, one of the joint-creators of the famous 'Mere paas Ma hai' film script gets ecstatic every time the image of Tendulkar with a bat flashes on his TV screen. Salim, who once played with C K Nayudu's brother in Indore and is otherwise a long-standing CK devotee, compares the cricketers of the previous generation with the big stars of Bollywood. He compares Vinod Kambli with Rajesh Khanna. Even though I feel the comparison is controversial, Salim does not seem to look burdened with the possible after-effects of his findings.

'Both were blessed with tremendous talent. But couldn't overcome their mental barriers,' he says.

He moves on to the next comparison. This is for the real achievers. 'Let's talk of Sachin and CK. The difference is that CK threw anger all around the bowlers at the nets. Sachin shows the same anger in match situations. He treats the bowlers mercilessly.'

|||||||| Sachin is the living symbol of the movie Three Idiots.

'Sachin is definitely a Rancho-type character who did his own thing and yet excelled in it.'

Chetan Bhagat

Salim ends with a definitive statement: 'Sachin is the undisputed angry young man of Indian cricket and from the film industry there is just one parallel – Dilip Kumar.

In India, Sachin's persona invites opinions across the country. And by and large, most share a common admiration for him. Surely a rarity amongst public figures!

From a tea boy to the Ambanis ... from a plumber to an auto-rickshaw driver ... from a senior airforce officer to a Bollywood actress ... they all have their own image of him. Sachin is de facto India's Macbeth, Arjun, Napoleon, Gandhi – all rolled into one!

He has a designated fan, one Sudhir Gautam from Bihar, who travels extensively with the team all over the country provided Sachin plays.

During matches you can see him anointing himself in the colours of the national flag and painting the jersey number 10 which is the Cricket God's own number. He doesn't have the means to support himself. So the players, including Sachin, have ensured during the last eight years that at least his railway and bus tickets are taken care of. Players also give him tickets to watch the matches. He is known in all the cricket stadia across the country. And at the gate, often instead of frisking him, policemen seem more interested in hearing stories about Sachin from him.

Has team sports ever invited such a euphoric reaction in a spectator? That too for eight long years? But then such is the power of Sachinmania in India!

The film industry grapevine claims that Asha Bhosle and Lata Mangeshkar, the two legendary sisters, have disagreed on 999 points from the start of their journey in Bollywood. They have, however, agreed consistently on one point and raised the same demand: to award Sachin the Bharat Ratna. That remains, arguably, one meeting point between them!

A few months ago, Asha Bhosle was in Kolkata performing Rabindra Sangeet in front of a packed Science City Auditorium. It was a rare day as Asha was finding

|||||||| With Lata Mangeshkar and Shah Rukh Khan

it difficult to find her rhythm. She clearly seemed to be struggling with some of her lines. Little did the audience know that she had still not recovered from the Bombay fever and was physically not fit yet. But after the break, it was a different Asha who faced the audience. She began with a very diffcult Rabindra Sangeet number *Esho Shyamalo Sundaro* ... The minute she sang the first few lines, the hall reverberated with applause which continued almost non-stop. This was the vintage Asha Bhosle. But what led to this transformation? Ashatai, as she is known in close circles, explained the next day over a cup of tea. 'I told myself: You need to perform. You need to sing better whatever the constraints are. And then I thought about people who motivate me. One of them is Sachin. He has an inspiring effect on me. Whenever he gets a hundred or hits a sixer, I feel very inspired. I tell myself if he can do it so perfectly on a cricketing field for twenty-two long years, why can't I do the same with my singing!'

To put it differently ... Tendulkar is the picture perfect Indian hero who incidentally plays cricket!

Years ago, Adidas ran an advertising campaign on Sachin which was unthinkable for any other Indian sportsperson. It still is.

When Sachin plays, big city roads are easy and trains and buses ply empty at rush hour and the markets take a beating.

When Sachin plays, busy, ambitious executives ignore their calls, and cancel their appointments, and avoid their clients, and miss their deadlines and put their careers on hold.

When Sachin plays, school yards are silent and playgrounds are deserted because those who normally make such a racket imitating their hero are all too busy watching him make batting look so ridiculously easy.

When Sachin plays, bowlers and fielders and opposing captains feel their incompetence and inadequacy like at no other time and curse themselves and wonder what they can do if anything to end the shame, the nightmare, the humiliation.

When Sachin plays, India forgets its differences and divisions and teeters between tension and exhilaration, and breathes and laughs and cries as one, as its heart fills with pride and joy and patriotism ...
When Sachin plays, all else is irrelevant ...

The campaign was obviously overhyped, overdramatic, over the top! But the central theme – that Sachin is the greatest 'impact individual' in this country – is not exaggerated. If Sachin reacts to an issue, if Sachin raises his voice, Kashmir to Jhumritalaiah reacts. Kanyakumari to Srinagar empathizes.

He is India's hero, the peoples' chosen one. Hamare Paas Sachin Hai.

In 1996, when Madhuri Dixit was at the height of her popularity, and the World Cup was taking place, Pakistanis were often heard saying, tongue-in-cheek, 'Madhuri do, Kashmir le lo!'

I was asked by the editor of an ABP group film magazine to take the views of Pakistani cricketers on this. I ran into Saeed Anwar and Aamir Sohail, the most destructive opening combine of Pakistan at the time. To make matters simple, both turned out to be film buffs. They, incidentally, were part of the joint Asian Eleven which had played a few weeks ago in Colombo. Despite the onslaught of the World

||||||| 'I will play fair and
square and smile ...'

Cup, both seemed to have still not recovered from the hangover of that particular match and one particular individual, as I was to realize a little later.

Instead of answering my question, they threw another poser at me (in jest of course!):

Sachin ke saath pehli baar khela
Oof, kya player hai
Aap log us ko de do
Kashmir le lo!

Take Kashmir! Give Sachin!

The poor film glossy editor! The next day, the story made prominent news on the Sports page! And Ms Dixit was put on hold!!!

All the more does one realize:
Sirf India ke paas Sachin hai.
Only India has Sachin.

|||||||| A very young Tendulkar (seated extreme right) with possibly the first team trophy that he was part of.

|||||||||||||||||||||||||||||||||||||||||||||||||||||||||||||||||||||||||||||||||||||||||||||||||||

CHAPTER 2

GANAPATI BAPPA MORIYA

|||||||||||||||||||||||||||||||||||||||||||||||||||||||||||||||||||||||||||||||||||||||||||||||||||

Mangesh Adhatrao is a tough, stockily built man. And the first impression he creates is that of a man who may have missed his profession.

Adhatrao may well have made it to the Mumbai soccer team, had he not instead tried his luck at the highest level of cricket. Fate took him only up to the Under-22 level and Club matches in Mumbai. Yet he will always be a part of the great Indian cricketing folklore as it is to him that the distinction of intentionally running out a teenaged Sachin Tendulkar goes!

If you think what he did was blasphemy, you have not heard enough. The primary and only reason was that Adhatrao the Captain didn't have enough confidence in Tendulkar's batting skills. As the team was chasing a stiff target which was threatening to climb up even further, the best option was to run the pencil-thin number three batsman out and then try and win the match.

What happened subsequently, according to onlookers, was that Adhatrao, the striker, called Sachin for a single that was non-existent and then sent him back.

||||||| Sanjay Manjrekar was once Sachin's friend and philosopher.

The young boy cried all the way back to the pavilion and even after the match, the tears didn't stop. Sitting in front of me in a roadside cafe in Bandra, frequented by the local cricketers, Adhatrao can still recollect, 'Woh bahut der tak roh raha tha.' ('He kept on crying for a long time.')

Twenty-six years have passed by since then. But the picture of a sobbing Tendulkar has still not been erased from the memory of the participating players and is now part of a legend. This was at the Khar Gymkhana. The year – 1985. India had just won The World Championship of cricket. And Ravi Shastri – his Audi. Cricket fever was running high in the country. The teams were battling it out for the Govardhan Das Trophy which hardly offered anything in comparison to the country's noteworthy cricket tournaments. But such is the tradition of Mumbai cricket that whatever be the standard, there is no lack of intensity. So you can't fault the captain for trying to win at any cost. And the opponents were no pushovers either. In their ranks they had a former India pacer, Ajit Pai.

After a fruitful first-wicket partnership was broken, the twelve-year-old, number three batsman emerged from the pavilion. The Captain, all of twenty-two years, and more importantly, on a roll, was hardly impressed. He had no confidence in Sachin but had to send him in at number three as he was part of a coach-driven system. The coach was the Ferguson in local cricket. He decided everything – from the time of declaration to batting orders. One Mr Ramakant Achrekar, whose dictate was very clear: 'This young boy will play every match and go at number three.' No one dared to change the all-powerful coach's order but within that framework, could always try and manipulate the coach's stricture.

Today, of course, this sweet, innocent incident of yesteryears assumes an altogether different perspective. Today Sachin is a batting legend comparable only to Bradman. So Adhatrao slightly fine-tunes his story by saying, 'Sachin could not run fast and that was why he got run out that day. He is now faster at thirty-seven plus.' But the local cricketing fraternity remembers the actual story. So does Sachin who, incidentally, has an elephantine memory about game situations, bowlers, his manner of dismissal.

'Who did you face in the very first over, the day you made the debut for CCI, in Kanga league?'

Pat came the reply: 'Sharad Rao.'

'What did you do with the delivery?' I asked Sachin, as the former Karnataka bowler had presented a different version to what I had heard from the then CCI Captain.

'Oh, first ball sixer over mid-off,' Sachin said, remembering the day as clearly as if it had happened the day before.

Mind you, remembering this was much more difficult than the final Adhatrao episode. The ending had as much an unreal touch as a masala Hindi movie. After winning the match, the Captain went to meet the coach with the trophy. In return all he got was a slap for running out the coach's favourite disciple intentionally.

|||||| Just being one of the boys!

Apparently the conversation between them went like this:

'What is this nonsense? You ran him out like that. You should have carried him with you,' Achrekar fumed. Whether the slap preceded this or came after the comment was not properly recorded!

But the startled team captain defended his case by saying, 'Sir, we have just won a trophy and you are still blaming me.'

Today, of course, he has only praise for his former coach. 'That is why they gave him the Dronacharya award. He could spot the Arjuna amongst all his trainees.'

While writing this book, I often asked myself if it was possible for a Sachin to have risen from Delhi! The hard Mumbai cricketing culture, the opportunity of hobnobbing with the India stars, the fight, the passion, the intensity – possibly shaped him all the more. But as you delve deeper into the Tendulkar story, you would think that a more pertinent question would be: Would a Tendulkar have been possible minus Achrekar?

Someone blessed with the kind of extraordinary talent and humility supposedly would have anyway conquered all grounds. Notwithstanding that, Achrekar should

|||||| Dronacharya and his Arjun

get the credit that he ensured the full flowering of a talent at such an early age. That he went beyond the boundaries of the age-old cricketing manual. Nine coaches out of ten would have changed the strong bottom-handed grip of Sachin. Erapally Prasanna still believes that because of Sachin's 'faulty grip' as a quality spinner, he would have fancied his chances of having him caught more times than a Gavaskar or a Vijay Manjrekar. Not many share Prasanna's optimism though. They think that Sachin's genius would have found a way out. But even they are convinced this was hardly the ideal cricket grip.

Today at most cricket coaching camps, this grip is in fashion. But way back in 1983, in Merchant's Mumbai, someone with the vision of not trying to disturb an unorthodox style was sensational. And then Achrekar's emphasis on match play! He instructed his trainees to play more and more if they were enjoying it. If they were not, he advised them to stop playing altogether. This was his mantra and the distinguished students all knew of this. It is against this ethos of training that a Vinod Kambli says very confidently, 'Sachin will surely retire the day he stops enjoying cricket. We Achrekarites were all taught that and took it to our hearts.'

|||||||| With Kambli — his childhood buddy

Emphasis on match play went to such an extent that on one given day, Sachin was playing three innings on three different wickets in three different parts of the city. Achrekar ferried him on his scooter. The coach's commitment was such that once, after attending the funeral of his new-born baby, he came straight to Matunga Gymkhana and began his usual routine.

Sachin was always his favourite pupil and possibly only once did he get a firing from Achrekar. This was when he and Kambli defied their Guru's instruction to declare in the Inter-School Harris Shield Semi-Final and carried on batting. The match was at the Azad Maidan against Sunil Gavaskar's former school, St Xavier's. The pair made a world record by notching up a 664-run partnership which subsequently, went on to create even higher run scores. Sairaj Bahutule, the Xavier's Captain who later went on to share the same Indian dressing room with

Sachin, recollects, 'They were just batting at will. Mind you, not slogging. Majority of the shots were good hits from the centre of the bat. Some of my team members were so demoralised that they didn't want to field.'

Kambli apparently gave a chance but got away. He remained not out on 349, Sachin – an unbeaten 326. Bahutule smilingly recalled that the Principal didn't chide him or any of the team members. Maybe because by then Tendulkar and Kambli were formidable names in school cricket and even principals knew that.

Around the same time the hugely traditional CCI relaxed its rules to accomodate Sachin as a playing member. Hemant Kenkre, who was leading the team in the absence of Sandip Patil, had been talking about this teenager for quite some time. Kenkre, a first cousin of Gavaskar, had once carried the master's leg guards to the teenaged sensation. But what made Kenkre's brief strong was that his Club President himself got a first-hand feel of the teenager's talent. This was at the Shivaji Park Gymkhana where the hosts, Shivaji Park Youngsters, took on CCI led by former Indian test opener Madhav Apte. Apte, a highly respected man in Mumbai's cricketing and business circles, was standing at slips when Sachin came out to bat. From his wicket keeper's position, Kenkre signalled that that was the boy! The wicket was terrible – in local parlance, an *akhara* track. Sachin missed a few shots and at the end of the over, while they were crossing over, Apte advised the youngster not to push but wait for the ball to come to him. The result was immediate. At the very next delivery he hit the off-spinner for a straight six. Scored a brilliant sixty-odd which stunned Apte. In all his years of watching and playing cricket, Apte had not seen anything like this from a thirteen-year-old. He reacted promptly by immediately convening a Committee meeting to pass a resolution allowing the fourteen-year-old a membership. Apte, who had the opportunity of opening with the great Vijay Merchant, told me, that he views Merchant, Gavaskar and Sachin on the same level. He explains it thus: 'To quote Cardus, they can commit an error of judgement. But never an error of grammar.'

Incidentally, my first meeting and an interview with Tendulkar took place in front of the CCI dressing room. There was a statutory restriction though laid down by the team manager Milind Rege. He had made it very clear that since Sachin would be going out to bat shortly, his picture could not be taken at that time. So the world's most photographed cricketer's picture could not be taken along with the interview. The interviewee spoke softly. So softly that I thought that the next time I interviewed him, I should bring along a pair of hearing aids.

By sheer chance, I had come to know of Sachin being there a little earlier than anyone else in Kolkata. I still remember the Sea Green Hotel on Marine Drive, where two of us Kolkata-based journalists were lamenting the farewell of the biggest superstars in world cricket – Imran Khan and Sunil Gavaskar. Imran's Pakistan had been knocked out the previous day in the World Cup Semi-Final at the Gaddafi. And the day we spoke, on 5 November 1987, Gavaskar played his last ever international match. That Imran would take back his retirement was obviously not known then. Sanjib Banerjee from The *Telegraph*, who is now a sitting judge in the Calcutta High Court, and I were lamenting that the game had lost its charm with the exit of two of its most colourful ambassadors.

This was when Makrand Waingankar, easily the most cricket-passionate journalist I have ever come across, brought up Tendulkar's name. He explained that there was no reason to despair. Whatever Makrand said about this new boy was enough to give me a single column item for the next day's sports page – a page which, following India's exit from the World Cup, was beginning to look like an obituary column. Now, at least, a window of hope, if not cheer, had opened.

The benchmark, of course, was Gavaskar. He was considered the ultimate. And my report began by saying that this new batsman had the makings of a Gavaskar. He seemed to possess the same appetite for runs. His average in the previous year's Harris Shield had been 1028. However, the next day's *Ananda Bazar Patrika* reported the average as 128. The sub-editor at the sports desk was so convinced that I had made a mistake following the Cup depression, that he corrected the copy

|||||||| First time ever in Australia, with a bang!

'Sachin under my captaincy ... Really ... he went in as a substitute, I never knew about this.'

Imran Khan

without even speaking to me. That incident however, signified the pattern in which Tendulkar's cricket was to unfold for the next quarter of a century.

He was perhaps destined to prove people wrong at all stages of his cricket.

While interviewing him, little did I know that the boy-wonder had served an hour's apprenticeship under the great Imran. This was during an exhibition match which the visiting Pakistanis had played in the mid-1980s at the CCI. They took on the CCI Eleven which comprised quite a few senior Indian cricketers, including Azharuddin. During the last hour of this CCI Golden Jubilee match, two of the touring cricketers went off the field. Some local players had been arranged beforehand as stand-by fielders. Out of that stock Sachin and a contemporary of his were sent in as substitutes. Come to think of it, this was the first real taste of big-time cricket for Tendulkar. His captain was Imran. He was playing for Pakistan.

No one, of course, knew of Sachin then. As was his usual routine after the match, Sachin returned home on the local train. His fellow traveller was an umpire called Marcus Kouto. Kouto remembers the train ride quite fondly as during the journey, Sachin kept on cribbing about his captain's field placings. Apparently Imran had placed him very deep in the field and because of that,

|||||| Sachin with his first unofficial captain – Imran Khan

||||||| With his first official captain – Krishnamachari Srikanth

he missed taking a catch of Kapil Dev in the outfield. How could a hungry achiever like him come to terms with non-performance! When this incident was narrated to Imran, he laughed un-controllably. First there was absolute surprise: 'Under my captaincy, Sachin ... really ... he went in as a substitute? I never knew about this.' When I told him that Sachin had confirmed this himself, Imran kept silent. One of the greatest spotters of cricketing talent was perhaps wondering how destiny had let him miss that one!

Twenty-eight months from that day, the scenario changed dramatically.

It was the turn of the man he had substituted at the Brabourne Stadium, Abdul Qadir, to grumble. It was not so much the Waqar Younis incident at Sialkot where Sachin stood up to brutal pace despite getting hit on the nose, that had convinced the then Indian superstars like Kapil about his competence. Sialkot had registered his bravery. Peshawar talked about his class. It was after the Peshawar game that the Indian captain Krishnamachari Srikanth, now the Chairman of Selectors, told Sachin in full public view, 'Bachcha, one day you will become very, very big. That day don't forget your first captain, K Srikanth.'

Srikanth today reminisces that the first meeting he had had with Sachin in New Delhi had impressed him very much. In those days Tendulkar's selection at such an early age did raise eyebrows. Not that his class was in doubt but the

'Bachcha, one day you will become very very big. That day don't forget your first captain, K Srikanth.'

K Srikanth

jury was divided as to whether it was prudent enough to expose him to the lethal Pak pace battery in Pakistan. The fact that Mohinder Amarnath was ignored for reasons other than cricket, and Vengsarkar himself had opted out from the tour, had helped the selection. Vengsarkar, sitting today in his plush chamber at the Mumbai Cricket Association office, still feels that it was a gamble that worked. But left to him, even today he may have waited for the Pakistan tour to be over. Incidentally, as the records suggest, Vengsarkar is one of India's most successful Chairmen of Selectors.

So, in hindsight, it required a maverick Chief Selector named Raj Singh Dungarpur to take such a gamble with Sachin.

Srikanth, however, thought the selection was only natural and very logical. For the youngster who had scored hundreds in all three of his maiden outings – Irani, Duleep and Ranji – had to be there. The Irani hundred had a sweet backroom story associated with it, like most of Sachin's heroic knocks, though in this case, it was someone else who played the pivotal role – a cricketer-turned-coach, Gursharan Singh. Gursharan had broken his right hand while batting in the first innings for the Rest of India. In the second innings, while Tendulkar was batting on 88, the innings collapsed. This was when Raj Singh requested him to go out, play with one hand and help Sachin get the hundred. Kirti Azad and Maninder Singh were bowling. Gursharan negotiated them with his left hand and helped Sachin complete his hundred. Sachin was so touched that till today he remains grateful. Not only did he appear for Gursharan's benefit match but also

||||||| Those days, Sachin looked up to Dilip Vengsarkar

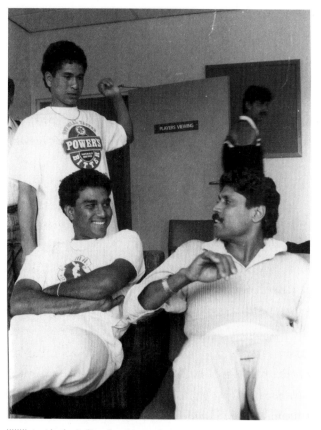

||||||| Inside the Indian dressing room

sent him a lovely message when the former wished Sachin on his completion of twenty years in international cricket. Sachin's message was somewhat like this: 'I still remember what you did for me at the very beginning.'

Pakistan, of course, presented such a huge challenge where no quarters were asked for none were given. Pakistan had prepared such a green top at Karachi that the great Qadir had been reduced to a Roger Harper, who during the reign of four fast bowlers, had hardly been given a decent number of overs. Karachi not only saw the debutant Tendulkar but also recorded one of the fastest ever spells in Indo-Pak cricket by a certain Wasim Akram. Sitting at the Karachi press box, which was then a fair distance from the ground, one was really worried about the safety of Sachin and his team members. Akram was at his fiery best during the series and initiated an incident which was as funny as it could get.

During the series, Imran was the first to notice that Sidhu and Manjrekar were often fighting with each other at the middle of the wicket. One felt that the other was tactically avoiding a single off Imran's fifth or sixth ball so that he would not have to play Akram. A beaming Imran announced, 'Both wanted to play me as by that time I had almost become a medium pacer. And both wanted to avoid Wasim.' The complete breakdown stage arrived when, during the third test, an angry Manjrekar told Sidhu, 'Before leaving the country I didn't sign a contract with the Board that only I was going to play Akram. Call the Captain and let him decide.' Sitting in the dressing room, Srikanth had to intervene before Manjrekar took his guard again.

This incident illustrates the backdrop against which Tendulkar played his maiden international series. The eleven who were to play in his maiden Test Match included Raman Lamba but not Azhar. However, Lamba ruled himself unfit on the eve of the test, prompting a senior Delhi-based journalist to write that Lamba had developed cold feet at the thought of taking on Pakistan's pace battery. Lamba was furious. He took on the journalist face to face and shouted at him. On the second day of the Test Match, where Sachin batted in test cricket for the first time, the dressing room was filled with Lamba stories rather than Sachin's debut. The team was also discussing the vital Shastri-Kapil partnership which had seen India out of the woods. Manoj Prabhakar became an exponent of reverse swing in this series and reportedly shared some secrets with Kapil who was to become an enemy in the years to come. There were allegations from the Pakistani dressing room about Prabhakar's alleged suspect action which had turned on the heat further. Manjrekar was, of course, the star of the series. He also sang melodious Pankaj Udhas numbers, thereby coming across as a complete package. And Sachin, in the midst of all these, remained like the loving youngest son, adored and protected by his captain. But not someone who was supposed to do the breadwinning bit for his cricketing family during a crisis.

Peshawar saw him assuming that mantle for the first time. Kapil Dev and Imran were not the best of friends in those days. But both admitted that Peshawar changed their opinion about Tendulkar completely. For some strange reason, Salim Malik was declared the Man of the Match but the unannounced critics' choice went to Sachin. Twenty-one years later, Imran was to remark, 'Of course I was teasing and egging on Qadir, whom I rate as great as Warne. Viv agrees with me on that. The difference was in those days umpires didn't give the batsman out if the flipper struck on the front foot. So Qadir was extremely unlucky and he suffered. If you take away all the flipper dismissals of Warne, one-third of his tally goes. And so to hit the same Qadir for towering sixes, I was amazed.'

Srikanth was batting with Sachin at the other end. When Sachin hit Qadir for two sixes, Srikanth went and told him, 'Relax. Take it easy'. But Sachin was

|||||||| Abdul Qadir: the one who conceded those 4 sixes!

hardly listening. He told his Captain, 'Don't worry, I will handle Qadir.'

Since it was unofficial, this match doesn't find a place in cricket history. But in Indian cricketing folklore, this is read in the very first chapter. Qadir's recollection goes like this:

'I had bowled a maiden over to Srikkanth. So while the batsmen were changing ends, I went across to Sachin and tried engaging him in a challenge. I told him to take the challenge. "Try to hit me." I don't think I would have done this if it was an official match. But also admit that Sachin played brilliantly. I got him bowled in the Lahore test match a few days ago. But here he was unstoppable. If you look at my career I have not conceded too many sixes. So years later when Sachin dominated Shane Warne to such an extent, I was least surprised.'

So many versions of this epic episode are now in circulation that it is difficult to get an accurate account of who said what to whom at the crease. All one remembers is that Qadir showed a lot of grace after such a beating. Despite one sixer breaking the windowpane of the Indian dressing room, the great sport that Qadir was, he told the visiting media, 'One day, this boy will become as big as Viv!'

Surprising that it was, even after such a knock, the teenager did not speak out publicly at all. But a few days after the match, once he was back in his hometown, he gave details of the exchange to his childhood friend Vinod Kambli. 'You know what! Qadir was teasing me – "Bachcha, tum dudh piyo. (Child, you drink your milk!)" So I decided to give him the milk bottle!' Both laughed uncontrollably.

So did Indian cricket. Ganapati's favourite son had arrived at the batting crease to look after Indian cricket. As the devotees say at the Ganapati immersion, 'Ganapati Bappa Moriya.' ('Ganapati, please come back next year.') Cricket devotees were to say the same for perhaps the next quarter of a century: Sachin, please don't leave us permanently. We would feel unsafe!

|||||||| (left): Packing his bags before the first ever international tour, (right): With Ravi Shastri — someone with whom he shares a deep, long-standing relationship

CHAPTER 3

THE CRICKET GOD'S ORIGINAL RESIDENCE

ahitya Sahawas is actually like a tiny little hamlet positioned in the shade, miles away from the crowded thoroughfares, from the din and rat race of urban Mumbai. There is so much greenery all around that it seems as though an invisible fencing has carefully kept modern civilization at bay. This part of East Bandra has also miraculously managed to keep some amount of pollution away. In terms of per square feet price, there is no comparison between Bandra East and the swanky Bandra West where Sachin now lives. The cross over from the East to the West symbolizes a shift from a middle-class milieu to the land of the rich and the famous. Almost like the old Virgina Slims ad which, after a successful crossover, announces, 'You have come a long way baby!' What if the baby had begun at the destination rather than at the starting point?

On entering Sahitya Sahawas Enclave, I was immediately reminded of a famous Tagore poem, *Two Acres of Land*.

The little hamlets resting in deep silent shades as havens of peace ...

My mind somehow wondered along those lines as I stood in front of 'Ushakal'– Tendulkar's first official residence. The first thing that came to mind was that, of course, he had to have been raised in a place like this to conduct himself in the humble, yet dignified manner that he did. Anywhere else, armed with that kind of talent, he may have still been a great player. But the human qualities that make him an exemplary package may not have developed outside the walls of Ushakal.

On the way to his house you have to pass Kalanagar on the right. This township for artists and performers was built on plots of land distributed to them by the Government of Maharashtra. At the further end of this road is Patrakar Colony, earmarked for journalists. Sahitya Sahawas is sandwiched between the two, to accommodate people associated with literature. Like Ramesh Tendulkar was. A teacher of Marathi literature at Kirti College who was awarded gold medals for his performances at the BA and MA examinations of the University of Maharashtra. Ramesh also wrote Marathi poetry and took part in literary discussions.

Out of his so many poems there is just one he has written in English. It was on his youngest son, written months before he died in 1999.

|||||||| Trademark Sachin shots

Perhaps may be because of you
But cricket to me
Dear Sachin is no more a game
But a poem
A lyrical poem –

Intensity, concentration, spontaneity
Moods and tensions and form ...
Rhythm and movement and composition
And flashes of imagination and talent ...
When the strokes go across
To the boundary
Of all the things, that string of
Uncertainty hanging all the time
Making moment of every movement –
A creative moment
And a challenge
What else can all this be
If not a lyric on the playground?
Hence this vocabulary
Rushing up to me
As I sit down, Dear Sachin,
To describe your game.

||||||| Ramesh Tendulkar's only poem on Sachin

|||||||| 'Team Tendulkar': (left to right) His mother, Nitin, Ajit, Savita, Sachin and his late father

When Sachin was building his own house, he wanted to have a special room in it for his father. A room with a writing table, book shelves, pens, writing pads … everything that Ramesh might need. But Ramesh Tendulkar died in his fifth floor apartment at Sahitya Sahawas in May 1999, long before the house could come up. Sachin moved to his new home only in 2002.

'My blood goes cold when I think of that day his father died. Sachin and his brothers were abroad at the time. Sachin was playing the World Cup in England, Nitin was in Chicago and Ajit in Paris. Their mother called me on the phone and asked me to come immediately,' reminisces Ramesh Pardhe, Sachin's childhood friend, now his secretary and an important member of Team Tendulkar.

'Uncle (Sachin's father) had had an angioplasty. The doctor had reassured Sachin that Uncle would be fine and he could go to England for the World Cup without any worry. But Uncle's illness suddenly took a bad turn. It was all over soon after I reached their home that night. A neighbourhood doctor tried to revive him by massaging his chest but it was already too late. We didn't even get the time to take him to a hospital. Soon it was there on television. Resulting in crowds … media … complete chaos,' Ramesh went on.

The moment Senior Tendulkar's death sequence and the drama started getting discussed, my mind was swinging back and forth to a cloudy afternoon in Bristol. Sachin Tendulkar sporting a stubble – looking miserable, yet determined, alighting from the team bus a day before.

India played Kenya in their World Cup Group League match. Twelve long years separate that incident from the present. Yet onlookers would feel as if it had happened twelve minutes ago! It was the kind of fairytale that you posssibly witness only once in your lifetime. And then keep on asking yourself for the rest of your life: Did you actually witness it? Or was it all an illusion?

Tendulkar alighted from the team bus first. And it still gives me goose bumps to write what he said. 'Mother has sent me back. She said, "Father would have loved to see you fighting for your country. Not mourning at home." ' Sachin suddenly started resembling a soldier who had to pack his bags despite an untimely death in the family. And now he had to guard the border.

The transformation from a cricketer to a soldier was completed twenty-four hours later. While India was struggling at 92 for 2, Sachin went out to bat. By this time, the press box was sure that the entire Sahitya Sahawas gang must have gathered in front of the TV to see their Tendla battling during his mourning period.

Asif Qarim was the left arm bowler he faced up to. He is the type of bowler who forces you to ask 'Asif who'? Again, as Rohan Gavaskar points out, the tragedy with his father and Sachin was the same: they couldn't afford to take even a Mickey Mouse bowler lightly. By doing so, if they gave their wicket away, the innocuous bowler would be credited with the story of a lifetime and instantly would earn a name for himself. There in Bristol, it was worse. Apart from the usual pressure of living up to his reputation, there were surreal factors involved too. And unreal that it was, Asif Qarim had silly points stationed for the first two deliveries against Sachin. Some observers made notes then itself that Qarim already had enough *masala* for his grandchildren.

As his partner Rahul Dravid was to confess years later, 'I didn't sense any pain in him while we were at the crease. He didn't give the slightest hint that he was emotionally troubled. And considering the state he was in, I found that remarkable.' The duo registered a third wicket World Cup Record. India won its maiden Group League Match.

But then, just about everything – the applause and the thrill – faded away before the sight of Tendulkar who, after completing his hundred, looked towards the heavens. His gaze continued for the longest possible time. Looking around in the Press Box, all one could see was moist eyes. I had enormous difficulty controlling my tears and beyond a point, just gave in.

In those pre-9/11 and match-fixing days, it was not very difficult to meet a cricketer during the break. I remember walking up to Sachin after lunch and enquiring what Rajani Tendulkar had said when he called home.

'Why call her now? The match is still not over.' Tendulkar gave me a look which was somewhere between being polite and stern! Of course I got the message. Only the first battle had just been won. Not the war!

|||||||| He gets the Bristol 100 and looks skywards in search of his father

Before that was achieved, why would a soldier call home?

The next day I got a call from the Chief Editor which, during a tournament, was the most unlikely thing to happen. He had a query. He wanted to know if, while writing the match report, I had been influenced by Cardus at some stage. Of course I had not.

There was so much material available to tap there itself that there was no need to look anywhere else for it. But the last paragraph that I wrote and which began: 'Beginning to think whether it was all dreamt on a midsummer's night ...' was similar. Of course it had seemed like a dream and it was mid-summer! I can still visualize the magical cricket Tendulkar displayed that day under such trying circumstances. It was so sensational that, for a short time, even the average cricket writer's mindset leapt to the formidable heights of the great Nevile Cardus.

'I didn't sense any pain in him while we were at the crease. He didn't give the slightest hint that he was emotionally troubled. And considering the state he was in, I found that remarkable.'

Rahul Dravid

I think that is what Sachin has done repeatedly during his career. Ever so often he lifts the journalist's pen-pushing spirits to such an extent, that the latter soars along with him. And in certain places like Bristol and at Centurion, while he demolished Pakistan, the take-offs were such that while he mingled with the stars of the solar system, those of us reporting on the same were hovering around the clouds!

While I was talking to Pardhe, a BMW pulled up by our side. There was a bearded man in the driver's seat. It was Ajit Tendulkar, whom I had been trying to get on the phone for long without success. Ajit is as reluctant to speak to the media as Sachin is to allow a cricket ball to go through his defence. But that day, Ajit was strangely voluble. He was ready to bathe in the nostalgia of his youth.

' ... The swing that you see over there, that used to serve as our Jungle Jim. I'm afraid the slide here doesn't work anymore. This is where that childhood

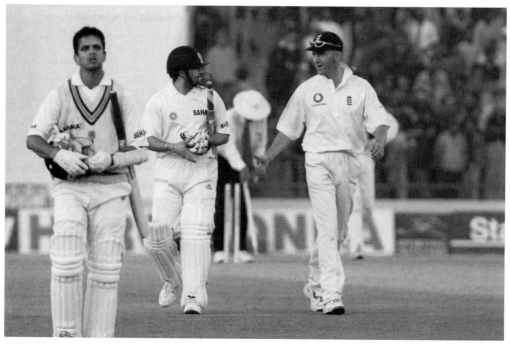

|||||||| With Rahul Dravid, his partner in many games

photograph of a wrong-side-up Sachin was taken. There was a mango tree over here, which was cut down. Cricket matches were often played near the colony gate. You must have noticed the bank there. Sachin would regularly break the glass panes of the windows. When the employees came in the morning, they would find shards of glass lying everywhere.'

If the remains of the broken windows were still there, perhaps a museum in Australia or England would have bought them at a premium! Anything associated with Sachin's past could surely have been a part of the Bradman museum.

But where is the field where the modern-day Bradman learnt his cricket? I was told that the 30ft/30ft patch of land partially covered with grass that lay ahead of me was 'the field'!

An old resident of the colony told me how the boys used to roll and prepare cricket wickets there. I wondered how they managed to play on that tiny bit of land with so many trees all around. A cricketer like Ishant Sharma would not even have space for his run-up there. It would have also been impossible to practise high catches.

For many children living in colonies and complexes like this, there is hardly any space to play. They have to restrict themselves to playing in whatever grounds and schools there are in their own locality. This is so common in India.

But it seems the seeds of Sachin's cricket up to the age of eleven were sown on that rugged little land mass. That was where Sahitya Sahawas felicitated its favourite *Tendla* after he returned from his 1989 tour of Pakistan. The residents of the colony had invited Gavaskar to hand over the memento to Sachin. Which he happily did.

Sachin was so attached to this little patch of land that he played there even after graduatiing to the level of a Test cricketer. Incredulous members of the media turned up to watch the spectacle and photographers took interesting pictures.

The neighbours had many interesting stories to relate about Tendulkar and his childhood exploits. I heard little of what they were saying. My mind had wandered to an obscure little town in Germany called Bruhl. I was ringing the front doorbell of a tiny house. The flat I wished to gain entry into was a pigeon hole of a two-bedroom apartment. Two tennis rackets and a stack of towels would have been enough to fill up its shabby interiors.

I wonder who lives there now but in the early part of the 1980s, a gentleman named Peter Graf and his family occupied it. During an exclusive chat I had with him in the early 1990s, the Senior Graf mentioned to me that he had put up a net in the bedroom so that his little girl could play tennis there. Whenever she hit the ball above the net five times in a row, she got an ice cream. The little girl soon began to get more ice creams than were good for her. Worried about her health, Peter kept raising the height of the net. This did little to stop the girl from achieving her goal. And sure enough, like any other exasperated parent would, Peter gave up the practice.

But ice cream or no ice cream, the girl went from strength to strength, honing her tennis skills, winning just about every tournament and proving the age-old theory that if you are good enough, you can shine splendidly without any solid financial backing. Steffi and Sachin – even if they don't know each other personally – somewhere deep down there is a similarity in their success pattern.

Just as the East Bandra colony reminded me of that personal experience in Germany, the trip to Bruhl had stoked memories of a debate one had with Chuni

|||||| The Steffi Graf story is somewhat similar to Sachin's

Goswami, the Indian ex-soccer star, at Kolkata's South Club.

The year was 1988. The Wimbledon Ladies Singles Final was being played between Martina Navratilova and Peter Graf's daughter. Goswami and I were watching it together at the club. After the first set, it looked as though Martina was slated for yet another victory. But Goswami kept repeating, 'You never know.' Steffi was tailing Martina till the second set.

I remarked, 'Steffi doesn't stand a chance. She is not getting her forehand drive right from the Left Court under such pressure.' Which afficianado of tennis didn't know that in the absence of the lethal Steffi drive, Martina was invincible!

It was exactly at this point that Steffi seemed to say to herself, 'Buck up, girl. Enough is enough.' She started playing some incredible shots and went on to win the championship. While dropping me home that night, Goswami said, 'Do you know why your match analysis was flawed? You are used to looking at sportsmen from the Third World. You understand their psychology and know how they might react to certain situations. But Steffi is First World. She got her forehand right when she needed it because she is free from the usual Third World inferiority complex which cracks under extreme pressure.'

I nodded and told myself that I would remember the lesson for the rest of my journalistic life. After having seen the original Graf residence, I revised the lesson.

The visit to Bruhl took place in 1997. There were no cell phones in India then. If there had been, I'd have dialled a Kolkata number straightaway. I would have said. 'Your nine-year-old analysis was completely wrong. You should have come to Bruhl. Steffi was nothing but Third World. I have seen her home which is a typical lower middle-class home in that country. Her father was the lone breadwinner in the family – an insurance agent who drove a second-hand car. But that didn't stop those bullet-like forehand drives that night. You know why? Because champions do not follow the beaten road. They are born winners. Things like circumstances and facilities are totally irrelevant in their scheme of things. They win because they are born to win. Period.'

That day at Sahitya Sahawas I kept on constantly cursing myself for not having visited Sachin's colony earlier. I had been writing about him and following his career chart for over two decades. Yet, had missed out on the one vital path that had been the start of it all – the missing link that

|||||||| Steffi's original residence in Bruhl – an average middle-class German residence

bespeaks the root of Sachin's genius! Surely all that is said about the requirement of the right environment, sports medicine, governmental support and sponsorship is only for the mediocre, the talented and the near-great. A champion does not need such support. Like Steffi or Sachin. A genius is born, not made.

Sahitya Sahawas is full of Marathi litterateurs. Growing up in 'Ushakal', Sachin had seen his neighbour Vinda Karandikar, a Marathi poet, win the Gyanpith Award. He saw the Maharashtra Government felicitate writer Arvind Gokhale, who lived a few floors below them. The media also came to interview the author Vijaya Rajadhyaksha who lived in another building within the same complex. The writer Subhash Bhende, Head of the Economics Department in Kirti College, was also a neighbour. I asked Bhende a simple question.

If Kambli had been raised in the same complex as Sachin, would he have become a Sachin?

Bhende took half a minute before answering. 'You know what,' he said, 'Kambli would surely have become a better Kambli. But becoming Sachin is out of question.'

Of course, none of these men have had the sort of international fame that Sachin has enjoyed. None of them is even a national icon. But they are highly successful people in their own fields, and have earned enormous respect in Marathi society. Their stature and unassuming ways have taught Sachin a thing or two about humility.

One of his teachers narrated an incident that took place while Sachin was studying in school. For promotion from the 11th to the 12th standard, as per the dictates of the Board, Sachin needed 75% attendance. He had, by such time, toured Pakistan, New Zealand and England with the senior team. He had been away for so long and, predictably, didn't have the required attendance. The Board informed the school that Sachin could not be promoted as the rule stated clearly that even if a student played the Ranji Trophy as a school cricketer, he still needed to have the necessary attendance.

Sachin's school authorities argued that he had not played for the Ranji Trophy but for India. There was no mention of that in the rules. Finally the rule was amended for Sachin. As a test cricketer he was given a special sanction to directly appear for the exam. Some of the teachers loved him so much that they recorded the lectures he had missed on an audio cassette and gave it to him. He was permitted to sit alone in front of the Principal's office and give his exams. One or two police security personnel provided him company for comfort. By such time, Tendulkar was already perceived to be national property. He was finally promoted to Class Twelve but that's where his formal education ended. Cricket consumed him completely and no one was complaining!

This, along with the influence of the father, has helped him to retain his balance despite the most outrageous demands on his time and attention – that too from the age of sixteen! While he was the Indian Coach, Greg Chappell had admitted that, at times, he used to get flabbergasted to see the kind of attention and respect Sachin enjoyed in India. 'Just a simple nod from him or a smile can change the mood of a person for an entire day,' Chappell observed in wonder.

Not many people would perhaps know how the after-effects of a Hindi movie gave Sachin a new direction in life. Strange as it may seem, in 1983, despite the

Bachchan wave ruling the country, the earlier generation of Tendulkars remained mesmerized with one Mr Dev Anand.

There was this Head of Department of Philosophy in Kirti College, M P Rege, who looked like Gregory Peck. And his colleague Ramesh Tendulkar was said to resemble Dev Anand from certain angles. Those were the pre-satelite TV days. Doordarshan still ruled the mind and hearts of people across the country. Be it the Vastraharan episode in B R Chopra's *Mahabharat* or the Sunday movie on Doordarshan, the channel enjoyed a monopolistic supremacy over the hearts of the Indian people.

And on one of those high TRP-filled Sundays, the movie *Guide* was being shown. Seeing that the entire family was glued to the TV, the errant boy in the family

||||||| The elusive Ajit Tendulkar with a trainee

|||||| The 'Achrekar Coaching School'

decided to raid the mango tree in front of the house along with his gang. Unfortunately, the tree was not strong enough and could not stand the assault of six boys. It crashed. 'Sunil, Avinash and I managed to save ourselves from falling. But Sachin and two others who were lower down, fell and hurt themselves badly. There was such a loud noise that everyone left the TV set to find out what had caused the explosion,' reminisces Ramesh Pardhe.

Ajit Tendulkar was most upset. His eleven-year-old brother was clearly getting out of hand and needed to be disciplined. He was always up to some kind of mischief – either up on a Jungle Gym or turning cartwheels on someone's jeep, or falling off trees. 'Can't take any more of this,' he said to himself and decided to take immediate protective measures. The next morning he landed up at a park a few kilometres away from his place and entrusted the younger one to the care of an elderly gentleman. 'He is hyperactive. Please look after him, Sir, and teach him some cricket,' Ajit was commonly believed to have said.

The venue was Shivaji Park and the gentleman – Ramakant Achrekar.

Little did Dev Anand know, sitting in his plush Juhu residence, how a silver jubilee hit movie of his was responsible for slamming the clapboard on the birth of another superstar!

Without the mango tree incident, the young boy may have still been Sachin. But you can't argue with certainty that he would have played for India at sixteen!

Even today cricket pilgrims visiting Sir Don Bradman's old house in Bowral check out the water tank where Sir Don had apparently given shape to his batting. He used a stump to negotiate a delivery thrown at the tank each time it rebounded on him. That is how the champion had sharpened his reflexes. Some say this unorthodox style of practising was the turning point in Don's career.

Armed with a camera, I ran quickly towards the mango tree that should logically assume as much immortality as the water tank in Bowral. There were several of them. Where was that particular mango tree? Ramesh, who narrowly escaped a fall that evening by holding on to the trunk of another tree, proceeded to inform me: 'It's not there any more. They cut the tree down soon after it fell.'

||||||| Here I come to steal your heart away!

|||||||||||||||||||||||||||||||||||||||||||||||||||||||||||||||||||||||||||||||||||||||||||||||

CHAPTER 4

GATA RAHE MERA DIL

|||||||||||||||||||||||||||||||||||||||||||||||||||||||||||||||||||||||||||||||||||||||||||||||

The protagonist of this song could never have guessed this one! That a landmark movie of *his* career would have also brought about such a significant change in the Indian cricket skyline! He was pleasantly surprised when the connection was explained to him. It took quite sometime for the legendary actor to actually believe that this was so.

Dev Anand did express profound happiness when it finally registered that in a subtle way he had played an important role in shaping Sachin Tendulkar's life. I told him that some of Sachin's close friends often jokingly said that *Guide* became the guiding light in Tendulkar's life. It ushered him towards an eternal journey of excellence. Dev Sahib broke into a hearty laugh over the phone and wondered how, during the few times that he had met Sachin and his family, no one had ever brought it up. 'Must mention this next time to them, when we meet,' he chuckled. Unmistakably the voice sounded happier.

The veteran movie star, now in his late 80s, is especially acclaimed for his *joie de vivre* and phenomenal energy. Generations have grown up watching and admiring the same. Even someone as respected and acclaimed as Asha Bhosle admits openly, 'Dev Saab is my idol. He never puts on weight. Doesn't fall. Doesn't show any sign of age. Yet he is so dignified.'

Sachin is no exception. He grew up in a house which made no bones about being a committed part of the Dev Anand captive audience. And in an unconscious way he had enlisted himself as well. Sachin has never made a secret of the fact that despite advancing years, Dev Anand's energy continues to inspire him.

And in Sachin, Dev finds the same admirable commitment to constantly unearth energy and preserve it carefully. He said, 'Everytime Sachin gets a hundred, he looks skywards and salutes the unknown force. That is energy.'

Dev Anand admirers cut across all cross-sections of the Tendulkar family – from Ramesh Tendulkar to Ajit, his elder brother Nitin and finally Sachin. In his heyday, Dev had formed a superhit combination with music director Sachin Dev Burman. And it was after the late music director that Ajit Tendulkar decided to name his baby-faced younger brother.

Little did he know that the inspiration of the music director's brilliance would indirectly flow into his baby brother, even though in another direction. And a time would come in future when music directors across the length and breadth of the country would be inspired by the same brother!

Shantanu Maitra, for one, does not stop at merely admiring Sachin, but thinks of him as his Dronacharya. It does not matter that without even meeting Sachin once, Shantanu has, on his own, assumed the role of an Eklavya, who, faced with a crisis, silently derived inspiration from his guru. 'I was shell-shocked when I didn't win the National Award for the Best Music Director despite our *Antaheen* team walking away with so many awards. Then after a day or so, I thought how Sachin would have handled the same disappointment. I told myself, he wouldn't have complained. He wouldn't have blamed external factors. He would have looked internally to find and correct his own faults if there were any. He would have answered through his performance. I decided to do the same.'

Mahesh Bhatt, the noted film director, often talks about accidental circumstances in life. Bhatt opines that without such defining coincidences, no person, however brilliant he or she may be, can succeed in life. Was the fall from the tree such an accidental circumstance? Or was that too minor? Would Tendulkar have become a Tendulkar with or without the fall? So many have said that he was destined to succeed and things just happened in his life as if they were all pre-arranged. We will never know the answer.

But in all fairness it should be said that the starting point was similar to the manner in which he would begin his innings. He wasn't a star son whose father had already come to an arrangement with a producer. Tendulkar's single-generation journey, like other self-made men before him, the likes of a Dhirubhai Ambani included, began with a big zero. The situation was such that every skirmish had to be faced. Every battle had to be won. Every challenge had to be met.

And he has done all that with remarkable resolve. His own city-based newspaper had questioned his fitness through provocative headlines. The biggest national daily had 'gifted' him with the front page headline 'Endulkar'. His own Wankhede crowd had barracked him. His own ex-superstar colleagues raised doubts as to whether he was still good enough to win matches for India. And he has handled all that with dignity and every time there has been a tirade, has invariably bounced back.

His life reads somewhat like a film script. In that, one self-made multimillionaire of India plays for another self-made billionaire's team – Mumbai Indians – at the IPL; but then, in Dhirubani Ambani and Sachin Tendulkar, you have two incredible MADE IN INDIA success stories. Incidentally, in the Indian

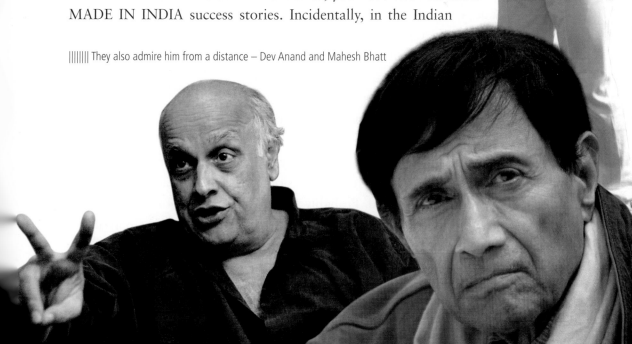

|||||||| They also admire him from a distance – Dev Anand and Mahesh Bhatt

|||||||| With Mumbai Indians and the 'Malkin' – Nita Ambani

dressing room, they refer to Sachin as the MASTER.

To go back in time a little, the Sachin journey began not so much with Sachin, as with his brother Ajit and his persuasive skills. Ajit tried to convince the local coaching fraternity about his eleven-year-old younger brother's outstanding talent. But Ajit's marketing skills were tested to the limits. On one occasion he met with a flat refusal. And even with Achrekar, he had to clear the initial doubts that the coach had.

As Ajit described the scenario later on, Achrekar was surrounded by a clutch of pupils and was clearly very busy.

When Ajit approached him, even without raising his eyes, he asked, 'How old is your brother?'

'Eleven,' replied Ajit, who hadn't brought his brother along. 'Only eleven!'

'Has he ever played with a proper cricket ball?'

That made Ajit nervous. What if the coach refused to coach his brother?

He was obviously a busy man who had every reason to turn down a fresher.

'Sir, he has never played with a deuce ball but I can assure you that he will manage fine.'

'Ok. But does he bowl or bat?'

'He bats and also bowls fast,' said Ajit. Those days, Sachin had a penchant for fast bowling too.

'Ok then. Bring your brother here tomorrow. Let him observe the practice session on the first day. The day after, he can do nets,' said the coach.

And that's how it happened. Probably for the first and last time in his life, a fully fit Sachin Ramesh Tendulkar just sat and watched while others played. He was not allowed to practise on his first day with Achrekar. On the way back, young

|||||| Sachin 'overseas' has been more successful

Sachin kept complaining to his brother, 'I can play better than all those boys. Still I wasn't allowed to hold the bat.'

He had, however, been called for high catching towards the end of practice. Achrekar's assistant, Shivalkar, was holding the session. Ajit was worried that his little brother would fail. He had neither played with a proper cricket ball before nor was he used to high catching.

The ground at Sahitya Sahawas was too small and full of trees for that kind of catching practice. But the youngster was okay. His coaches liked what they saw. It was time for net practice at seven o'clock the following morning.

Everybody at home wished him luck before he left. It was the beginning of a great cricket life, but Sachin had no proper clothes to wear! Dressed in a T-shirt and jeans, Sachin arrived at Shivaji Park with a bat his elder sister had brought him from Kashmir. On the way to Shivaji Park, Sachin kept bothering his brother, 'What do you think should be my approach? Should I hit out or be defensive?'

Ajit wasn't sure. For starters, he didn't know what kind of players Achrekar liked to have in his camp. A hard hitter may get dismissed from the team. But, playing with a rubber ball, Sachin had almost deleted the word 'defence' from his game plan. He either pulled with a cross bat, or hit out as soon as the ball came on to him. Defence, for him, was a flick of the wrist.

Aggressive from the beginning, he was already a huge fan of the ever-aggressive John McEnroe. While most of his friends admired Borg, Sachin fell for McEnroe.

And it is ironical that for the next two-and-a-half decades, all across the globe, he would be a *Borg* and never ever a McEnroe. Sunil Gavaskar possibly pioneered the school of thought of never letting the fast bowlers know that you are wounded. Gavaskar said: 'If you convey to the opposition that the injury is hurting, then you are dead.' Sachin has taken it to another level. At times after he has been hit badly, he behaves so normally that an onlooker would think what he had seen a few minutes ago was perhaps an optical illusion.

It is easy to sit back today and proclaim that Sachin has evolved modern Indian batting. Young aspiring cricketers in satellite towns continue to draw inspiration from his aggressive attitude. They try to hit out like him. But in the Mumbai of 1985, aggressive cricket was an absolute No-No. The batsman's rulebook, written by Gavaskar, instructed him to save his wicket before initiating the attack. Breaking the rule would be as serious an offence as that of a recalcitrant member of the communist party going against its canon.

When he saw Sachin bat, Achrekar said nothing except that he had been selected and would be required to play a 50-over match the following morning. The camp was divided into two teams to play against each other. This was the first time Sachin would be playing a competitive match. His entire family was excited.

After Sachin returned, they heard that he had been out for zero. And so it was that Sachin's cricketing life began with a duck. He took to maintaining his own scorebook, recording his runs in it. 0. 51, 38, 45, 47 ... and so it went. A pleased Achrekar soon asked Sachin to come for practice in the afternoons as well.

Thus ended Sachin Tendulkar's childhood. He would no longer have fun the way other kids his age did. He even lost touch with his friends.

|||||||| The hour of triumph!

|||||| Bowler bowls; Sachin improvises

Every morning and evening of his life was dedicated to the sport. Two important decisions were taken in the next few months:
A) The distance from his Bandra home to Achrekar's camp was too much to negotiate everyday and so he started living with his uncle in Dadar.
B) He had to change schools. Achrekar wanted his gifted student to play for the school team that he was in charge of.

So far, Sachin had been going to New English School in his Sahitya Sahawas neighbourhood. Now he had to be put in the Shardashram Vidya Mandir which offered a much more improved environment for cricket.

Many other families would have been loath to change the child's school. They would have insisted that he played cricket at Achrekar's but continued in his old school, where his father Ramesh had been a gold medalist. It is rare for a middle-class family to pin its faith on the talent of an eleven-year-old, believing that his future lay in cricket and not in the pursuit of education. It was while collecting information for *Sach* that I realized why Sachin always says, 'My father was far more successful than I am.'

A brief meeting was organized in the Tendulkar household to decide on Sachin's future. Sachin was asked what he wanted to do. His brothers half expected Sachin to relieve them of the responsibility of taking a decision on the matter by saying, 'I cannot play for the school after such strenuous practice sessions all day. That would leave me with no time to see my friends.'

But the eleven-year-old said nothing of the sort. 'I want to play cricket seriously. I'm sure I'll find time for my friends,' he declared. The family then focussed attention on procuring a cricket kit for him. It was not easy for the professor who ran a family of six — three sons and a daughter — on a meagre income, supplemented by that of his wife who was an insurance company clerk. Acquiring a kit with a good quality bat was not any less expensive than admitting a child to a medical or engineering college.

And then there was this huge difference between the two: The future in this case was as uncertain as that of a small dinghy fighting the vagaries of the sea. One doesn't usually make a one-dimensional investment in a boy who has just crossed his teens. No one in the Mumbai cricketing circles had ever done that – neither Gavaskar's family with its cricketing background, nor Sardesai's. Wadekar took up a cricket bat for the first time when he was in college. There hadn't been any cricketer in Sachin's family before him, unless you counted his grandfather Achyut Tendulkar's dalliance with the sport in the company of his friend, the district collector, while he lived in Alibagh. Subsequently the family moved away from Alibagh and thus the earlier generation's connect with cricket also went out of the window.

The three older children too, despite the usual enthusiasm for cricket, showed no great talent there either, though Ajit represented his college and was a dependable middle-order batsman.

Many years ago, Sachin's older sister Savita had opened an account with the State Bank of India because she wanted to lay her hands on the miniature bat with Wadekar's autograph on it that the bank was giving out to its customers. Sachin's brothers and sisters studied in Balmohan Vidya Mandir in Dadar, where

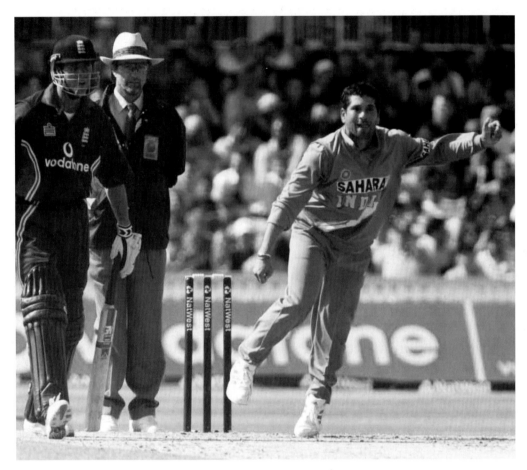

||||||| The bowler – Tendulkar

the blackboards displayed the scores of one of its cricketer students everyday: Sandip Patil. They watched in awe as Patil made his way through the crowds to go for practice.

Little did they know that in a few years' time, Sharadashram Vidyamandir in Dadar would display huge hoardings advertising the name and photograph of their youngest brother. They did not ever dream that some day their brother would have the duty of passing a verdict on Patil's retention as the Indian team coach!

They could not have known at that stage that Sachin, with his defective grip, would some day become the world's best. Even today most captains place a fielder in the short point or short extra cover region when Sachin is batting. Erapally

SACH

|||||||| The opponent is invariably on Cloud Nine when he gets out

Prasanna still claims he would have been far surer of getting Sachin out than he was of getting Gavaskar. 'I would have got him out trying to play the off drive,' says Prasanna. This is not mere bragging. The right hand grip so close to the handle is a sure recipe for a catch in the short extra cover region.

Thanks to Sachin's genius, he has been able to overcome this flaw, just as Bradman's footwork and reflex more than covered up for his unorthodox stance. Neither the Don's stance, nor Sachin's grip is classical. A lesser cricketer would never have been able to deal with such a shortcoming.

The interesting part is that today the bottom-handed grip is in fashion. If you go to any cricket coaching camp across the country, you will see the same grip in vogue. Through his performances, Sachin has now raised a debate as to whether the MCC Coaching Manual had overemphasized the importance of a classical grip!

But quite expectedly, at the beginning of his career, the loving elder brother would worry incessantly about this grip. It was Sachin's impishness as a child that had given birth to the flaw.

He would often steal Ajit's heavy bat — his eldest brother is 11 years older than him — and grip it close to the handle for balance while wielding it. By the time this trait was noticed, it had developed into a habit.

It was at this point that Sachin was excluded from a cricket team for the first and last time in his life. Not as a batsman but as a bowler.

In October 1986, Sachin had gone for a trial at Dennis Lillee's MRF camp in Chennai. He was still planning to be an attacking batsman and a fast bowler rolled into one. But as luck would have it, he failed in the trial. Sairaj Bahutule, his friend and cricketing colleague, still can't understand the logic. 'He used to bowl really well. Everything was so good. Why didn't they take him?' questions Bahutule.

Rejection embraced another medium pacer from Bengal. His name was Sourav Ganguly. Strange are the ways of destiny. Sourav and Sachin were roommates the night before the trial. They didn't know each other well and there was hardly any conversation between them that night.

'Both of us were disappointed. Lillee rejected us immediately after seeing us bowl. He advised us to try our hands at batting. He thought that way we would be better off. ' Ganguly looks back with amusement.

Two decades thereafter, these unsuccessful roommates were destined to open for the Indian One Day team for a period of six long years! Both also had a face-off with Lillee's close friend, Greg Chappell.

'Both of us were disappointed. Lillee rejected us immediately after seeing us bowl. He advised us to try our hands at batting. He thought that way we would be better off. '

Saurav Ganguly

Sourav was not half as depressed as Sachin at the elimination. Sachin had packed in his bat and pad on this trip to Chennai, with the hope that he would get a chance of some batting practice against the legendary Lillee. Plan B failed as well, with Lillee announcing unambiguously that he would only give batting practice to boys from Chennai.

A photograph of a miserable Sachin boarding the Mumbai-bound train would surely have great value today. No one knew back then that Chepauk would turn out to be India's greatest ever batsman's favourite hunting ground. No one knew that his masterly knock of 155

||||||| Dennis Lillee – the man who rejected the bowler Tendulkar

against Shane Warne would prompt the same Lillee to say, 'If I've to bowl to Sachin, I'll bowl with my helmet on. He hits the ball so hard. Thank God I have retired.' One wonders if Sachin has ever reminded Lillee of his rejection as a bowler.

It is in the nature of geniuses. Rejection breaks them only so that they can fight back. They change all equations, showing the world that they're made of sterner stuff than others. When Ajit Tendulkar sought Sachin's inclusion in the Under-19 trial, the authorities baulked at Sachin's youth.

'How old is he?' asked the coach.

'He's fourteen and a half. He's scored a lot of runs in school cricket. You may take a look at him,' replied Ajit.

But the coach was adamant. 'I can't do that. How can he play Under-19 at his age?' he said. As a result of the rejection, Sachin never played Under-19 cricket. At 15, he played for Mumbai and at 16, he was selected to play for India.

The Sourav-Sachin friendship finally began from the Indore National Camp. Sourav can still recall how after the end of the practice sessions, Sachin and Kambli still stayed put. They kept on practising with the tennis ball. For the other trainees at the camp, this was a revelation as they were too tired after the usual sessions.

Sourav's first ever international series was in 1992 in Australia. This is where he got his final confirmation about Tendulkar's genius. Sourav still can't forget the Perth hundred. He rates that as his former opening partner's best innings ever along with the One Day double hundred.

While being interviewed for the book, Sourav said something he had never said before. While talking about partnerships they shared on the crease he said, 'Sachin and I had a mutual agreement that we would not backbite about each other. We would not backstab each other. Only then would our understanding grow. Only then our on-field coordination would improve.'

I wondered when this particular MOU had been signed between the two greats of Indian Cricket! Or did the move become a necessity during Chappell's regime? The answer is possibly Yes, though a confirmation can't be expected on this controversial issue.

What were the fine little things Ganguly learnt from his batting genius friend while standing at the non-striker's end for so many years?

He lists six of them: Bat flow. Bat speed. Body positioning while playing strokes. Concentration. The art of relaxation between deliveries. Inner toughness.

Such a list is fairly telling in that it shows that even for a player of Sourav's calibre, there are so many things to fine tune and learn from Sachin. No wonder he is called the God of cricket inside the Indian dressing room.

Sachin's passion for cricket is just mind-blowing. Even the best of cricketers get consumed by cricket so much, that at some point of time, they start getting bored. Towards the end of his career, Sunil Gavaskar used to openly admit that post-tea, he would start looking at the clock.

During an Irani Trophy match in Nagpur, Gavaskar was requested to select the Man of the Year for the special supplement of Kolkata's *Telegraph*. We are

ANIL KUMBLE SETS A FIELD FOR HIS DEAR EX-COLLEAGUE

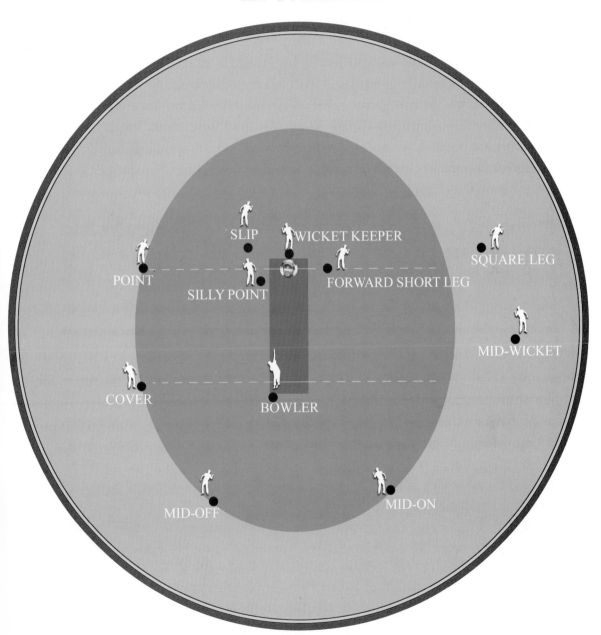

Situation: Team 20 for 2. Sachin arrives

talking about late 1985. He assured the correspondent around tea time that by the end of the day's play, he would have the name ready. But he was getting ready to go out into the field. 'How and when would he think?' the reporter wondered. Gavaskar smiled while replying, 'Don't worry. While standing at the slips I will think.' Clearly it was the voice of a man who found it hard to remain charged continuously in those days unless faced with top-class opposition.

Kapil Dev was another victim. There were several occasions when it seemed that he was not enjoying cricket at all. At times even victories meant little.

Sachin has never shown any such symptoms and that is astounding. Tomorrow if he agrees to come to your colony and play gullie cricket, even there he will look at scoring runs and winning. Gavaskar finds this quality of Sachin, 'absolutely

'Absolutely amazing. For twenty-two long years he has played so much cricket and yet to retain the youthful enthusiasm for the game is just unbelievable.'

Sunil Gavaskar

amazing. For twenty-two long years he has played so much cricket and yet to retain the youthful enthusiasm for the game is just unbelievable'. He rests his case.

Sachin's psychology, therefore, should be analysed alongside the stroke play. This would help in developing the temperaments of future Indian sportsmen. At the beginning of his career, his plumpness and cherubic good looks led people to tag him as a 'chocolate hero'. This was in the post-Bachchan age when chocolate heroes were making their mark in Bollywood.

Now that Sachin is moving towards the end of his career, who remembers the chocolate boy image? According to Salim Khan, he could well be called the 'angry young man. As with the bat he destroys.' Some call him the 'Concrete Hero'. He truly seems to be made from concrete.

Otherwise how do you explain his performances at the time of death of a close one? Geneticists believe that some people possess something in their genes called 'Tough gene'. Such people have better developed muscles. DNA tests have

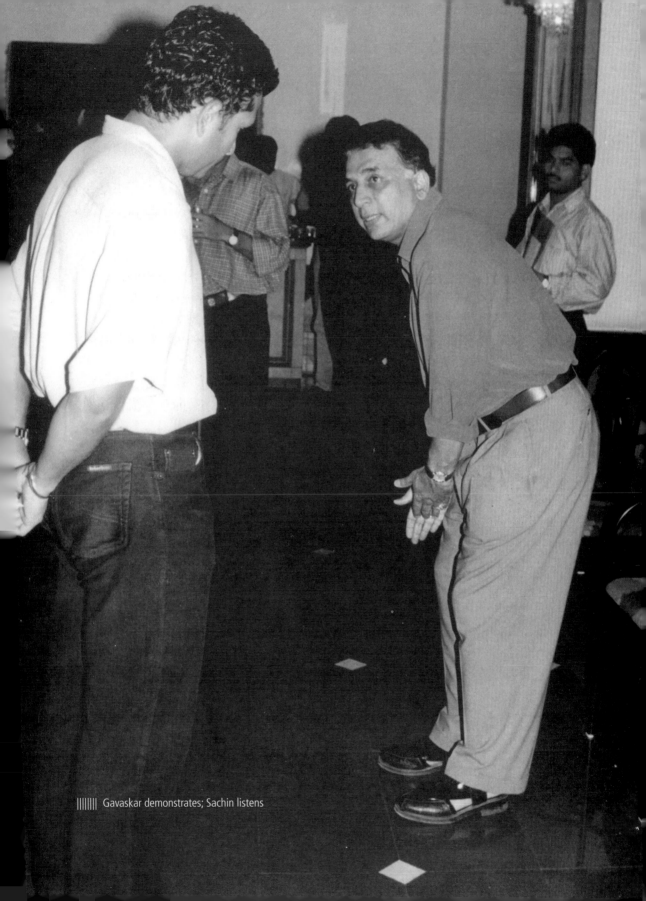

|||||||| Gavaskar demonstrates; Sachin listens

revealed that they have far greater endurance for physical and mental pressure. In the words of the famous physician from Kolkata, Dr Sukumar Mukherjee, 'There is no definition in medical science that would fit Sachin. Watching him from a distance has led me to believe that he has a creative ego. He is not reckless enough to try and win a match at whatever cost. He is someone who would rather win using his determination, perseverance and struggle. For him only winning matters. Nothing else. But he is the type who wants to win fair and square. He hates short cuts.'

This is 'Sach', though it seems like a fairy tale. If Sherlock Holmes was asked to investigate the phenomenon, he would perhaps have said, 'My dear Watson, a genius is what genius does. I cannot take up the case for the fear that it might make me miss the end of the Sachin show on TV, which will not be repeated. I would rather sit at my Baker Street residence and watch ESPN.'

|||||||| He is always involved!

||||||| The baton is passed
on to the next generation

|||||||||||||||||||||||||||||||||||||||||||||||||||||||||||||||||||||||||||||||||||||||||||||||||||

CHAPTER 5

SUNNY SETS, SACHIN RISES!

|||||||||||||||||||||||||||||||||||||||||||||||||||||||||||||||||||||||||||||||||||||||||||||||||||

Sachin Tendulkar:Born 1949.

Sunil Gavaskar: Born 1973.

What would have happened if the years of their birth were reversed by some strange turn of fate? The gentleman sitting next to me in that 15 x 15 feet corner room at the Nagpur Cricket Stadium was of the opinion that their roles might have got completely reversed. He felt, both were the 'societal expressions' of their times on the cricketing field. That is why their temperaments differed. While one was careful and defensive, the other seemed aggressive and liberated.

To put it simply, had Tendulkar, 24 years his junior, preceeded Gavaskar, in all probability, he would have played the same brand of cricket. And Gavaskar would have played like Tendulkar. As Pritish Nandy described in one simple sentence: Both were products of the Marathi Brahminical society that dictated the sporting expressions of their times.

||||||||| Those were the 'good old days'

||||||| These are the 'good new days'

Peter Roebuck analysed it most dispassionately and also provided some food for thought. Let's hear him out:

... Each post-colonial nation needs a post-colonial warrior. Gavaskar was that warrior. He had to prove a point through his cricket that Indians were not scared of fast bowling and by extended logic, not scared of anyone in this world. Brown. Blue. Black. White. His battle was to establish an identity for his nation. Even now he fights his battle. Notwithstanding that the battle has already been won!

Tendulkar's generation is not post colonial. It is neither tormented nor troubled by history. It is quite comfortable being East and the West at the same time. Tendulkar, through his cricket, embraces the modern and the ancient together. Tendulkar is at ease with the world. He is not fighting the world. There is no anger. No torment. No baggage in his approach. He is in his times has a nuclear bomb. Is aspiring to become a member of the UN Security Council. Tendulkar is an expression of the happy, liberated India ...

Meanwhile, the gentleman sitting next to me in the 15 x 15 room, was on a nostalgic plane. I travelled with him to the India of the 1950s – an unsure, uncertain country – about to lose the battle against poverty. His recollections were so real that this listener got somewhat moved. The main purpose of collecting the source material for this book went out of the window. It was like not just listening to a cricketer but embracing an era where an achiever – if he was an Indian – had to walk that extra mile to prove both his worth as well as the identity of a destabilized nation. I must admit here that I had no business getting emotional. But then, the Sunil Gavaskar story is an emotional story despite the obvious success quotient.

And more so if you were hearing it from the person himself in flesh and blood – GAVASKAR HIMSELF!

Q: Being born in 1973, do you think you would have played a different style of cricket?

SMG: I think I would have. If you are brought up in a generation which has seen only test cricket, if from your childhood you are told to play risk-free cricket, if you are warned never to lift a cricket ball six inches off the ground, then it becomes part of your upbringing.

These were the factors that shaped my cricket as I went along.

Q: Being born just two years into an independent India, you had this aversion towards the Whites. You took great pride in fighting them.

SMG: It could be that when India went overseas, you read all sorts of things in the foreign media. It was terribly one-sided with no adequate response from our side. It is an accomplishment of the British media that they have managed to project their institution as the best in the world. I didn't fight battles for anyone. I spoke for myself. I, personally, do not get sufficiently enamoured by Lords. I think Eden Gardens is the best cricket ground in this world. And I say it.

Q: The youth of the India of the 1970s got its self-belief from primarily two individuals. On the silver screen it was Amitabh Bachchan, who played the angry young man. On the cricket field it was you, who apart from scoring consistently, exploded every time you saw any injustice.

You were someone who had the courage to take on the mighty Board officials and still win. Did you watch the Bachchan movies in those days to keep your blood boiling all the more?

SMG: No. Of course I watched some of his films. I used to watch Marathi theatre as well. But I didn't see them to get angry. And I don't think anger was a very conscious part of my package.

Q: Please answer this simple question. Can Sachin be compared to Bradman?

SMG: We would never know. The cricket you display on the ground, your particular style is only a product of the times that you live in. On a subconscious level, that plays a very important role. So it is not fair to compare people from different eras. My mental make-up, for instance, was shaped by what I saw and encountered in my growing-up years. When I was growing up, India didn't have even one billionaire. I don't think we had a nuclear bomb then. There was so much poverty. We had a severe shortage of food grains. The then Prime Minister Lal Bahadur Shastri was compelled to appeal to people to forego one meal a day. We had a meeting at home about this. The family decided we would not forego a meal. But instead of having rice and chapattis for two different meals, we would only have chapattis for both. We would forego rice. Since then the habit has stayed on with me. Even today I eat chapattis for both meals.

This was the juncture which made me emotional. Sunil Manohar Gavaskar was almost saying: You wanted me to play and express the joy de vivre of a Sachin! But how could I? My generation of middle class couldn't afford to eat a decent rice-and-chapatti meal during a day. So to win I had to be extra watchful. I had to eliminate all the possible 'chance' factors. I had to play risk-free cricket as I was also playing in an ambience of a discontented, unsure nation simultaneously.

I must admit I had goose bumps sitting across the man inside the Nagpur Cricket Stadium. Mentally, I was transported to Shastri's India of 1965. I was imagining an evening meeting in a tiny household where a grim-faced elderly gentleman, after a meeting with his family, decided not to bring home rice anymore from the local grocery shop. Even the World Wars had not been so hard, he thought.

Gavaskar grew up in the heart of South Mumbai, in one of those simple middle-class localities – Chikalwadi. From there, against the backdrop of the severe economic crisis and gloom prevailing in his country, he fought his own battle. Gavaskar didn't have an Achrekar. Neither did he have a brother like Ajit Tendulkar. If Sachin is the story of a genius honed by a happy, protective family, Gavaskar was the champion who wrote his own dialogues.

Taking into account all forms of the game, Sachin assumes a bigger space. Perhaps, between the two, Sachin is more talented. The steadiness of his purpose is unprecedented not only in India but also in world cricket. Not only has Sachin shown more durability but his achievements in one-day cricket are way ahead. His range of shots is more in numbers. He also mastered T-20 which is as different from test cricket as soccer is to rugby. But if you take into consideration test cricket exclusively, Gavaskar compares favourably with Tendulkar.

Gavaskar scored 10,122 runs in 125 Tests. He made 34 hundreds averaging at 51.12. Tendulkar, in his first 125 Tests, scored 10,281 runs. He made 35 hundreds at an average of 57.12.

||||||| Gavaskar – the then monarch of Indian cricket

Gavaskar, however, has 45 half centuries to Sachin's 41. And if you consider that in his time the bowling attacks were relatively stronger, wickets were kept uncovered for quite a number of years in his career, that he had no helmet for protection and that there were no restrictions on a bouncer, both appear somewhat equal.

It is just that Sachin remained much more focussed on his job. An element of tranquility has always characterised his persona. The award-winning filmmaker

Gavaskar scored 10,122 runs in 125 Tests. He made 34 hundreds averaging at 51.12. Tendulkar, in his first 125 Tests, scored 10,281 runs. He made 35 hundreds at an average of 57.12.

Rituparno Ghosh finds a strong similarity between Sachin and Rajiv Gandhi. 'As a filmmaker, Sourav would appeal to me much more. His persona will be very useful in movies. Sachin won't appeal to me if I was only looking for an actor. But outside that, Sachin's tranquility is a huge turn-on,' says Rituparno.

Gavaskar was, in sharp contrast, a trade union-activist-cum-lead-performer all rolled into one. He could jolly well dedicate a particular Tagore number to Sachin. At least a few lines ...

Oh, daytime traveller remember
That I walked through darkness
with only a lamp in hand ...

Gavaskar's India was unsure as to whether the path she had chosen was the road to prosperity or if she was walking into the sunset. This was where Gavaskar emerged as a picture of assurance. An imagery of hope. Not just in cricket. Even on a social level, Gavaskar was the Indian *aam admi's* first ever Swiss bank account – as every win of his was also their victory.

Ajit Wadekar has had the unique experience of watching both SMG and SRT grow in international cricket. In different capacities though. He was the Indian Captain in 1971 and in Tendulkar's third season he became the National Coach on a long-term basis. Wadekar can't separate the two. To him, Gavaskar is the Raj Kapoor of Indian Cricket and Sachin, an Amitabh Bachchan.

Wadekar lists the following similarities in them:
* **Mentally tough.**
* **Extremely brave.**
* **Solid technique.**

* Ability to concentrate for long hours.
* Supreme self-confidence.
* Always up to a challenge.
* Both do a careful study of the opposition and its bowlers.
* Never frightened on seeing big names.
* Hungry for big scores.
* Goal oriented.
* Absolute team players.
* Pranksters and good mimics! Both play pranks on left-handers: Sunil on Ekki Solkar; Sachin on Kambli.

Wadekar narrates a story involving Sachin and Kambli. Those were the days when the Pager had just arrrived. Kambli was presented with one by his Mumbai teammate Sishir Hattangwadi. Once, it so happened that the minute a beep was heard on the pager, Kambli was jumping with excitement, 'Oh that was Mr Birla ...now it's Mr Ratan Tata ... Ah, I knew it would be Mr Ambani.' As this drama went on for a while, Sachin finally got up and said mischievously,'Mr Kambli, you are now showing off your pager. Did you read the history pages when you were in school?' The whole dressing room erupted in laughter.

To Wadekar goes the credit of establishing a middle-class connect within the Indian team. In his predecessor's team, there was a clear divide between the elite and the lower-middle class. Most of the former group were English-speaking

|||||||| Ajit Wadekar would have wanted both of them on his shopping list and then propose to go off to sleep in the dressing room

|||||||| Tiger Pataudi and his better half

and convent-educated types. For every Borde, there was always an Engineer. For every Viswanath, there was always a Jaisimah. Groups and camps were part of the package.

Pataudi remained neutral. But he had such a stand-offish persona that not always were the junior players at ease around him. As a captain he stood out to his generation. And as a batsman he was terribly unlucky.

As Sharmila Tagore was telling me, 'It is a miracle that even after the accident, Tiger could play fast bowling with one eye. If he had two eyes, who knows where he would have stopped. Before the accident, Tiger had an 80-plus average which shot down to 30 after the mishap.'

Sharmila never feared for her husband's safety when he went out, one-eyed and without a helmet, to face Andy Roberts and Vanburn Holder. But she kept on wondering how he managed to bat against them.

Sachin doesn't feature in Sharmila Tagore's list of favourite modern-day cricketers. It goes in this order. Kumble, Dhoni, Dravid … But she has profound respect for Sachin's genius. 'Sachin with the bat, to me is like Naseer in front of the camera. Or a Farida Zalal. Everything comes so naturally to them. They don't seem to be making any effort. It just flows.'

Her husband unhesitatingly declares Sachin as the greatest ever Indian cricketer for the sum total of his achievements. Pataudi thinks that for achievements on the field, for his sense of fair play and off-the-field humility, Sachin is the biggest role model. However, if he is asked to nominate the greatest innings ever played by an Indian, the Nawab goes for Gavaskar's 96 in Bengaluru. However, despite their long association over the years, the cricketing grapevine hardly declared them to be sms-sharing buddies. But Pataudi clearly has a lot of professional admiration for his ex-deputy.

'Gavaskar could read a contract prepared by the Cricket Board like a top lawyer,' he had once written in his *Sportsworld* editorial.

The greatest USP of Gavaskar is his incredible record against the West Indies. He has thirteen hundreds against them and I have attended enough cricket functions in the Caribbean to know who they rate as the greatest ever Indian batsman. Sachin has only three centuries against them. Peculiar as it is, he has not played much test cricket against the West Indies. Out of his twenty-two year run, only an eight-year period marked his test appearances against the West Indies – from 1994 to 2002. David Frith, the former *Wisden* Editor has watched cricket for the past fifty years and according to him he would not care to separate SMG and SRT, in terms of capability against hostile fast bowling. Again the benchmark was those thirteen hundreds which, according to Frith, 'are the most impressive statistics in Test history' - a statistic which for once certainly does not deceive! For the ordeal of going out to bat against those fearsome fast bowlers was possibly the toughest. Imran Khan said recently, 'People talk about Bradman's 1948 side, Steve Waugh's side of 2000. But to me the all-time best team will always be Llyod's West Indies of the 1980s. People playing them got crushed not just technically but also mentally. I have seen even the great Richard Hadlee taking months and months to recover from a Windies tour.'

To be fair to Sachin, he cannot be faulted for what was not available during his time. Just as Diego Maradona cannot be faulted for Pele not being in the opposition at that time. For Sachin's generation the biggest test was Australia. And he has performed outstandingly well against them. Eleven test centuries and some murderous assaults in one-day matches hardly tell you the story. Sachin has been the cricket-monument that the world champion Aussies have always feared. If Gavaskar averages 65.45 against West Indies, Sachin is also in the 60-plus category against Warne's country. He averages 60.51 in 31 tests against Australia. According to Malcolm Conn, Chief Cricket Writer of *The Melbourne Age*, Sachin

|||||||| Gavaskar was one of Sachin's two idols

is a rare international cricketer about whom opinions in Australia are not split. He is universally admired and respected.

In the 2008-09 tour of the Down Under, every time Sachin went out to bat, it seemed the crowd was cheering the arrival of a Bradman. It carried on for so long that Sachin must have been taken aback as to whether he was playing against or for Australia.

Though it is purely a scenario of a cricketing fantasy, and not even really a fruitful exercise, I wonder how Tendulkar would have fared against the likes of a Holding and Marshall operating from both ends. And then Garner and Roberts? The Indian cricketers who have played them are very confident he would have handled them successfully. Everybody from Kapil to Shastri, or from Mohinder to Gavaskar, is convinced Tendulkar is the complete package to handle them. Mohinder, one of the most successful batsmen against those quickies, said, 'It was not as if you were playing all four at the same time. You played one at a time. To handle them you needed to be brave. You needed a perfect technique. Sachin has all of that.'

Vengsarkar rates Sachin as one of the cleverest batsmen he has ever seen. 'Someone who makes the bowler bowl to his strengths. Even with a reverse swing you find difficult to unsettle him. He knows which side of the ball is shiny, which side is getting rough. And even when the bowler changes his grip he is smart enough to find out which way it would go.'

Kapil Dev, who batted with him during Sachin's maiden test hundred at Manchester, still can't forget what he saw from a distance of 18 yards. 'He was playing those Yuvraj-style shots with minimum backlift just with sheer timing. And then also the classical shots, the perfect coaching-manual types. Standing there I felt, my God, he has two different styles of game in him!'

But what possibly makes a majority of the team of the 1980s convinced about his class was Sachin's 100 at Perth. It came in 1992 while some of the seniors of the earlier era were still playing. Ravi Shastri, for one, was sufficiently impressed earlier in the series at Sydney. When he was on his way to a double hundred, Shastri was under the siege of a full-fledged Aussie barracking. Sachin, all of 19 years, came and assured him, 'Let me get my hundred, then I will give it back to them.' Shastri did not know what to say as the scorecard said Tendulkar was batting at 5. Eventually he did score the 100 but more than the 100, what struck the Indian Vice Captain was the lad's confidence.

If Sydney was all about confidence and stroke-making ability, Perth displayed great technical skills. For a typical Perth wicket which opened up after the third

'Someone who makes the bowler bowl to his strengths. Even with a reverse swing you find difficult to unsettle him. He knows which side of the ball is shiny, which side is getting rough. And even when the bowler changes his grip he is smart enough to find out which way it would go.'

Dilip Vengsarkar

day, cracks had developed soon. One of the players in that team had told me that it was so bad that if you put your little finger on the pitch, it went inside. When the ball pitched on the crack it was going anywhere. Bruce Reid and others were just aiming for the cracks and it became almost impossible to bat on. On the fourth day, it got from terrible to worse. And on that very day Tendulkar scored a hundred. This possibly convinced the Indian dressing room for the last time that they were dealing with an exceptional talent. With a once-in-a-century cricketer!

Tendulkar's life changed permanently with that one innings. The entire country has since then looked up to him to provide them with happiness, self-belief and glory. Since then, every time he has gone out to bat, he has carried the aspirations and dreams of a developing nation. Most have looked up to him as a superhero who is supposed to win any tough battle, without realizing that the cricket field is not a make-believe world. It is not scripted. As Sourav says, 'Actors have an advantage we don't. Their best shots are taken with the advantage of retakes. In a cricketer's life there are no retakes. It is a one-ball game. Your worst shot is recorded. A first ball duck.' But who wants to listen to all that. It is much easier putting up a hoarding that says, 'God wanted to play cricket, so Sachin was born.'

Considering the pressures and expectations that he has handled, Tendulkar should have had grey hair all over his body. Or a muscular disorder. That he could protect himself under such exceptional public glare is a great tribute to his family and the upbringing with which he was raised. He is recognized in most parts of the world. Though when he travels to some of the non-cricket playing countries, he enjoys not being recognized. He can move around happily there. Just like any other hotel boarder, he picks up the luggage himself to take to the room and plays video games with the children. Sanjay Narang, his restauranteur friend, has accompanied him on a few such tours. Narang can recall the experience of sitting at a Barcelona cafe with Tendulkar. While eating, they figured out that a waiter was constantly staring at Sachin till he mustered enough courage and asked, 'Sir, you look like Sachin.'

Tendulkar, enjoying his privacy, was in no mood to relent. So he told this enthusiast, 'Mujhe sab log aisa hi bolte hain.' At the time of settling the bill, however, what happened was the usual scene – 'Let me take it, no, no, this time it's me.' Finally, after a bit of arguing, Tendulkar handed out his credit card for

SACH

||||||| Gavaskar and Sachin always exchanged cricket notes

payment. The very next minute the same Pakistani waiter made a re-appearance with some of his friends.

And immediately there was Little India manifesting itself in Barcelona!

This syndrome of an entire country going out to bat had begun with Gavaskar in the 1970s. In a relatively dark period of poverty, unemployment and price rise, Gavaskar's hundreds were the healing touch that India desperately needed. Each time the public looked up to him to get a century as if that was going to solve their own personal problems. On the face of such unrealistic demands on his performance, Gavaskar remained immersed in his family and close friends. Going out for a movie or lunch with his wife were the sort of things he did to keep himself relaxed. That helped him to take his mind off the game. And beyond that he looked up to the Almighty to guide him towards his journey.

||||||| Left to right: Sachin, Rohan and Agarkar

Sachin does the same. That he comes from a religious family perhaps also helps him to retain his balance. And what makes his case slightly different from Gavaskar is Sachin's insatiable appetite for the game.

In Gavaskar's case, as well as in Kapil Dev's case, the law of diminishing marginal returns took its own course. Sachin doesn't seem to have any time for economics and its famous principles, as he keeps on enjoying the ride.

While he was the Indian coach, Wadekar told me that he often felt sorry that he did not have Sachin in his team when he had been the Indian captain. 'Arrey, if I had had him and Sunil both in the side, then I had to just look for a strike bowler to complete my shopping list. Then I would simply have gone off to sleep and not bothered about the match score.'

Only two years separated the exit of Gavaskar and the entry of Tendulkar. And when Gavaskar retired, it was not as if he was forced to retire. His last five-day match score was 188. His last Test innings score was 96. And his penultimate one-day knock boasted a hundred which was one of the fastest in those days. He could easily have played for another two to three years.

Didn't he ever feel tempted to bat with Sachin?

'Never. Once I was finished with cricket, I was done with it completely. Never ever did I think of coming back. Nor was I missing anything,' replied Gavaskar.

And in a fitting manner he did pass on the baton to the future generation.

Gavaskar passed on his own pair of pads that he wore at the Bicentenary Test to the new wonder kid in Mumbai cricket. A first cousin of his who knew Sachin well enough, delivered the same. So, one day, a tiny, teenaged Tendulkar landed up at the Gavaskar residence to say thank you in person. Gavaskar was not at home. His wife called him on the phone and informed him of Tendulkar's arrival. Gavaskar enquired: 'Is he the same chap?' Marshneil replied, 'Possibly, I am not very sure. Since coming here, rather than raising his head and talking to me, he has figured out about his toes.'

Gavaskar walked in soon. Learnt it was the same Tendulkar who had come with a printed 'Thank You' card. Gavaskar insisted that Sachin must sign the card if he was giving it. So Sachin scribbled. It was possibly the first time in his life that he was giving an autograph. That too to one of his idols! He must have been a little unnerved. What he wrote was not exactly legible.

So Gavaskar, the perfectionist, set out to address this in the future monarch. He told him, 'If you see the autographs of great cricketers like a Bradman, Merchant or Hazare, you will see they are extremely legible. Fifty years down the line, people will be looking at your autograph and will say, "Oh, that was him". But for that, people must be able to recognize your handwriting. So please sign for me again.'

So Sachin signed again. What a moment it was! Acceptance of that one stroke signature possibly signified that the baton was passed on to the next generation. And the two men stood there. One guiding and advising the other, twenty-four years his junior. Thankfully, there were no TV cameras. No still photographers. No print journalist to spoil the innocence. It remained a private moment. A moment in eternity.

||||||| Cracks were
always visible!

CHAPTER 6

GURU GREG AND HIS TUTELAGE

 raham McKenzie was livid and wanted an immediate answer! During his playing days, the Perth-based fast medium bowler didn't have the pace of a Thommo or a Lillie. But at this moment, his expression belied that. As if he had suddenly been put on a fast forward mode. McKenzie wanted to know why the little Tendulkar was being used so indiscriminately by the Indian team. 'He is batting to make them win. He is bowling to get them wickets. But cricket is played by eleven people,' McKenzie professed; 'if the trend continues, very soon this talented lad will be a burnt-out case.'

This remark provided a completely different dimension to the thinking that was revolving around this very special talented youngster. He was all of 19 then. The sporting world was also very familiar with the deadly phrase. It was as much feared as HIV. Thanks to one Mr Bjorn Borg. It was of little surprise, therefore, that McKenzie's observation was the headline on our sports page the very next day.

This was 1992. India had just won her World Cup match against arch-rivals Pakistan. Sachin was declared the Man of The Match for bowling well and for scoring an unbeaten half-century against Imran's Pakistan, whom he was playing for the first time since his debut series three years ago. And wherever you went in Australia-New Zealand, the countries that were jointly hosting the Cup, experts were all talking about him. Most of them had precautionary words about Tendulkar as they were supremely convinced about his talent. The tall, bespectacled gentleman I was trying to interview since the beginning of the tour was an exception. The day after the Pakistan match, luckily I found him at the Sydney press box. He was at his analytical best and I quickly jotted down the pearls of wisdom he was offering. 'I rule out the chance of a burn-out completely as sports medicine has improved so much in the last ten years. But Sachin, the volcano of talent that he is, will have to pick and choose his matches carefully.' Cut to. This was Gregory Stephen Chappell whose voice marked the love and appreciation of an older brother. He was rarely heard in the Indian media as satellite television had not yet opened up in this part of the world. Former cricketers travelled less to the subcontinent. Quite naturally, there were zero interaction opportunities with him.

Cut to. August 2006, Colombo. The day after a tri-nation One-day series. The gentleman sitting next to me at the Taj Samudra Hotel lobby coughed to clear his throat and then dropped a bombshell. 'After Sourav, now Sachin has to watch it. His fitness is not looking any great.' It was almost impossible to believe what I had just heard. But having heard it from the horse's mouth itself, anyone would have taken half a minute to understand the coach's mindset. In my mind it was impossible not to do a flashback and return to Sydney of 1992.

Sadly the flashback kept repeatedly overlapping with the current scenario, as Chappell kept on explaining that Sachin's fitness and fielding skills had deteriorated. Since he believed the World Cup would be won by the best fielding side, the Coach was reviewing how to accomodate only a limited number of seniors who were not agile anymore. The hint he dropped was very clear that somewhere, there was a bit of discord between the direction in which the team wanted to go and where Sachin wanted to travel. It was not well spelt out but not very difficult to sense either. I got completely stumped as my own queries were mostly about Sourav and whether he had a chance to claw his way back into the Indian team. Having dismissed Ganguly's chances in one, rude sentence, the coach was talking about someone else being under the scanner. That was something that had not crossed my mind at all.

SACH

|||||||| Sourav and Sachin feared for their safety

One was further flabbergasted about whether this was all printable. At no point during our discussion did the coach say it was off the record. Was it meant to be understood that way? Or could I safely write about it? Everything that relates to Tendulkar is so sensitive! Supposing the coach denied it later! What made the situation more complex was that I didn't even have a recorder with me and would have no means of proof. Burdened with thoughts and doubts, finally I took the 'An important senior cricketer being closely watched' line. Mind you, this was a year before the Cup. And unmistakably the cracks had started appearing then.

In another four-five months, the battle lines were clearly drawn. The coach was gunning for Sachin-Sourav. And the duo, with the support of quite a few players, had sufficiently armed themselves for the contest. It almost came to a stage as to who would fire the first bullet. Out of Chappell's twenty-two month stint, Sachin remained involved in eighteen. The rest was spent in nursing a tennis elbow and rehab.

||||||| Does the gloomy mindset adequately explain the 29.67 average during this period?

The first match Sachin played for Team Chappell in Nagpur – he walked away with the Man of the Match. He did pretty well in some other one-dayers too. Yet the honeymoon ended abruptly. To the public at large, it was Ganguly versus Chappell. But any insider would have told you the philosophical and real battle was Sachin versus Greg. Many felt that Greg was forcing them to embrace the Australian cricket culture overnight and a perennially talent-driven Sachin's India was resisting the change.

Chappell had taken over the reigns of Indian Cricket in June 2005. His contract was up to March 2007. However, post the World Cup disaster, this hugely controversial twenty-two month tryst wasn't extended any further. Majority opinion however suggested that there was a powerful section of the Board that wanted to retain him. This section had been taken up by a presentation Chappell had made post the World Cup humiliation. The presentation talked about infusing fresh blood at the expense of jaded seniors. It talked about how Australia, burdened with similar problems in the past, had taken measures to invest in the future. To quote Chappell from one of his most controversial interviews:

'In Australia we have a system in place which will reject you the moment you slip below the mark. You need to do a reality-check (in India) and take a few hard decisions.' His 'Commitment to Excellence' document talked about a cricketing reform which had never been attempted earlier in India. And now that India had failed so badly in the premier sporting event, Chappell wanted to come clean on the 'roadblocks' that he faced. He hinted that the time had come for the system to reject some of the seniors. Even a school kid understood that his list didn't exclude India's biggest ever cricketer. There were also unconfirmed reports that he had called some of the seniors in the team 'the cricket mafia'. Chappell may not have had actually said it, but news reached the seniors that he did.

So the following day, possibly for the first time in his life, Tendulkar came out in the open and defended his case. A stunned nation read with interest as he told a national daily in an exclusive interview with Ajay Naidu: 'I am shattered beyond words and I feel helpless. I have never felt so bad in my entire career. We do realize that we played badly as a team and take full responsibility for that. But what hurt us the most was that the coach has questioned our attitude. I have given my heart and soul for the team for the last seventeen years. No coach has even mentioned in passing that my attitude was not correct.'

Chappell may not have expected this serve and volley style from India's most loving son. With those few lines Sachin created such a nationwide impact that the 'Commitment to Excellence' document paper was thrown to the wolves. Chappell beat a hasty retreat. In the following years, he did work with the Rajasthan Cricket Academy but the doors of Indian cricket were permanently shut on him.

Greg has not spoken on this forbidden chapter for the last four years. He has turned down innumerable requests for interviews on Indian cricket. In this book he finally broke the long silence and presented his side of the story. Which is not

'In Australia we have a system in place which will reject you the moment you slip below the mark. You need to do a reality-check (in India) and take a few hard decisions.'

Greg Chappell

'I am shattered beyond words and I feel helpless. I have never felt so bad in my entire career. We do realize that we played badly and as a team and take full responsibilty for that. But what hurt us most was the coach has questioned our attitude. I have given my heart and soul for the team for the last seventeen years. No coach had even mentioned in passing that my attitude was not correct.'

only interesting but adds a further twist to the whole episode. I have retained it verbatim.

This is the Greg Chappell account. Unedited. Uncut.

'... At the outset let me clarify I never ever doubted Sachin Tendulkar's commitment to the side. The only time I talked about him was in relation to the team's World Cup venture. If you talk about a breakdown in relations, that possibly happened only around this time.

'Basically we differed on his batting order in the West Indies. We had toured West Indies the previous year and noticed that on the slow tracks there, you desperately needed a power hitter in the middle overs. Someone who would control the most vital part of the game from 20 to 40 overs and also hit the ball through the field. It wasn't just me alone. Rahul Dravid was also involved in the thinking which felt the matches were going to be decided in those middle overs and you needed the brilliance of either a Sachin or Sehwag to play in that position.

'Sehwag didn't seem very keen. So we sat down with Sachin who, in any case, was the first priority. We put it to him and he seemed reluctant. He thought, top-of-the-order was the best place for him as it has always been. But we were still in the discussion as Rahul and I were convinced no other batsman in the team would be able to do it. Sachin finally agreed the next day and informed Rahul. Though he made it known that he was not happy doing it. He felt that his reputation demanded two places higher in the order. You must understand the scenario in that prevailing context. Before I took over as the coach, India had lost about 22 One-day games, including a few important finals. The team was especially getting panicky while chasing. Through careful consideration of the failure pattern we suggested certain changes. We did reverse the trend (as records would show later) and subsequently won 17 consecutive ODI matches while chasing. It was some kind of a record. Strategy with Sachin was only an extension of the radical strategic moves we were making. Had the World Cup been held anywhere else —Australia, England, India, Pakistan – there would have been no discussion. Sachin would open. Always. But here in West Indies, we badly needed a power-hitter in the middle overs and looked up to him to fill that vacancy. I even assured him that once the World Cup was over, he would revert to his original position. But to be honest, that experience has taught me a lesson. Today, confronted

|||||||| The Three Musketeers of Indian cricket – Sachin, Rahul and Sourav

with a similiar situation I would still put the idea across to him and explain. But if he shows any kind of discomfort, I won't push. I would let Sachin decide.

'Later on, I had a face-to-face chat with Sachin. There was an issue about a write-up which had come out in the Times of India. We spoke the next day in Mumbai and I would like to believe, parted on good terms. As I said earlier, the only disagreement we had was over his place in the batting order which is now a thing of the past.

'If you talk about a historical perspective, I won't jump out of the window and say – Hey, Sachin is the best after Sir Don. Graeme Pollock averaging sixty in test cricket played a lot less. But played under much more trying conditions as a batsman in England and South Africa. skill-wise, of course, Sachin is brilliant. In my all-time-best World Eleven, he will surely be there but I may not put him at No 4. Though I must admit here that he has handled greater expectations than Bradman over a longer period of time. During my years as the Indian coach, how people vied for a minute's attention from him irrespective of wherever he went! Emotionally and physically it must be very draining to cope with that sort of attention day in

||||||| Are we reading too much into the picture?

and day out. But he has handled it remarkably well. He must be the most single-minded devotee cricket has ever seen. Cricket has taken up so much of his life that at times you wonder what he is going to do once he gives up the game! I believe, as long as he can keep himself mentally fresh, he can play international cricket. I can see him playing till forty if he can refresh his mind again and again. Because his technical skills are fine and he will be able to meet the relevant demands. He has to only cope with the mental part.

'I remember having a discussion with him in Chennai. This was a phase when he had just come back after an injury and begun doubting himself. Around that time we had a long chat on batting. He rang up later to say that that was the best cricketing conversation on batting he had ever had. I had told him that as one grew older, one experienced more. But because of the experience, one also became more cautious. More apprehensive. I told him that he had to recreate in his mind the imagery of a young batsman all over again. The same freshness.

'I am sure he remembers the discussion even to this date. As last year or may *be the year before, I read an interview of his on the net where he talked about the mental part associated in batting. And he repeated exactly the same things that we had discussed that night. I have also read interviews of his where Sachin has talked about a happy environment in the dressing room. I am willing to believe that just up to the lead-up to the World Cup, we had a fairly happy environment. I thought it was quite happy. Now Dhoni, as a captain, has contributed towards that enormously. He has the special ability and is quite an unflappable guy. Dhoni, during my time, was acceptable in all quarters. He could mix with both juniors and the seniors. Dhoni keeps a very calm demeanour around the group and that has an effect on the dressing room.*

'Contrary to what people may think, my decision to relinquish the post of the Indian coach was made much before the World Cup. I had presented the BCCI my roadmap for the project Commitment to Excellence and they had approved it. Yet there was a clear philosophical clash as to which direction the group needed to take. I, for one, wasn't prepared to compromise. If I had conceded then, there would have been no fight. But I wanted to remain true to my beliefs and cricketing thoughts. Bottom-line – it wasn't going anywhere. And whatever I had set out to do remained unattainable. That is why I decided to quit and this was much before the World Cup. So to set the record straight once again – Sachin's statement in the press against me had nothing to do with my discontinuing as the coach. As I said earlier, we had parted on good terms ....'

Hmm ... what the ex-coach says is sensational ... that after the Sachin outburst in the media which, many believe, sealed Chappell's fate, he and the Little Master had a private one-on-one meeting. And that they parted on good terms. Was there actually ˆsuch a meeting? Or was it a figment of Chappell's imagination? Ratnakar Shetty, the man incharge of administering the Tenth World Cup, is someone who enjoys Tendulkar's confidence. Shetty has been observing him since the Shardashram days. Shetty is also a Board bigwig and had perfect knowledge of the tension between the two. Apparently, a night before the Vadodara One-day International against the West Indies, Tendulkar brought to Shetty's notice that he was not exactly happy about the way things were going. It was very unusual for a patient man like him to lose his cool and complain. But things were going out of hand as Chappell had told Sachin, 'You will have to think of the needs of the team. For that, if necessary, you will have to bat low.' This particular bit of advice of keeping in mind the needs of the team had hurt Sachin, who, in his own eyes and in front of the millions, has always been a team player.

Although surprised with the turn of events, Shetty advised Sachin to keep his cool and remain focussed on the game. As is quite normal in a cornered Tendulkar scenario, he scored an unbeaten hundred. That too, when he was forcibly sent at number four. Eventually, Sachin walked away not only with The Player of the Match, but also Player of the Series.

But even when he was back in his house in Mumbai, Shetty could not stop recollecting what he had heard from the wounded national hero: 'I have done so much for the team. If after all these years, someone tells me that the team's interest comes first, then it really hurts.' Looking back, Shetty attributes the problems regarding Greg's twenty-two month rule in one simple sentence – poor man manangement.

It is difficult to refute the argument. The essence of Tendulkar's cricket has always been romance. And the creator of this magic required soft handling, a special yet delicate assurance from the powers that be that they were all happy and enjoying themselves. From the very first series in Pakistan, he had been handled with special care and he has never abused that fondness towards him.

Sachin did not see eye-to-eye with Azhar on many occasions. But Azhar never dealt with him rudely. This was the first time he had been treated like an average Australian cricketer playing for his bread and butter. For Sachin it was clearly like being driven out from his own house to stay with the stepmother!

Dilip Vengsarkar, the then Chairman of Selectors, was one who had opposed Chappell tooth and nail. Sensing that the players were uncomfortable and a major breakdown in relationships was on the cards, Vengsarkar decided to remain in close touch with some of the seniors. He took it upon himself to put forward strong views at the Selection Committee meeting. Most of what he said was directed at Chappell's philosophies. Vengsarkar felt that the dictatorial style of a football manager was irrelevant in cricket and openly criticized the Chappell moves.

Very soon he emerged as the parallel power force. According to him, 'Sachin was put under pressure intentionally during this regime.' Vengsarkar concludes by saying, 'Chappell wanted to get rid of Sachin. But his game plan failed.'

'Chappell wanted to get rid of Sachin. But his game plan failed.'

Dilip Vengsarkar

During the Greg regime, Tendulkar averaged an abysmally low 29.67 in test matches. Most people I have interviewed related this phase with Sachin struggling to overcome a tennis elbow injury. But during the same period, he averaged 40 in One-day cricket.

Sourav Ganguly, who still retains the candid freshness of speaking his mind, spells it out in this uncensored tête-à-tête:

'... Sachin felt, as if someone was trying to pull him down. Though the coach had personally assured him that he was with him. I had no such confusion or illusion. I knew I had no backers and I had to do things on my own. But Sachin got thoroughly confused. He didn't quite understand whether the coach was for or against him. He did hear that the coach was talking against him to a select part of the media. I thought his mind got clouded and that affected the performance. I feel, batsmanship is all about clearing your mind. Keeping it free of anxieties and worries.

'Look at what Sachin advised Pietersen recently. He has told him to keep his mind free. Why has the Indian team been performing so well for a period of almost two years? Because Gary Kirsten has managed to create a happy dressing room atmosphere where the players are mentally fresh ....' Ganguly's statement discusses the Chappell regime in general and is not World Cup specific. Also from what Shetty said, it clearly emerges that Sachin's problem did not originate at the World Cup. It started three months before that. During the World Cup, even a loss against Bangladesh hadn't made the team management revise its batting order. And in West Indies, the Sachin-Chappell relationship had touched rock-bottom. Tendulkar, arguably the best ever One-day batsman and the highest scorer in the World Cup, was sent at number six to bat against lowly ranked Bermuda. For the Master perhaps, this was the ultimate humiliation. The team, of course, scored 400 plus and set a record, but its premier batsman suffered in agony. In an all-time best Australian team, could anyone think of sending Allan Border, Greg Chappell and Neil Harvey ahead of Bradman unless the idea matched the Don's sentiments!

'... Sachin felt, as if someone was trying to pull him down. Though the coach had personally assured him that he was with him. I had no such confusion or illusion . I knew I had no backers and I had to do things on my own. But Sachin got thoroughly confused. He didn't quite understand whether the coach was for or against him. He did hear that the coach was talking against him to a select part of the media. I thought his mind got clouded and that affected the performance. I feel, batsmanship is all about clearing your mind. Keeping it free of anxieties and worries.'

Sourav Ganguly

For anyone covering the last World Cup and particularly the Indian team, it was crystal clear that the team was divided into three groups: pro-Chappell, anti-Chappell and completely neutral. It was not because of the divide that the team lost out so early.

Apparently the World Cup winning Indian team of 1983 had also had its share of problems and divisions. But everything was forgotten the moment Kapil lifted the Cup at the Lord's Balcony. Anyone who saw Dravid's team celebrate after recording its maiden victory on South African soil only four months earlier at Johanessburg, was sure about one thing – that this was the most united and peaceful outfit in the world. Sadly, a defeat brought out the cracks much more than what would have remained well covered in a victory. It did not help matters that Dravid, caught between the coach and his long-time friends, didn't show the diplomacy that was required in this kind of a situation. Quite often he symbolized the helpless husband torn between the mother and his newly married wife.

Dravid, possibly this generations's finest batsman after Tendulkar, has throughout his career appeared like a Karna to Sachin's Arjuna. A team player to the core, Dravid wanted to take the team built by Ganguly on to the next level. He shared the coach's vision that importing the selfless baggy green mindset was that level where individuals only shine to the extent the team allows them to. That they don't play for personal records and centuries. That the star system of the old must make away for the team system. That ultimately, team play must prevail! But given the conditions it was too idealistic and predictably, met with a premature death.

Ganguly's team had an incredible run. But they couldn't get it beyond Australia and thereby remained a good Number Two. The coach and the captain agreed on a point that if they improved the team's fitness, thinking pattern and emphasised on team play, Mission Australia would be achievable. They decided on a certain team ethos – for instance, naming the final eleven very late to keep the opposition confused! They also changed the age-old thinking that batting orders were like safe deposit lockers that remained forever with the batsmen who were allotted the locker keys. Dravid's India minimized the role of a specialist batting order, especially in One-day matches – a trend that Dhoni has happily continued in his regime. That it did not meet with the required success was only expected.

Unlike Ganguly, who was a smart, hands-on captain, Dravid was too idealistic. Too romantic. He is the sort of a man you take home to your mother. The kind who believes in moments. The sort who would think, the moment you got a hundred – that was the optimum high. Anything beyond that – the clinching of the fist, the celebrations, the prize distribution were only secondary and just followed the high. As a poet he would perhaps outdo Ganguly eleven times out of ten. But as a hands-on Indian Captain, Ganguly was much smarter. It showed in his results notwithstanding the fact that Dravid's contribution in them was immense.

Ravi Shastri was a part of the three-member panel that handed over the job of coaching India to Greg on the very day of the interview. When the news was finally conveyed to Greg, he expressed happiness. But no delight. Sitting in his room at the Taj Palace Hotel, New Delhi, I found him a little anxious as he had still not heard from Ganguly. His favoured son-in-law. Mrs Chappell may have differed then. She felt Sourav was their son. Not son-in-law. She had told Dona Ganguly, a year ago in Brisbane, that when Sourav went out to bat, Greg was as nervous as if his son was going out to face the Aussie quicks.

What happened later became part of Indian cricket history. But what led to Chappell's relationship becoming stiff with Shastri was not known. To many, the tall, former all-rounder is the Voice of Indian Cricket and possibly what may have made the voice bitter was Chappell's handling of Sachin. Shastri, over the years, was possibly the closest cricketing confidante of Sachin. And he was candid enough to say, 'Sachin was not happy with the environment that existed in the team. He was not treated well. His body language suggested he was not internally happy.'

To the old-timers, the Dravid-Greg regime brought back memories of an earlier experiment undertaken by Bishan Singh Bedi in the 1990s. Ganguly's former teammate, an ex-India international player from Kolkata, had attended Bishan's fitness camp before the England tour. On the very first day, he wrote a poem, the contents of which reached the coach the same evening. Just a one-liner:

'Bishan, on a mission to kill.'

Needless to say he didn't find a place in the team to England which was captained by the Dravid-like introverted Azhar. Faced with the team management's rapid-fire thinking and mysterious ways, Ganguly and Sachin formed a self-protection group. Quite a few seniors like Sehwag, Harbhajan and Zaheer rallied around them. Juniors like Dhoni, Raina, Pathan remained neutral. In a no-war zone!

Why did the Chappell experience backfire? Because it ignored the practicalities of a change. In an individual sport, it may have been easier for Chappell to do what he did. But for a sport that is followed with almost religious fanaticism, you have to be careful. You can't shift the capital to Daulatabad just because *you* think it makes sense. You have to carry your team with you. In the 1990s, they said Bishen Bedi was the Mohammad-bin-Tughlaq of Indian cricket. Chappell assumed the same mantle with increased hype and hatred.

As Ganguly admitted when I interviewed him for this book, he and Sachin formed an understanding between the two of them when they were cornered by powerful forces within the team. 'We were good friends even from our under-15 days. Subsequently, we formed a mutual trust-based equation that we would not backstab each other. Or backbite against each other.'

Jagmohan Dalmiya, who controlled Indian cricket for nearly two decades, was the man behind the appointment of Chappell. Today, however, he is pretty sore. If Dalmiya was to sit down today and make a final assessment of Guru Greg's

|||||||| How would Chappell have handled the temperamental Lara? We will never know!

contribution, he would term it as 'poor'. Today Dalmiya regrets that they ever made him the coach and opines that they ought to have picked a 'better alternative'. According to inside information, Dalmiya had received intelligence reports of Chappell's poor man management skills which he had believed. But his captain could not be dissuaded. Ganguly wanted him at any cost, a move that he was to regret for the rest of his life.

Was Chappell actually that bad? If you speak to the players, including some of his favourite ones, there is widespread resentment. He apparently foul-mouthed Sehwag in the media ... expressed dissatisfaction with both Zaheer and Harbajhan. As it turned out, only a few years later, the duo played the most important role in plotting India's elevation to the top spot in ICC rankings. Chappell was all for youth and promoted them to the core. The likes of a Raina, Munaf or Irfan were continuously pushed. But four years down the line, how many from the

|||||||| With Jagmohan Dalmiya, who today regrets having appointed Chappell

youth group made it? It is still the good old, senior group helping India to win, mocking the 'youth theory' in a skill-intensive, non-body contact sport.

Cricket historians in future will surely research why the Chappell model failed in India. Poor man management skills must have been a primary reason. Not to forget the fact that he also had similar problems dealing with the South Australian players years ago. But his technical understanding, attention to details and explanatory skills were awesome and attracted admiration. Sourav still rates a certain Greg Chappell as the best cricketing consultant he has ever come across – 'the one who would examine your problem and suggest ways of immediate rectification'. But as you look at him in wonder, Sourav finishes the paragraph – 'But always on a one-on-one basis. Not as the group consultant'. Greg Chappell now has as much chance of taking over again as the Indian coach, as Obama has of becoming the Indian President. But hypothetically, if he did, what would be the changes that would comprise his new vision document?

Talking to him, I got the impression that he would have been more patient. He didn't realize then that he was trying to enforce rapid change in a society which only adopts something new after careful consideration. He would have also understood that in cricket, the buzzword is skill. Not age or fitness. In a physically violent body-contact team sport, you need to have strength and fitness along with skills to survive. Not in cricket. A Tendulkar might not finish among the first three in a 100-metre dash. But that doesn't stop him or a VVS Laxman from consistently winning matches against top teams.

By all accounts, Sachin won this cricket philosphical war against the Guru in Indian conditions. He is now threatening to win the war in Guru Greg's own country. A selection panel powered by Chappell, continued to face pressure and public criticism to include an aging 40-year-old leggie during the last Ashes series. 'Bring back Warne!' was a template which actually meant something else: Skill is permanent, age is temporary. Even the Australian system could not unearth players to arrest the Ashes slight, proving yet again that skill wins you matches. Not necessarily the system. Young age. Or fitness.

Gary Kirsten, the current Indian coach, is not involved in such philosophical debates. But he remembers clearly the first meeting with Tendulkar at a Perth hotel after taking over his new office. 'Sachin, what do you expect from me?' 'I want you to be a friend,' came the almost immediate reply.

Kirsten felt he had just heard a profound statement. The first and very first line of his coaching model was ready – Thou shalt always be a friend and not betray their trust!

||||||| The bowling machine is his friend

CHAPTER 7

THE CHAMPION'S PRIVATE LAB

What were Virender Sehwag and Sachin Tendulkar, the opening pair discussing while they went out to bat against Pakistan's daunting target of 273 at the Centurion?

There are various stories. One suggests that Sehwag asked Tendulkar, 'Paaji, kya karna hai?' ('Paaji, what is to be done?') To which Sachin replied, 'Kya karna hai – marna hai un logon ko.' ('What is to be done – we have to thrash them.') Then they went and hammered Pakistan at the crucial World Cup Group League match in 2003. Possible? Yes, of course!

There is another story. Story number two: That both got off from the stairs discussing, 'This is Pakistan. Agar jan bhi chale jaye to ...' ('Even if we have to give our lives ...')

Though I must admit this sounds too dramatic.

Story number three: Going down the long staircase at the Super Sport Park, Sehwag suddenly turned to his partner for help. He said, 'Paaji, will you please take the first strike? I have never played Wasim Akram before and am a little scared.' Sachin said, 'Don't worry. I will.' That was it. No further game plan was discussed. This version is equally difficult to believe as Sehwag is the most unlikely batsman on earth to be scared of any bowler. Usually it is the other way around!

But the man in whose Nagpur hotel room I had been sitting for the last half an hour, confirmed during the interview that version number three was the correct one. There was no point in arguing. This was straight from the horse's mouth – Sehwag himself! I was only left thinking: wouldn't most other batsmen in Sachin's place have said, 'Sorry, you are telling me at the last minute to take the first strike. Right through the tournament I have begun as the non-striker. Now suddenly you are asking me to handle, of all people Akram. Veeru, I hope you understand ...'

But then, Sachin Tendulkar's confidence levels are legendary. That historic day at the Centurion, Sehwag saw his own initial apprehension disappearing very early. After taking the strike, Sachin plundered nine runs off Akram's first over itself. According to Sehwag, the Pakistan team soon took to abuse. The two batsmen had a meeting at the middle of the crease. It was decided that no counter abuse would be resorted to. But at the same time the run rate would be maintained. Around this time, Tendulkar hit a sensational sixer off Shoaib over third man.

There was a study much later in a British journal that this particular shot signified the liberation of Indian cricket from the clutches of Pakistan. But no study ever recorded that despite the alert stump microphones, the Pakistanis had begun a verbal war.

Sehwag can remember another incident during the Adelaide test match, the last time India toured Down Under, where Brad Hogg and Michael Clarke were continuously sledging at them but Sachin remained unfazed. He didn't counter-sledge but just kept on doing what he knows best – scoring runs.

My own assessment is that more than handling sledging, the real story lay somewhere else. That pitted against varying cricketing challenges, Tendulkar has never backtracked. I was reminded of an earlier story of his life narrated by Kiran Mokashi, his former Mumbai

|||||||| No wonder he is called Arjun!

teammate. 'Sachin was destined to be great. Even at the age of 14 he had so much confidence in his own ability!'

The Mumbai team had gone to Vadodara. Sandip Patil was the captain. He thought he should protect Sachin at the nets against Raju Kulkarni, his side's tearaway fast bowler. Though Kulkarni was playing for India only on and off around that time, he did bowl a good pace. Sandip had asked him to bowl a little slow at the nets. But Tendulkar wanted him to bowl as fast as he could. The moment he started

||||||| With Sandeep Patil, his former coach

hitting those somewhat slow deliveries, an angry Raju measured his full run-up and started bowling quick. This was exactly what Sachin wanted. 'He seemed so happy,' Mokashi recalled.

A few months later, it was Dilip Vengsarkar's turn to be surprised by the same confidence. Mumbai was playing the Ranji Trophy Quarter Final against Hyderabad in an away encounter. It was a predictable rank-turner which the hosts had prepared to suit their spinners, namely Arshad Ayub, Venkatapathy Raju and Kanwaljeet Singh. Sachin was to come in at number five. Since a wicket fell on the last over of the day, Vengsarkar choose to send in the night watchman Kiran Mokashi. As luck would have it, Mokashi was bowled. At the end of the day's play, a fifteen-year-old boy confronted his skipper who was leading India then, 'What was the need to send Kiran? I could have easily handled that.' The next day Vengsarkar shared a long partnership with the boy on a vicious turner. All along he couldn't stop thinking about the boy's confidence level. He told himself, if everything went well, this boy would become India's greatest ever batsman. He was someone special. Even more talented than Gavaskar.

As the owner of a few academies located in different parts of Mumbai and Pune, Vengsarkar finds Sachin's batting only comparable to Viv Richards. 'Sachin's ability to read the bowler's mind beforehand is amazing. Because of the special ability some

Anyone who has watched Sachin up close would have learned a very important lesson in life – that no one has an Alladin's Magic Lamp. The only lamp in life are two four-letter words – work hard.

||||||| When he bats, India comes to a standstill

of his shots look pre-determined.' The veteran of 116 tests finds Sachin's straight drive exquisite. The head is still. The body is supremely balanced. The bat comes down straight. There is an initial front foot movement. 'You can't get any more perfect than that,' says Vengsarkar with a look of approval, something that is a rarity in that man.

But Vengsarkar was only one of the many who had at that stage been pleasantly surprised with this wonder boy's confidence. The 1990s team of Azhar also got a first-hand feel of the same confidence, when in a pulsating Hero Cup Semi-Final at Kolkata, Tendulkar snatched the ball from a hesitant Kapil Dev and bowled India to victory. At that stage, South Africa required only five runs. It had two wickets in hand. Srinath, Jadeja and Kapil had not completed their quota of overs. A huge discussion was going on as to who should bowl the last over. Sensing the indecision, Manager Wadekar promptly sent a note through the twelfth man to Azhar. 'Bowl Kapil,' it said. But Sachin insisted he would bowl. The South African tail-enders found his slow leg-cutters very difficult to slog. And India snatched an incredible victory from the jaws of defeat.

Kapil presents an interesting twist to the story by saying that getting Sachin to bowl was a conscious decision. As he and Azhar discussed, five-six runs off a pace bowler might not be difficult but since the South Africans did not play leg-spin well, a chance could be taken with Sachin's slowers. According to the World Cup winning captain's recollections, it was a calculated gamble. Though I have reasons to believe, as do the majority, that the gamble only followed Sachin's initiative to confront a huge challenge.

It is pointless trying to find out after fourteen years what exactly happened. In any case, the essence of the story does not change much. That in front of a boisterous crowd of one lakh people, a 20-year-old showed enough courage to take the ball in his hands and bowl the final over in a Semi-Final. It was such an unnerving thing to do, considering the pressure and the fact that he was not a specialist bowler. But the confidence Sachin had in his cricket all along explains why he did not chicken out. Again, in Auckland, just before a One-day against New Zealand was about to start, Sidhu, the regular opener, expressed his inability to play. Kapil, Azhar and Wadekar were discussing the possible replacement when Sachin went up to them and voluntarily offered to open. His enthusiasm was such that the management of the Indian team didn't refuse.

From that game, Indian one-day history was never the same again.

Teammates witness Sachin's confidence every day and never fail to be affected by it. Harbhajan says, 'I have seen the best of them in my time. Steve Waugh, Lara, Ponting, Warne, Kumble. They were all greats and I don't mean any disrespect to them. But the truth is Sachin begins from a point where these people end.' The Sardar first came to know about

|||||||| He has bowled his team to victories

'I have seen the best of them in my time. Steve Waugh, Lara, Ponting, Warne, Kumble. They were all greats and I don't mean any disrespect to them. But the truth is Sachin begins from a point where these people end.'

Harbhajan Singh

Sachin's magical technical brilliance from his Punjab teammate Vikram Rathore. Rathore told the team, 'Yeh ladka kya player hai. Aap sirf dekhte jao. Kamal ki adjustment.' ('What a player this boy is! You keep watching. What adjustment!') According to Bhajji, experts in the media still haven't figured out a very significant part of Sachin's success at the crease. To quote the off-spinner, 'His adjustment skills – how, at the drop of a hat, he changes the game plan. When he plays the ball, there are so many varying movements. Most of the time the movement being practised currently differs from the movement of the previous delivery. How many times have you seen Tendulkar getting beaten by two successive deliveries?'

You can't say he is talking like a fan. Because then what would you call a VVS Laxman! He is equally charmed.

The wristy Hyderabadi still can't forget the minutest details of the triple century partnership they shared in Sydney. Laxman felt honoured that he could watch some of Sachin's masterclass knocks standing at the non-striker's end only from a distance of 18 yards. But the triple century partnership in which Sachin got a double hundred, stood out in his mind for the absolute control he had over his mind and body. 'He had decided not to play the cover drive as he was getting out to this shot. But even if you decided beforehand, at some point of time, your reflexes and body take control over your mind. I was amazed to see an exception from so close. Despite playing so well, I don't think he played a cover drive till he completed a hundred.'

If you deconstruct Sachin's success, talent of course emerges as the number one component – the primary component. He was born with more talent than others. And a very close second would surely be his work ethic, which is simply

|||||||| Supreme talent also requires computer analysis

awesome. It is so intense and unwavering that even the Gavaskars and the Kapil Devs suffer in comparison. Outside the twenty-two yards he has hit more deliveries at practice than anyone dead, living or yet to be born. The most fascinating story about Sachin's genius is that he doesn't take the genius at all seriously!

Well, the confidence he displays in hours of crisis is not just mental, but technical and is hard earned. As if to say: I have prepared well enough. Now I am ready for the battle.

Two months ago, I was in Mumbai to begin preparations for the book. I knew Sachin would be in town and practising. I presumed that getting him to talk exclusively would be child's play. Not too many media people would be there at the practice sessions. So I would get the required time and attention. I asked Prashant Shetty, who at times helps him at the nets, if I could meet Sachin. And the smooth talking, pleasant person that he is, Prashant did not seem very enthusiastc. 'He works like an office-goer. Gets inside at 9.45 am. Leaves at 6 pm. It might not be very easy meeting him. And when he comes out he is so drained that he mightn't be in a mood to talk,' Prashant had warned me gently before.

He was absolutely right. This was before the start of the 2010 Australia series. Sachin responded to a text message the same day saying that he would rather see me in Chandigarh – venue of the First Test match, rather than in Mumbai. The SMS came a few hours before I was to board the Mumbai flight. So I couldn't cancel going to Mumbai. There I spoke to everyone else on Tendulkar, but couldn't speak to the man himself. This is how seriously he takes even a pre-series practice session.

What does Sachin do inside the practice arena for such long hours? I was curious. The thinking behind this, of course, was that if after scoring fourteen thousand runs and so many centuries, you have to slog for seven hours on a non-match day, is it worth it? Sachin, of course, thinks it is worth every bit of it. I learnt that he doesn't simply practise. He practises with purpose. If tomorrow he started training for the World Cup, the preparation would be completely suited towards one-day cricket. He would have targets then, while practising. He would imagine real match situations and adapt accordingly.

Is it the first or second power play? How is the field set?

Who is bowling? Will he face a pacer or a spinner? He will, of course, practise with white balls.

What is the imaginary situation? Is it say – 10 balls left? 25 runs to score? Sachin will then ask the net bowlers their individual field and beat them. In between it is more or less mandatory that he would have worked out at the gym for one and a half hours. And batted alone with the bowling machine.

There is clearly a lesson from this for all of us – for professionals in diverse fields: that you should not take anything for granted. That you should not take sunshine for granted even for a single day in life.

Instead prepare yourself for complete darkness. Then in darkness you will be more visible than others. And the day the sun comes out, you will look like the sun king.

Tendulkar's whole preparation in cricket is for a period of relative darkness. And that is why it takes so much sacrifice out of him, so much commitment, so much intensity of purpose. It is not just spending long hours at the nets or at the gym. It is also knowing what he needs to do and when. If tomorrow he is to play

|||||||| Stretching is vital for fitness

||||||| He goes to the gym religiously

Sri Lanka, it is unlikely that the net bowlers he would carefully shortlist would not include an off-spinner. Despite the runs, despite the talent, despite the experience – he never ever takes anything for granted. He does not allow himself to sit on a high horse even for a minute though he deserves to sit on one. Tendulkar knows that batting is a cruel, one-ball game and unless you keep on searching for perfection, it is likely to move away like a butterfly.

Possibly that is the greatest lesson from a Tendulkar story. And a lesson that needs to be learnt well. As life quite regularly presents itself on a similar footing. Life is also a one-ball game. Hit or miss.

If you train like and believe in the Tendulkar school, you might still miss. But if you consider the overall percentage, the chances of missing will decrease a lot.

Take a simple example: Sachin still approaches a test match as if he is going out to play his first one. He prepares so diligently for a match that a day before the test match, his bag is packed first and kept outside the room for the team luggage man to pick up. Invariably, he goes off to sleep by 10 pm before the first day's play. Tendulkar is not just passionate but meticulous.

His story also shows that you should always retain the ability to do a brutally strong self-analysis – that you must not forget who you are and why you are here. It is perhaps not surprising to see so many youngsters drunk with the IPL money. But what is surprising is that even after seeing Sachin from such close quarters, they don't follow even some of his traits. Anyone who has followed Sachin closely would know he doesn't compromise with his cricket. If cricket beckons even after twenty-two years, everything else takes a backseat. Wife. Family. Friends. Media. Contracts. Commercials.

Everything.

Hemant Kenkre, the former CCI Captain and one who saw Sachin's growing-up years from very close quarters, still remembers with fondness that every season Sachin would bring in something new. Some new shot. Some new technique. Some new thoughts. Which invariably made him a better player than what he had been the previous season.

Sachin doesn't need to sing out aloud about his achievements. He knows make-believe does not translate into success. Nothing goes well without doing homework. You not only have to keep on practising constantly but at the same time, add variations.

The package that Tendulkar presents in terms of stroke play is unparalleled in cricket history. No other player including Viv and Bradman ever had so many different shots. For instance, Tendulkar plays four different types of sweep shots. Then the scoop shot over the wicket keeper … the upper cut … If you make a video of Tendulkar at his prime in 1998, you won't find half of these shots. That alone explains his continuing genius.

He keeps on inventing new strategies. He thinks about them constantly as he knows, in a ruthlessly demanding professional world, even if he stops for a minute,

|||||||| Practising with a tennis racquet is innovation

it may well bring his journey to a halt. That would be too big a price to pay. And in any case he needs to be alert. All over the world the coaches and captains are only plotting a terror attack on his wicket!

Five years ago India was playing Pakistan in a Kochi One-dayer. Practice was almost over. I had gone to meet Dravid and was standing near the practice arena when I saw the unusual sight of Tendulkar batting at the nets. Unusual, as all of us had seen him batting an hour prior to that. And then he had batted for a long time. What was he doing again? That too batting left-handed. I was curious. To make the scene a little more absurd, Sachin was displaying power-packed left-handed batting. One delivery that he hit cleared at least 70 yards and nearly broke a TWI camera which was stationed to capture the practice frames from a seemingly safe distance. Arun Lal, standing next to me exclaimed, 'Even with his left hand he could have played for India.' But I still didn't know why he was doing that and Arun was also unable to provide an explanation. Sachin is not the sort who would waste time at the nets like that. There is no phrase in his dictionary called 'time pass'. So batting left-handed must have been for a specific reason.

Sachin put an end to all my speculation by smiling a lot and saying, 'Oh! Left-handed batting. That was fun. *Mazak se* (For fun).' I not only believed him but was scolding myself deep inside that years of cricket reporting had reduced me to looking for stories in everything. In the process it may have taken away the fun and innocence of life. A few days later, sitting in front of the TV in a Kolkata household, I got a shock to see that I had been correct! And that I had been stupid enough to let go of an excellent story. I also realized that I had been misled by the creator of the scheme, one Mr Tendulkar!

What I saw on the screen was that Afridi, while bowling to Tendulkar, had pitched one well outside the leg stump on the rough. It pitched on what would be a right-handed batsman's blind spot. But Sachin quickly turned left-handed. Now he could clearly see the ball turning inside and with his left hand, hit it so hard that it just fell short of the deep point boundary for a one drop four. It now dawned on me that that was what he had been practising for. Mind you, this was much before Kevin Pietersen thought about his switch-hit. In those days, no one prepared himself for such a shot. I confronted the man soon and alleged that he had taken away an important story of mine. What I got was laughter and possibly – I would say possibly, a sharp hint that I should not have expected him to talk about his new strategies beforehand to the media. No professional worth his salt would ever do something as suicidal as that.

The team members are privy to so many such innovations that they will always keep faith in Sachin even if you talked about an imaginary crunch situation. For instance, Gatting's dismissal on the last ball of the day to Warne: a delivery pitched well outside the leg stump had turned sharply to take the leg stump. Later it was to be termed as the Ball of the Century. How would Sachin have faced the same delivery? I asked some of his teammates.

HARBHAJAN SINGH: He would have paddle sweeped the delivery for a boundary.
ANIL KUMBLE: Difficult to say. He may have got out. He may have defended. Don't forget Warne too was a great bowler.
VIRENDER SEHWAG: He would have played a sweep. Straight four.
RAVI SHASTRI: Difficult one. Gatting was a formidable player of spin.

But then, with Sachin, you never know.
The teammates have such confidence in Sachin that according to them, nothing

is beyond him on a cricketing field. A lot of respect is based on his intense preparation for any given match. And that he is capable of such varying feet movement inside the batting crease.

In Gavaskar's era they used to talk about his detailed preparation.

Sachin has taken that to another level. He has solutions for every cricketing problem, tempting people to write, 'Genius is the art of finding solutions in a crisis'.

His approach towards detailed preparation has not escaped the eyes of another living legend, though from another industry. Dilip Kumar, in his advancing years, has been away from the public eye for some time now and keeps a low profile. But for Tendulkar he decided to make an exception. Here is what he had to say in a special just for this book:

'... It is certainly very inspiring for any new entrant to the game to hear the scores Sachin has notched up, the records he has broken, the awe he has inspired in his contemporaries, and if I may say so, some of his seniors. I would like to point out to them they should also observe the tireless practice and perseverance that has yielded each outstanding performance. I don't think he has ever gone on the field without preparation, which includes a sensitive awareness of the opposing team's strength and weakness. You can easily sense the intense preparedness, especially when he is facing a Shane Warne or a Shoaib Akhtar.'

Nothing exemplified this better than his duels with Warne. Sachin had practised specifically for the duel by inviting a retired Laxman Sivaramakrishnan to bowl at him in the Chennai camp. Siva did get surprised when Sachin phoned and requested him to join the practice. At first he thought that perhaps Sachin just wanted to have a crack for one or two days. But much to his surprise the same routine was followed for five days – half an hour's intensive practice session each day; but quite innovative. The idea was to create spots outside the leg stump and bowl there. Siva would pitch there and turn in a manner that at some point of time the ball would altogether disappear from the batsman's vision. Then Sachin would practise the inside-out shot. Looking back, Siva can recall two things very clearly:

A) All possible chance factors were taken care of.

B) At no point did Sachin show any tension if the plan did not work.

All along his thought process was so positive that it only dealt with dominating and winning against Warne.

In the first innings of the Chennai Test, Sachin was out for four.

But in the second, he just murdered Warne. An innings, Kumble says, that was possibly the best he had ever seen Sachin play. Sitting in the pavilion one person was hardly surprised though – L Sivarmamkrishnan, who knew this had to happen at some stage. Around that time, Siva had given up playing for Tamil Nadu. He only managed the odd match for Vadodara. Sachin could easily have trained with bowlers who were regulars at the time – his childhood friend Sairaj Bahutule or his Indian team colleague Kumble. Why did he pick the ex-Tamil Nadu leggie of all people? Because case-specific Siva was the best choice in the country. He too was a classical leg-spinner in the Warne mould who turned the ball much more than any other leggie in the country. He alone could have made the practice against that particular delivery meaningful.

If smart, relentless preparation distinguishes him from his esteemed colleagues, then Sachin is also characterised by another benchmark. He has always believed in a zero compromise theory when it comes to his cricket.

Atul Kasbekar, the well-known photographer, is a close friend of Sachin's and shoots him for various clients. Pepsi wanted him to fly down to London and shoot their commercials with Sachin who, in any case, was there in England during the Natwest Trophy. Now in terms of commercials, Sachin has two fixed principles: A) He won't do an alchohol advertisement irrespective of the money on board. B) He won't shoot during a series. During a tournament, the slightest distraction is DISTRACTION for him. As has been written and discussed earlier, in a one-ball

In terms of commercials, Sachin has two fixed principles: A) He won't do an alchohol advertisement irrespective of the money on board. B) He won't shoot during a series.

sport he wants complete focus and not even a 0.01 per cent diversion is tolerated.

Kasbekar checked in at the same hotel in London. Sachin was pleasantly surprised to see him. Anyway, pleasantaries were exchanged. Dinner plans were made. Then Sachin asked the ace photographer the reason for his arrival in London. Kasbekar replied that he had only come to shoot him. Little did the photographer know that Sachin had already told the Pepsi bosses he wasn't going to do it and yet they had just decided to take another chance. But Sachin explained that he would stick to his ground. So, though Kasbekar is Sachin's close friend, to Sachin, cricketing principles are principles to be followed, regardless of who is involved. So Kasbekar, one of those close, hand-picked friends returned empty-handed from England with all his heavy camera equipment. On the long journey back, Kasbekar

||||||| With Sanjay Narang, his friend and business partner

was constantly thinking of how remarkably Sachin still retained the balance; How he does not for a minute forget the fact that what he is today is because of his cricket. So there is a zero tolerance policy on compromise with that.

Sanjay Narang, another close family friend of his, knows more than anyone else, how meticulous Sachin is when it comes to any kind of preparation, be it related to cricket or anything else. Sanjay is a big name in the hospitality industry and has interests extending across the hospitality spectrum. While their joint venture, the Super speciality restaurant 'Tendulkar's'was coming up, Sachin would even think and contribute his views on the colour of the stitching on the apron the stewards were going to wear. He would give an opinion on the shades of table cloths and the kind of cutlery to be used at the restaurant. Narang's experience with him suggests that Tendulkar is never ok with just anything; he is very specific about what he wants. 'Wherever he went, if he liked a dish he would get the recipe; we would try them out in the kitchen here before approving it and putting it on the menu,' Sanjay recalls.

Sushmita Sen, who was romantically linked with Narang at one stage observed at the time that her close friend was under tremendous pressure. She asked him, 'You have done so many big restaurants and hotels internationally. Why is it that here you are displaying such a sign of nerves?'

Narang replied, 'Because I am dealing with a name and an image as big as Tendulkar's.'

As his business partner on an outside batting crease, Narang's experience has been that Tendulkar has never believed in taking short cuts. If necessary he will go round and round. Work extra hard.

But no short cuts please! And everything with a straight bat. He has a simple rule that everything should be done as per the book. There are quite a few restaurants all over India who manipulate their sales figures to bring down the sales tax amount. Sachin clearly laid down his conditions beforehand that nothing that is not upfront should happen there; that in terms of employees, legal dues and sales tax, everything should be above board. 100 per cent. Not even 99 per cent.

Anyone who has watched Sachin up close would have learned a very important lesson in life – that no one has an Alladin's Magic Lamp. The only lamp in life are two four-letter words – work hard. He slogs day in and day out. So much so for anyone who questions: What is the point in being born a genius if you have to work so hard? The best *slogging* stories of Sachin are currently with the Indian Coach Gary Kirsten.

He occupies a ring side seat in Sachin's private laboratory. If you attend any Indian team training session, one picture is always constant. Kirsten continuously throwing balls at Sachin. This is not conventional net practice and a huge diversion if you think of the methods great batsmen of the past used to prepare themselves at practice. Kirsten throws at least four to five hundred balls at Sachin per session. This practice began in Adelaide. Kirsten was very nervous. He had just taken over the reigns of the Indian team after a stormy Greg Chappell era. Sachin and Kirsten together on a cricket turf. One-on-one. Both were gauging the other. Kirsten, especially, felt a little awkward. As a player he used to throw lots of balls to his erstwhile teammate Herschelle Gibbs.

Throwing is mainly done for a batsman to practise his skills. Kirsten knew all about this business. But in front of Tendulkar on a cricketing field, whoever you

|||||||| The unbeaten combination: Sachin and Gary Kirsten

are, you do get a little nervous. The first 25 to 30 deliveries he threw were not exactly up to Sachin's liking. They put a little extra pressure on the batsman who did not seem immensely pleased. So Kirsten decided to go back a little and throw slightly slower. Later on, he realized the hiccup had occured as he was trying extra hard to impress Sachin. Even to throw properly, you need to be relaxed. Neither of them, however, realized at the first meeting that an illustrious partnership had just begun. That if the Greg Chappell era marked a period of cold, relentless winter, this was the spring Sachin's heart had longed for.

From day one, Sachin has praised Kirsten for creating a family atmosphere in the dressing room. Sachin is not the sort who says the same thing again and again – unless he really feels like doing so. By saying it so many times, he has made clear the deep-rooted appreciation he has for the former South African opener. And also dropped more than a minor hint that in the previous dressing room, this *family atmosphere* did not prevail.

In return, Kirsten says that Sachin is the most likeable person he has come across in a professional world. He maintains that in all his years of playing, coaching and observing professional sports, there has never been a bigger role model. It is quite amusing that despite being the coach, Kirsten calls Sachin the *Professor* of the Indian team. He and Dhoni both feel that Sachin can stay as long as he wishes to, inside the Indian dressing room.

But how did someone who averaged 29.67 during the Chappell regime, bounce back so spectacularly in the new order? Kirsten offers his own explanation which not only sounds logical but offers interesting food for thought for cricket coaches all over the world.

... He is a great player and the best thing about his greatness is that he is ever so willing to contribute to the team. He wants to be made comfortable. If you can create that happiness around him and an enjoyment factor, he performs at his optimum.

I realized soon that for him to perform, I needed to set up an environment where he would feel comfortable. I knew all about the cleanness and purity of his technique. As for South Africa I used to field at either mid-on or mid-off and the number of balls that went past me at lightning pace suggested that he presented the full face of the bat to everything. When I turned the Indian coach and came in closer contact with him, the other aspects of his batsmanship were thrown open to me. I understood that he wants a certain peace of mind to be derived from the practice session.

Throwing practice for a long time gives him a certain mental feel. He locks that mental feel within his subconscious, so that the next day when he goes out there in the middle, he has no worries. He has to just remain focussed on the ball. Everything else has been taken care of.

Physically you have prepared well. You have been to the gym. You have taken adequate rest. Mentally you are happy. So your whole system is in place.

Kirsten, for one, doesn't want to equate Sachin with a poem. For him, Sachin is huge and rock solid – 'More of a New York skyline than poetry in motion.'

Again interesting. But to an Indian, possibly another description given by one of Sachin's close friends seems more appealing. 'He has proved that you can rise from the lowest of the low, without a godfather, without pulling strings; you can climb to the heights through sheer determination and hard work.'

Hearing them all, I honestly feel it to be a humbling privilege to visit the great champion's private laboratory through the minds of such wonderful people. Being able to write about it is perhaps a bonus!

||||||| Anjali, the sheet anchor of his life

CHAPTER 8

A⁺A WHOLE SQUARE

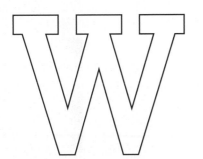ho is the best batting partner Sachin ever had? If you are ever asked that question in a cricket quiz, just safely answer: FAMILY!
You will walk away with the winner's cheque.
So many people have experienced this first hand
This author also did.

After attending the wedding reception of Sachin Tendulkar about fifteen years ago, I was tempted to write an open letter to his father, Mr Ramesh Tendulkar. As per the usual practice with open letters, I did post the same. Though I still have a doubt whether it reached him. Incidentally, just before the most celebrated marriage of the year took place, I had done an extensive interview with Sachin at the Eden Gardens. He talked about a lot of things in that apart from his impending marriage and kept emphasizing that his father was a bigger success than he. Of course I completely disbelieved him. But subsequently, the reception experience and the stories that I could gather, made me believe that Sachin was perhaps right.

In Sachin we have seen and praised the lovely flower. But forgotten to acknowledge the all-important seed. The idea of an open letter was perhaps an extension of the thought.

Mr Ramesh Tendulkar
Ushakal
Sahitya Sahawas,
Kalanagar, Bandra East
Mumbai

Dear Sir,
I would have loved to have engaged in a tête-à-tête with you at the Jade Garden party last Friday, even though I know of your aversion for publicity and the media. After all, the occasion was very special. We were there on your invitation. You could not have avoided talking to your guests, however much you may have preferred to.

On a four-foot high stage in front of us stood your newly married son and daughter-in-law. His black Italian three-piece suit and her off-white salwar kameez grabbed eyeballs. The guests at the party were largely divided into two groups. Those like Gavaskar, Shastri and Patil were seen chatting with one another. The rest of the crowd kept gawking at a tall, lissome, light-eyed beauty with lustrous long tresses. I have a feeling you didn't know who she was. She was Kimi Katkar, an actress who quit films some two years ago. But obviously her glamorous image still grabbed eyeballs.

But believe me, a Marathi journalist who sat next to me and I kept our eyes trained on you all the while. You sat quietly in a corner, not letting the crowd disturb you in any way. You were calm and composed, only speaking occasionally to give instructions to people. It was as though you were remote-controlling the whole event from where you sat inconspicuously.

A former professor of Marathi literature and a poet, Sir, you are regarded by your youngest son as the most successful man in your family.

Observing you from close quarters for nearly three hours that evening, I came to the conclusion that it is from your genes that Sachin gets his calmness, depth and cautious nature.

Your younger son has unmatched courage and self-restraint. After your family had decided that a wedding was a private affair and thus must not be allowed to get into the public domain, all the members adhered to the privacy policy. Your fort was impregnable.

I'm not sure you would have been able to pull off the function in such privacy in England, thanks to the aggressive efforts of the over-eager tabloid journalists in that country. But the combined strength of the Indian press that day was pretty formidable too. Here's what I saw outside the Jewel of India Hall on the morning of the wedding: About a 100 photographers agitatedly paced the field outside while the event was taking place within. The members of the media could see nothing except the shadows of some of the guests on the glass walls of the venue. Teams from Doordarshan and 'The World This Week' also waited outside. They too had been refused entry.

The police did not let anyone enter the hall, even though the photographers kept trying. Eventually, one of them, an energetic photographer from Kolkata, managed to get in. He took exclusive pictures of the wedding garlands being exchanged, only to have the offending reels confiscated by security personnel on his way out. So much for the exclusive photographs!

Right after the wedding your son and daughter-in-law stepped outside for a brief five-minute photo session for the press. Of course, no one was allowed to go anywhere near Sachin and his bride. A rod was used to fence off the photographers from approaching the couple at close quarters. The ensuing pandemonium was not like anything I have seen before or since.

If I had had a proper camera, I would have only clicked pictures of the tussle between star power and the photographers and the total helplessness of the latter in the unequal battle. It would certainly have made a more interesting picture than that of the newlyweds.

Apparently a few had resented the inclusion of the line, 'Please bring this card with you', on the invitation letter. During the last ten years only one other family in the subcontinent has dared to add this line to an invitation. That card was issued from a certain 70 Cliffton Road address in Karachi in 1987. After the Bhuttos, you were the first to insert this line on a wedding card.

In this age of media explosion, you probably didn't have a choice. Ajit Wadekar and Ravi Shastri felt that you did the right thing. If the stipulation had not been laid down, uninvited members of the media and the general

||||||||Glowing at their wedding night 15 summers ago

public might have spoilt the party for you. How could you take the risk?

This act may have made you look a little pretentious, but nobody would ever have held you guilty of opportunism. I have seen many Indian celebrities readily give in to the demands of the Western media. But at the Jade Garden reception, one saw the BBC crew and other sundry white journalists being driven out because they had not been invited.

This made me realize that some people are very different to others. Or else, you would not have been able to say NO to Star TV's offer of Rs 1 crore in exchange for a live coverage of Sachin's wedding function. One crore! Who in the subcontinent has ever received such an offer?

Most people thought that the wedding would be swathed in glamour, and gods and goddesses would fly down from space to land on the roof terrace of Jade Garden. They were disappointed. There was neither the Prime Minister nor any Bollywood star. Filmstars were conspicuous by their absence, which is what I thought was the spectacular thing about the event. A few delicious dishes such as the Illahabadi Alu apart, there was nothing exceptional about the dinner menu either. I was constantly struck by your family's sense of moderation and reluctance to show off. Your middle-class foundations are obviously too solid to be shaken by the waves of superstardom.

Your wife seemed as self-effacing as you. She had worked very hard for an insurance company to supplement the family income.

And now that the family is affluent, your wife continues to be a quiet, unobtrusive person. Only a mother like her could have given birth to children such as yours. Your elder son, Nitin, is a poet with published books to his credit. He has a plum job with Air India. And yet he prefers to stay away from publicity. Your second son, Ajit, has given up half his life and his cricket to look after the well-being of his younger brother.

When all of you were posing with the newlyweds for a picture to be taken by a hired photographer, it occurred to me that everybody in your family was a Sachin! The argument that a champion absorbs all the ingredients he requires from society to create himself is the West's recipe for success. In an underdeveloped country like India, things are fundamentally different. In such countries, the champion has to engage in constant warfare with a lack of infrastructure, and depends on family and society for sustenance.

Your support of Tendulkar has been unstinting.

The opponents may have technology on their side, but when has technology been strong enough to beat the power of a family-centric society? You should have let those BBC guys in that day. You know why?

So that they realized that India is not just about exotic rope tricks, elephants, snakes and poverty. So that they saw that India is about you, and families like yours.

Sir, the best course on your menu that night clearly was Family.

Best wishes

Gautam Bhattacharya

From all counts Ramesh was a remarkable man. Extremely kind-hearted. With his meagre income (pre the huge salary hike Government teachers and professors enjoy now), it was not easy to support a family of three sons and one daughter. Yet he stood straight and looked for social causes like bringing up the gardener's son. There was more than one occasion when he ended up paying from his salary for broken glasses. The glasses had been broken due to the batting fury of his youngest son. Angry neighbours who occupied the opposite ground floor flat demanded money and the gentleman that he was, the Senior Tendulkar obliged. He did bleed but didn't show it!

When a documentary on Sachin was being made a few years ago, one of his neighbours told me that the same people who had been so angry then, and had demanded immediate compensation, were now showing a lot of pride before the camera. They described in detail as to how the ten-year-old broke their window panes regularly. The only thing the cameras didn't capture was someone up there smiling big time!

Sachin is still led by the principles and ethos his father has ingrained in him. Apparently when he was becoming famous, his father had advised him that no matter how big a reputation he earned, he should never ever endorse a tobacco brand or an alcoholic product. Till today Sachin refuses such offers despite being offered crores and crores to do the same.

In a manner of speaking, Ramesh Tendulkar may have been Sachin's *first captain*. But along with him, Sachin was also privileged to enjoy other huge emotional supports – the kind of support that ensures complete peace at home, enabling him to concentrate on what he does best – scoring runs. And currently, it is the letter 'A' that has a much greater significance in his life.

A for Ajit and A for Anjali. And they form the most important equation in Sachin's life. A plus A = Whole Square.

A for Ajit and A for Anjali. And they form the most important equation in Sachin's life. A plus A = Whole Square.

There is a common truth about geniuses: They require an additional runway in their life where the excess energy that they hold within themselves can land and park. Or else the energy, instead of helping them, boomerangs to burn them up. It is said that Rabindranath Tagore was protected by his profound faith in the Brahmo religion. For Viv Richards, it is said to have been his Catholic conviction. And for Sachin, it has to be his innate ability to remain rooted to his family. If you find his humility very touching even today, then a bow is due in front of Tendulkar Family which taught him the basic values in life so well.

It is not easy to handle champions of Sachin's stature. Every move of theirs is scanned for imperfections. They have to answer a barrage of questions at every juncture in their career: What is your opinion on this matter? Why did you say what you said? Why couldn't you perform on the field? Why did you include another Mumbai cricketer in your team? Was it because you're too upset with cricketer B to let him play? Are you nursing an injury which is slowing down your game? If so, where is the injury? Why didn't you report it to the team physio? Is it because you are a holy cow called Sachin Tendulkar? What does the orthopaedic surgeon have to say about your tennis elbow? Will it get better or will you have to retire from cricket as a result of it?

The stage is now set for the 7 p m bulletin flashing this piece of breaking news: 'Sachin's about to Retire'. An excellent hour, given that no rival channel would be able to pick up the story from there at that time. It would be too late. With bytes from the doctor, and further validation from sundry indifferent performances from Sachin in recent times, using excerpts from an old article by Gavaskar, a killer package is carefully put together. Running a story on heavy bats the following day would strengthen the campaign. 'It was his bat that finished him,' it would contend. A question the story would invariably need to raise: Who advised him to use such a heavy bat?

What does Achrekar have to say on the matter? An OB van is seen at Shivaji Park … some gritty bargaining with Vinod Kambli at the studio to have him air his views … There would be spokespersons from the brands Sachin endorses, saying, 'We're not sure at this stage whether we'll renew our contracts with Sachin'. By late night, a piping hot headline would be ready:

Sachin's Contracts Are in Grave Danger.

What keeps Sachin going, in spite of all such odds, is the invincible fortress that the 'A' square in his life has constructed around him. One of them handles the outside world and absorbs all the pressure imposed on him by his cricket. The other takes care of the home and heart.

Normally, the Tendulkars are shy, fiercely private people who take good care to stay away from media glare. In spite of the reams written about him and the numerous shows on television, have you ever seen someone in his family on stage, or holding forth on television? There's no such possibility.

||||||| The ever reclusive Ajit Tendulkar

Sachin has two brothers, Nitin and Ajit. His sister Savita, who got him his first cricket bat from Kashmir, now lives in Pune with her husband. Even journalists who are particularly close to Sachin, have never seen Savita. Nitin loves writing poetry like his father. But he seems to have no interest in getting his works published. One word from Sachin and any newspaper in the country would have been ready to publish his works. But Nitin would never even make such a request of Sachin. Nor would he talk to the press himself. On the many occasions that we've met, my introductory 'How are you?' has elicited nothing more than a courteous 'Fine, thank you'.

Recently, at Gavaskar's 60th birthday celebration, I spotted Nitin's wife standing quietly in a corner. I overheard the organiser Pappu Sanzgiri go up to her and say, 'Come, I'll take you to him.' It so happened that Nitin's wife was keen on meeting Amitabh Bachchan. At a programme where Sachin was expected in a short while, his sister-in-law was waiting for a journalist to introduce her to her favourite screen idol! That's exactly how the Tendulkars are: normal people, as far away from the glare of publicity as they can be.

Ajit is even more private than the others. He does not meet anyone. Nor is he ever seen on stage. Media interviews are an absolute no-no for him. His public profile is all about the one book that he released 13 years ago: *The Making of a Cricketer*. His sabbatical from the press since the release of the book has not ended till date. But since the day he took his younger brother to Achrekar's camp, Sachin has never taken a step in his life without consulting his brother. Each time he has thought up a fresh strategy of combat for a new opponent, he has shared it with his brother.

Mumbai's cricket world feels that if there is one quote from Vinod Kambli worth taking note of, it is when he famously said, 'I had everything. But I didn't have a brother like Sachin's.' Bollywood is rife with examples of the love between brothers. But the Sachin-Ajit story is more astounding than anything in films. Even a Salim-Javed, within the realms of commercial cinema, wouldn't have dared to write such a seemingly unbelievable story. Ajit has given his life for Sachin. He has remained a bachelor and gave up his job. He still lives in their old flat in Sahitya Sahawas. His long beard disguises the fact that he is a reasonably good-looking man and a stylish batsman at that. Ajit looks after some of Sachin's business interests while his pre-occupation with cricket takes up the rest of his time.

But he never sits before a television set when his brother is batting. He is far too nervous to be able to do that. Instead, he stays away from home and comes back only when his brother is safely back in the pavilion. I saw him accompany a sixteen-year-old Sachin in Pakistan on his first tour. He was only there for three weeks and missed his brother hitting Qadir for those towering sixes by a few days. Ajit has travelled with Sachin on other occasions too but I don't think he has ever stayed in the same hotel. He's never seen anywhere near Sachin in public. Whatever conversations they have, take place in the privacy of Sachin's home, La Mer, in Bandra West or when Sachin visits him at their old Sahitya Sahawas residence. Though he was always reticent, Ajit has now become an even more private person than before. Forget talking to the media, he doesn't even want to be photographed.

During a Test Match, it is impossible to get through to him. He becomes completely incommunicado. Appears before friends only the day after the Test Match.

Do you find this strange? Then read this story ...

India was playing her inaugural match of the 1999 World Cup at Hove against Hansie Cronje's South Africa at the Sussex County Cricket Ground. While entering the ground, I thought I saw someone like Ajit standing outside the main gate. But convinced myself that I was wrong – why would Ajit be standing there instead of going in? The match was about to begin. And with Sourav and Sachin coming out to bat, it occurred to me that it might be interesting to include the first-hand excitement of the Indian supporters outside the ground in my match report. When I stepped out, I noticed with some surprise that the man who looked exactly like Ajit was still standing outside the gate. This time our eyes met. He smiled. And I realized that he did not *look like* Ajit. He was, in fact, Ajit!

'Why are you standing outside,' I asked.

'I don't have a ticket for the match. I'm waiting for someone who is getting one for me.'

'You don't have a ticket!'

'No. Actually I was in Paris and I got a friend to collect the match ticket from Sachin last night. But my friend hasn't arrived yet.' Then he added his bit of caution, 'You must not talk about this to anyone inside. Sachin should not be disturbed before he goes out to bat. That would be quite disastrous.'

Now can you imagine how outrageous the whole thing was! Sachin Tendulkar was at that point touted as the main attraction of the 1999 World Cup, and the man who is singularly responsible for making him what he is today was standing outside among a motley crowd of ticketless cricket fanatics!

I asked him whether I could speak to an Indian Cricket Board official, who would immediately organize a pass for him. But Ajit was adamant. He would not accept a pass from anyone. He would wait for his friend. I never did find out when he finally entered the ground but Sachin and Sourav shared a long first-wicket partnership that day. Ajit must have seen some part of his brother's innings. Many years later, when we met again, all he said was, 'This incident would never have happened in the age of mobile phones. I would have only had to check with my friend when he would arrive.' That's all.

Showing off is not in the Tendulkars' blood as I had realized fifteen summers ago at a wedding reception. They're quiet, unpretentious and God-fearing, like most Marathis. The family worships many gods, including Ganapati and Satyanarayan, and several fasts are kept by the family members through the year. They observe the Savitri *vrat* and practice the north Indian ritual of Karwa Chauth too. As Saraswat Brahmins, the Tendulkars are devotees of Mangesh or Lord Shiva. There is a temple in Goa called Mangeshi which they often visit. This lies twenty-two kilometres from Panaji in the neighbourhood of the Mangesh village, where the legendary Mangeshkar sisters come from. I visited the temple located near the Pandit Dinananth Mangeshkar Road more out of curiosity than as a place of worship. But finally was left with no other option but to step aside and admire the serenity of the place. There is a complete lack of hustle-bustle that characterizes so many Indian temples. A complete calmness, like that which is reflected in Tendulkar's mind, envelops the place. Most of the priests there know him personally. Mangesh is their Kuladevata (Family god) and one is reasonably certain that in some form or the other, Tendulkar contributes towards the well-being of the temple.

Ganeshtikri in Nagpur is also a stand-alone place of worship Tendulkar visits whenever he is in the city. Again, like the Mangesh Temple, it is very clean, calm and quiet. I feel the serenity of such places provide a lot of sustenance to Tendulkar who has been the subject of the most unrealistic expectations ever since the age of sixteen. On entering his hotel room during a tour, you're sure to come across three pictures on the table – Ganapati, Mangesh and his father. He is the visible face of a deeply religious family. For someone, with whom the country has been going out to bat for the last two decades, understandably requires a supernatural anchor.

According to close friends of the family, Anjali Tendulkar provides the touch of reality and helps her otherwise humble husband to remain grounded all the more. She is a very important stabilizing factor.

Anjali shares a vegetarian meal on Mondays with the rest of the family. The media gets to see her only once or twice a year, and that too when it is completely

|||||||| On a cricket tour-cum-family vacation. No escape from the paparazzi!

unavoidable. That is when she and the children accompany Sachin briefly on tour. In her fifteen years of married life, she has actually spoken to the media just once. She didn't show much interest in speaking to this author as well. And I thought her privacy must be respected.

Given Anjali's background, it is a surprise that she adapted herself so easily to the conservative Tendulkar household. Anjali's upbringing was entirely different. While her mother is an English lady, her father is a well-to-do, truly cosmopolitan man of the world. Anjali went to school in England and later won a gold medal in paediatrics. Her parental home is an opulent mansion near Breach Candy Hospital in Mumbai. Under the circumstances, the way she merged into the middle-class Sahitya Sahawas milieu is quite extraordionary. Close friends of the family have told me that the sheet-anchoring role Anjali plays, perfectly compliments the on-field performance of her husband. They got married in the mid-1990s but had apparently been seeing each other from 1990. To their credit the affair was kept away from the prying media.

Well-wishers had advised Anjali against completely giving up her career. It is better to stay in touch with the profession, they had said. 'Sign up with a hospital,' said some. In the early days of their marriage Anjali was attached to a hospital but quit when she had children. She feels that, as a paediatrician, she has to be available to her patients day and night. But with Sachin being away on tour for the better part of the year, how would she step out of home at odd hours leaving her children to themselves? She did, of course, make a few rounds to the hospital in case of an emergency. Once, Sachin's close friend Atul Ranade's newly born daughter was in a serious condition. The child had to be put in the ICCU. Sachin asked Anjali to immediately make a visit to the hospital and monitor the treatment. A grateful Ranade recalls she went twice every day, till his daughter stabilised.

The family has its share of superstitions surrounding Sachin's cricket. There is a small temple of Lord Ganapati right next to the Bengali Cultural Association at Shivaji Park. Sachin goes there as often as he can. His runs are like the family treasure. Everyone looks forward to that. Anjali remains glued to her TV when Sachin is batting. She does not make calls, preferring to keep her phone switched off through the innings. Nor does she budge an inch.

In 2008 Sachin was facing a rough patch during the One-day series in Australia. His family had begun to get worried about him. Some of Sachin's friends, members of a musical band, were doing a show which Anjali was attending. During the show one of the musicians announced, 'Sachin is not getting runs because he is in the grip of an evil spell. The next song will help him steer clear of it and then he will score a century.' The band's choice for the next song was the famous Mohammad Rafi number from *Sasural*: 'Teri pyari pyari soorat ko nazar na lage, chashme buddoor'. As luck would have it, Sachin did score a century in the following match. He devastated Australia in Australia, beating Ponting's boys to pulp. Australia lost both the finals.

Next up was the IPL. Even after starting off well, Sachin's team was not going anywhere. Questions were being raised about the captaincy of the Mumbai Indians. Sachin's musical friends were once again doing a show in Mumbai. Anjali arrived at the concert. After a while, she asked, 'Can't we have that song, *Chashme buddoor*, once more?'

The band was in trouble. On the earlier occasion they had the track with them because they had come prepared to play the song. But they didn't have it this time round. However, they honoured Anjali's request and though the Mumbai Indians did not make it to the semi-finals on this occasion, Sachin's form definitely improved. These incidents have never been made public as both Ajit and Anjali prefer to keep family matters to themselves. Sachin too knows how much they value their privacy and tries to keep them away from the public eye.

Like most women whose husbands are away on tour, Anjali has to shoulder all the family responsibilities during Sachin's absence. Sachin is particularly attached to his uncle Suresh with whom he stayed while serving an apprenticeship under Coach Achrekar.

His uncle's home was tiny and they had to share a common toilet with other tenants in the housing society. Today, the uncle is physically in terrible shape. And Sachin, despite his schedule, takes care of his uncle's treatment. He cannot forget that his cricket training period was served out while living in his uncle's house which was a *chawl* (accommodation on a community-sharing basis). When he is away for a long time, it is Anjali who looks after the uncle's treatment-related needs.

A close associate of Sachin's maintains, 'Anjali's greatest contribution lies in not trying to displace Ajit from Sachin's scheme of things. Nine out of ten women

|||||||| This was at a function to honour him

in her place would have resented her brother-in-law's control over his life. They would have taken pains to poison the relationship. But, instead of doing anything of the sort, Anjali created her own dignified slot within the family.'

It has often filled me with wonder to think that the person whom the whole of India relies on, only depends on religion for sustenance. Is it possible to survive so much tension by dedicating oneself to the service of God? There must be some other anchors in his life.

The more I have tried to probe into his life, the more I have been convinced that A Plus A whole square is the real sheet anchor in his existence. It is the core of Team Tendulkar. Ajit and Anjali.

Gavaskar never had a team like this, though he had close friends like Milind Rege and Sumedh Shah. He always went back to his wife Pammi for emotional support. But in the ultimate analysis, Gavaskar, a devotee of Sai Baba, always depended on himself for everything. Kapil Dev too took all his decisions himself, for better or worse.

But times had changed by the time Sachin arrived on the scene. Life had become more complicated with the media hogging the lives of public figures. Now there is more money and more technology. There are innumerable 24x7 news channels. There is Twitter. There is Facebook. There is You Tube. The consequent problems are also more complex than ever before.

It is mandatory for a contemporary icon to have a team around him. Unlike in the past he cannot afford to be a soldier and commander rolled into one.

Sachin knows that his family is one of the buildings in his complex cricket structure. Cricket and family share the same pin code. It is only when he retires that he can think of having separate pin codes for the two. He had once jokingly said in an interview, 'Everybody thinks I can handle pressure quietly, all by myself. Actually, I lose my temper pretty often at home. Poor Anjali has to bear the brunt of my anger on these occasions.'

He draws sustenance from his family in the same way we charge our cell phones from time to time. He constantly looks for new things that have nothing to do with cricket, like music, Thai cuisine or even his son Arjun's school books.

The moderation that the family practises is reflected the manner in which Arjun is being brought up. He practices at the MIG Club, Bandra, which by any stretch of imagination is far from flashy. Unlike some rich sons, Arjun doesn't enjoy the liberty of personally not carrying his cricket kit. He has to carry it himself. Even his birthday parties are not held in five-star hotels or in upmarket places. But at the MIG banquet. Being Tendulkar's son, of course, has its own pressure and even his scores in insignificant school matches are up for discussion in the media.

'Everybody thinks I can handle pressure quietly, all by myself. Actually, I lose my temper pretty often at home. Poor Anjali has to bear the brunt of my anger on these occasions.'

Sachin Tendulkar

Rohan Gavaskar was in the same boat almost two decades ago. And he left a very important piece of advice for the teenaged Arjun: 'Just be yourself. Don't play or behave in a manner to satisfy others. Just be the best that you can be.' Rohan Gavaskar and Abhishek Bachchan are close childhood pals. While their fathers were busy representing the hopes and aspirations of their millions of countrymen, these two must have had a few notes to exchange. People had such unreal expectations from them that they had to bear a cross all the time. In a few years Arjun will be at that stage and then Rohan's advice will come very handy.

Unlike a competent actor who can afford to switch off from the role he is playing and quickly transform himself into the person that he really is, Sachin remains focussed on his cricket. In this he is similar to Sir Don Bradman. They are both family men. But they are family cricket men.

Families play a very important role in the lives of many contemporary Indian cricketers. Rahul Dravid, Sourav Ganguly, Anil Kumble and VVS Laxman are among them. Cricket journalists often say, 'There are only two cricketers who will ask you about your family after they've enquired about the health – Sachin and Sourav.'

Sourav has said over and over again that he owes his captaincy skills to the way he was brought up in a joint family. Handling different kinds of people has taught him to understand characters and helped him figure out ways of motivating them. When Sachin was the Captain, Sourav was the Vice Captain. Whenever he was travelling abroad, Sourav's shopping list always included gifts for all the 51 members in his family. He would get some present or the other for everyone.

Anil Kumble too has his own team comprising his wife and older brother Dinesh. But the difference with Sachin lies in the fact that Dinesh is seen and heard in public much more than Ajit. The other difference is that, in spite of winning the greatest number of matches for India as a bowler, Kumble has never been hounded by the twin worlds of entertainment and advertisement to this extent. He has not been in the public glare from age 16. And yet, Kumble has felt the need to have a family wall to keep him safe. Dravid has required one too. No wonder Sachin has always needed a fortress to slip into.

The other day a well-known Mumbai journalist was saying that Dravid's determination reflected that of his mother, Pushpa Dravid. She is a person of rare spirit who had always wanted to get a PhD but never had the time or the opportunity to work towards it. Finally, however, blessed with both, she began her research at the age of 57 and got her doctorate.

Sourav, on the other hand, has inherited his father's knack for standing tall even under pressure. Anyone familiar with Chandi Ganguly's game in local cricket remembers his ability to bowl the right length at any stage of the game. In the next generation, Sourav has obviously become heir to this spirit.

Sachin's college-professor father and insurance company executive mother have passed on their prudence, calmness and ability to struggle into Sachin's DNA. Along with this, his limitless talent and the support of 'A' square have made him invincible. Who can hold back someone with so many gifts from God?

One school of opinion suggests that Brian Lara on song is more artistic, more lethal than Tendulkar. Despite that, the fact that he's had to permanently give up the position of the contemporary world's finest batsman to Tendulkar is probably because Lara never had a mast to help him sail through life. He is an audacious swimmer who has crossed many seas. But he has not been able to pass the test of reliability or consistency. Lara's been in an ICCU of a Colombo hospital one afternoon and at a shopping mall at night, all in the course of a single day! This, when he had not even been released by the hospital.

Sachin is not one to fritter away his energy. If Lara chooses to squander himself away in spite of his huge talent and prefers to live like Kambli on a bigger scale, it's none of Sachin's business. Bradman still lies way ahead of Sachin with an average of 99.94. But then a century of centuries is such an extraordinary feat that if it happens, it will be as spectacular as 99.94.

And the day that happens, may be 'A' Square will find a good enough reason to break their silence and happily part with some more interesting details about the family's proudest possession! Who knows!

||||||| They were that close – once upon a time

CHAPTER 9

KUCH TO LOG KAHENGE

The eternal story of Ram aur Shyam! Two made-for-each-other friends and their journey!

Both were real. Both were huge fans of Amitabh Bachchan. Shyam, incidentally, was a great mimic. Ram particularly liked the manner in which he imitated Bachchan's voice in *Agneepath*. And the modulation he brought into that particular line, 'Main Vijay Dinanath Chauhan ...'

Both were in the same school. Both played a little bit of cricket at the expense of their studies. Both were known for their famous pranks.

One day, while crossing the road off Azad Maidan, Ram noticed a fat, dhoti-clad gentleman making his way on to the ground. He immediately placed a bet with Shyam.

If Shyam could lift that man's dhoti, Ram would pay for the movie they were planning to go and see. Shyam, as usual, reacted lightning fast to such an attractive challenge. He went and lifted the man's dhoti immediately. But was not prepared for the 'fatso's' quick response. Shyam got a royal slap, the impact of which hit him so hard that he took well over a minute to regain his senses. By the time he turned back, Ram was nowhere to be seen. He was next seen inside the movie hall. Shyam was to remark later, 'I never saw him run that fast between the wickets!'

Had it been a movie, the scriptwriter may have named them thus. In real life, Ram was Sachin Tendulkar. Shyam, a certain Vinod Kambli.

Between them, during childhood, they had jointly created, apart from a world record, more than a dozen prank-stories worth recording! They batted together. Scored together. Moved around together. Created records together. Usually bowlers hunt in pairs. This was a classic case of two friends, both batsmen, hunting in pairs. To use that cliched phrase – Sachin and Kambli were the inseparable twins!

However, at the end of the day, their story ran like the antithesis of a Manmohan Desai film. Not lost and found. But found and lost.

As their respective careers started taking completely different directions, one achieved the pinnacle of glory and fame while the other reportedly drowned his miseries in alchohol and various forms of self-abuse.

The biggest pointer, of course, was the interview in 'Sach ka Saamna', the reality game-show that all of 2009-India could not stop talking about. The show which was all about spilling the beans on your personal and professional life, had Kambli alleging that his childhood friend didn't do enough for him. People in television circles and the participants knew very well, that even though the show was presented in such a manner that looked like everything was happening live and impromptu, that was not the complete truth. A small yet important part of the show was designed and agreed upon beforehand.

Kambli speaking out against Sachin on national television happened nearly eighteen months ago. However, for the devastation that Kambli's disclosure led to, it could well have occurred eighteen minutes ago. The cricketing fraternity is still stunned that Kambli could resort to such a dastardly act of accepting money to speak against his childhood friend on a TV show. Had it been an ordinary newspaper interview or even a television chat, the impact would have been much less. For all you know, people who speak ill against a seventeen-test veteran like Kambli today, may have sympathized and 'understood his frustration'.

But in 'Sach ka Saamna', the star participants were paid handsomely and if they were prepared to say nasty things about someone as big as a Tendulkar or a Dilip Kumar, their bargaining power would have shot up all the more. A Tendulkar abuse, that too by a fellow cricketer of his ilk, is such an unlikely event that aired at any given time of the day, it was bound to attract huge TRP ratings and newspaper headlines all over. A common childhood friend, Atul Ranade, feels 'betrayed by Kambli with a massive sense of being let down'. He says, 'The channelwallahs used Kambli to enhance their ratings. And the worst part was that he knew he was being used.'

But the emotional scar remained irreparable. Sachin did not react much. But some of his close friends felt this was a blatant lie and amounted to stabbing him in the back. They were not prepared to dismiss it as the drowning of miseries by a frustrated individual. They viewed it as the calculated assault of a self-seeker, an opportunist. One who was prepared to reduce a long-standing, innocent friendship on a weighing scale of currency notes!

That's what the show eventually achieved. Kambli possibly laughed all the way to the bank. The show's producer possibly strengthened his market share.

But the emotional scar remained irreparable. Sachin did not react much. But some of his close friends felt this was a blatant lie and amounted to stabbing him in the back. They were not prepared to dismiss it as the drowning of miseries by a frustrated individual. They viewed it as the calculated assault of a self-seeker, an opportunist. One who was prepared to reduce a long-standing, innocent friendship on a weighing scale of currency notes!

I heard stories subsequently as to how Sachin had offered to help Kambli financially or otherwise, when he was out of the Indian team.

The Mumbai cloudburst of 26 July 2005 had kept the city under water for a few days. It had also flooded the area in which Kambli lived. Sachin immediately called his friend, inviting him to come and stay in his own house at Bandra West which was not situated on a lowland area, for a few days. But Kambli preferred to check in at The Taj Land's End Hotel, hardly a kilometre away from his friend's place. There was always a miniature Lara in the fun-loving Kambli and it was no surprise that his not coming to the Tendulkar household was viewed as staying away from a disciplined regime.

Speaking to both at any given time of life, anyone would come to the conclusion that it was inevitable their worlds wouldn't meet finally.

The fallout was only too natural. Sachin is the intense perfectionist, decidedly ambitious and has prepared himself for the pain that comes with it. Kambli is fun-loving, a 'live-for-the-moment' type. Incidently, a small but significant example perhaps illustrates the different attitudes towards life of these two erstwhile friends: Sachin does not have a ring tone on his phone. Because, I suspect, cricket is his unmistakable ring tone. On the other hand, if you call Kambli, you will be greeted by a funny ring tone: 'I am Quick Gun Murugan. I am not your father's ancestral property that I will call you back.'

Kambli, the holder of two double hundreds in Test cricket, is quick to dismiss this 'He was serious, the other chose to be fun-loving' generalisation about them. 'People have always misunderstood me,' he says. 'I was as serious as Sachin. Just because I was joking all the time they felt I was not intense. They were wrong. Perhaps my style was different. And then destiny made a further difference.'

Kambli also tried hard to dismiss the belief in certain circles that he was envious of Sachin's standing in the game. He puts up a defence saying, 'We never had any jealousy problems between us. We used to compliment each other. I was at the non-striker's end when Sachin completed his first ever One-day hundred. I hugged him and was so happy.'

But if it was not jealousy, then what made him speak against his friend in 'Sach ki Saamna'? Kambli offers his own detailed explanation, possibly for the first time since the controversy. Some may agree. Most may not. But this is his account of the story:

'It is all about motivation. Not anything else. People again misunderstood me. All I wanted to say was motivation can do wonders.

'In early 2000, I visited a cancer patient at the Nanavati Hospital. The doctors told me the boy would live for another two days only. The boy also knew he would go any time. But I cheered him up. I said, "You are perfectly fine. Stand up and fight the disease." He seemed motivated. Finally, he lived for eight more days. That is motivation for you. I thought Sachin would provide me the same. I did not blame him. I only expressed my sentiments which were later twisted ...'

There will possibly be few takers for Kambli's explanation. He did definitely say on the show: 'Sachin didn't do enough for me'. That, to many, is difficult to comprehend. In Indian cricket circles, particularly the former national selectors will tell you how hard Sachin used to try for Kambli while he was the Captain. There were stories that one particular selector who was trying to push a much more deserving southpaw had told Sachin in anger, 'We are not choosing a Mumbai side here.'

Talking to Kambli, I got the impression that irrespective of whatever he said in his own defence, given another opportunity, he won't do a 'Sach Ka Saamna' again. Today, he says fondly, 'I will tell my son – when you grow up, try becoming a Sachin. You may not ever become one. Chances are that you won't. But if you try as sincerely as he did, you will certainly become someone in life.'

Very early in their cricketing careers, Kambli had compared his status to a staircase and Sachin to an elevator. 'I am taking more time to reach where he has already reached because I am using the staircase. He has got an elevator.' Kambli, incidentally, made his Indian debut three years after Sachin.

'It is all about motivation. Not anything else. People again misunderstood me. All I wanted to say was motivation can do wonders.'

Vinod Kambli

Now that he is leading an almost seven-year-old retired life, Kambli puts an end to this analogy by praising Sachin profusely, 'He showed great resolve to lift himself back from the staircase to the elevator. A tennis elbow and other injuries had taken their toll. For a short time that took him outside the elevator. People were even suggesting that he must retire. How well he got back! And I must admit that throughout his life Sachin has worked extremely hard inside the elevator.'

Words well meant. Well put. But it is unlikely that they will reach his friend's ears as they did in the past. The doors of friendship once found and lost will possibly remain lost. As a betrayed Tendulkar has shown tell-tale signs that it was all over .... Though to his great credit, he has not displayed this publicly and has attended functions with Kambli.

Quite a few in Mumbai cricketing circles used to say jokingly that this Sachin-Kambli pair was the nearest to the Veeru-Jai friendship in *Sholay*. But now the crack is so wide that they don't have to come and tell you 'Yeh dosti tut gaye'. This friendship is over for life. Unless something extraordinary happens!

Sachin's relationship with Sanjay Manjrekar looks like it is headed towards the same direction. Which is not only sad but difficult to digest for people who had seen their initial bonding in international cricket. If Ajit Tendulkar was the brother at home, Sanjay seemed the cricketing blood-brother of Sachin. During the 1989 tour to Pakistan which happened to be Sachin's maiden international outing, you could see a Manjrekar in almost every frame. Not only did Vijay Manjrekar's son dominate the series with masterly performances; he also sang lovely Pankaj Udhas numbers at the Sunday Club (which used to be the informal meeting place between the media and the team), and looked like guiding Sachin at every stage. There was a calypso made on Gavaskar when he stormed the cricket fields in the Caribbean with an aggregate of 774 runs. For the Sunday Club in Pakistan, Gavaskar recorded the same song with a slight difference. He replaced West Indies with Pakistan. And Gavaskar with Manjrekar.

> **Pakistan could not out Manjrekar at all,**
> **not at all you know ...**
> **Pakistan could not out Manjrekar at all ...**

||||||| He plays the tabla; Manjrekar plays the harmonium and sings

So sang Sunny. If one recalls correctly, the song was played on the third meeting of the Sunday Club. Everyone clapped, but Sachin clapped, cheered and rejoiced. Sanjay had topped the series averages with 90 plus and scored 569 runs from four test matches. But Sachin seemed immensely happy as if a calypso had been recorded on him. The relationship continued for quite a few years till Manjrekar played his last test for India and bid an early farewell to international cricket.

From there we got transported to a rude awakening of July 21, 2006.

Tendulkar, in an unusual counterpunching interview given to Vinay Naidu of the *Times of India* just tore into Manjrekar. Incidentally, the day before Manjrekar had written a stinging by-lined piece in the same daily, alleging that Tendulkar's body had aged and he was not ready to accept this fact of life. Manjrekar wrote,'I have found the scenes prior to his recent, long absences from the game quite strange. The Tendulkar of today gives me the impression that his main focus is not to fail! And he wants to give himself the best shot at that by competing only when he feels he is in his prime, physically and mentally. In comparison, Lara's success has a lot to do with his failures. Lara is not in fear of failure. Lara knows that with advancing years, failures will mount. So while Lara is staying realistic, Tendulkar seems to be chasing a ghost.' The article was headlined, 'Sachin, Don't Be Afraid of Failure'.

The day Manjrekar's article appeared, quite a few phone calls were exchanged within the Indian cricket fraternity. The tone of Manjrekar's article had surprised many as it smacked of vengeance. But the raised eye brows went up further when Tendulkar gave an equally stinging reply the very next day. Especially the members of the media were taken back. That someone, who even after spending seventeen years on the circuit, had never ever reacted to press criticism of any kind, had finally come out to defend himself!

Tendulkar said, 'I don't want to comment much. But I feel sorry that an ex-India player has made statements without checking the facts and without talking to people concerned. I also find it surprising that he has made these statements without being in the dressing room and knowing the true situation.' The physios who used to work with the team at that stage came to Tendulkar's defence.

'I have found the scenes prior to his recent, long absences from the game quite strange. The Tendulkar of today gives me the impression that his main focus is not to fail! And he wants to give himself the best shot at that by competing only when he feels he is in his prime, physically and mentally. In comparison, Lara's success has a lot to do with his failures. Lara is not in fear of failure. Lara knows that with advancing years, failures will mount. So while Lara is staying realistic, Tendulkar seems to be chasing a ghost.'

The article was headlined, 'Sachin, Don't Be Afraid of Failure'.

Sanjay Manjrekar

They cited instances when Tendulkar had endured pain and trauma to deliver his best for India. They were not exaggerating as Tendulkar did play in several series with an injury. The most notable one was the World Cup of 2003 where, quite incredibly, he lifted the Man of the Tournament with a broken finger.

Four and a half years have gone by and Manjrekar is still an outcast as far as Tendulkar is concerned. According to reports, from Sanjay's side there were attempts to clarify his position – that as a professional media person, he had only been doing his job. But it did not meet with the desired response. Someone very close to Tendulkar told me that Sachin realized where all this was coming from. And from then onwards he has just shrugged it off and moved on in life. Manjrekar, in his capacity as a top-quality media professional, works around all the teams in world cricket and does player interviews. But he is never seen in the close vicinity of a Tendulkar and vice versa. I am yet to see a cricket function in the last four and a half years attended by both. Journalists from Mumbai tell me that such an occasion may have taken place only in Mars! But on this planet there has been none!

How does a Manjrekar feel currently? With Sachin climbing so many peaks in the last two years, does he think he was a little hasty in passing a judgement? Does he acknowledge that before writing on something as sensitive as a career-threatening injury, he should have checked with Sachin himself? Access was no problem. Come on, he was no ordinary journalist. But currently, Manjrekar doesn't seem too keen to comment on this. And if someone is that reluctant, it is no use stretching him beyond a point.

Tendulkar has an enviable track record that during the last twenty-two years that he has spent in public life, he has attracted controversies in such small numbers that they don't measure up to double digits. But the Multan post-194 declaration controversy will surely count as a major one in his life. His relationship with Manjrekar, reportedly started losing its flavour since the 194-declaration controversy.

Insider information suggests that Kambli's disclosures in 'Sach Ka Saamna' came as a shock to Sachin. However, with Manjrekar, he saw it coming. Sachin's counter punch came as late as 2006 and yet the discord had become wide open since Manjrekar's strong views both in print as well as on TV were publicised after the Indian captain brought an end to the Indian innings with Tendulkar remaining not out on 194.

|||||||| A waste of energy for the fast bowler

Having been present at that day's press conference in Multan, I can still term the incident as almost make-believe. Tendulkar expressing dissatisfaction over a team decision, during an important Test Match, that too against Pakistan, on Pakistani soil, was simply incredulous! Unless you were physically there and thus can vouch for the fact that it actually happened. The Multan press box is just opposite the pavilion. And when three of them turned up for the press conference including Sehwag, Media Manager Amrit Mathur and Sachin – no one had any clue as to what was going to happen. Sachin's body language hardly suggested any disgust and I, for one, thought that perhaps the decision to declare with him standing at 194 had been taken mutually.

This was when Sachin was asked by a lady television journalist from Delhi as to why the innings had been closed with him just six runs away from an important landmark. Everyone expected him to be the ever-so-politically-correct-and-proper Tendulkar. What they got instead was a volcanic eruption. Mathur, one of the senior cricket board functionaries at that time, had pre-empted such situations before, including that of vice captain Ravi Shastri's exclusion from vital World Cup matches in Australia.

But here he was clueless as the damage took place even before his reflexes could work.

From the Tendulkar interview elsewhere in this book, it is quite apparent that the man has still not recovered from the incident. And that till today, he does not regret the outburst. Incidentally, for the record, the jury was divided about whether the declaration was the right decision or Sachin should have been allowed an extra over. Manjrekar remained the flag-bearer of the 'right decision' school of thought. It was not certainly music to Sachin's ears when he heard that Sanjay had gone live on TV and hailed it as the 'greatest ever team decision in Indian cricket'. He wrote about it as well and shared his thoughts with some journalists in the press box who went and relayed them to Sachin.

To be fair to Manjrekar, there were others like an Imran Khan who also welcomed the decision. Imran compared this to his own declaration in Karachi years ago, when Javed Miandad had been 20 runs short of his triple hundred. He sang the same tune that it was high time in the subcontinent's cricket that individuals went beyond their personal milestones and looked at team interests. But Manjrekar, or for that matter, someone close to Tendulkar, saying something adverse on the public platform without sharing his thoughts with him personally, was different to what an Imran said. All through his life Tendulkar had characterized himself as someone who did not react to media criticism.

The trait was quite extraordinary as during such a long and high profile cricket life, he had never ever got into arguments with any presswallahs. He just got on with his game. Tendulkar only bled in private when someone close to him wrote or said something nasty without caring to check the facts.

Why wasn't Sachin allowed to score those six runs? There are various theories. One is a purely cricketing one. That India needed to declare fast, so that she could give her bowlers enough chance to get Pakistan out in the second innings and ensure a victory. Understandably, the idea was to declare after the drinks' break and allow Sachin one full over to complete the double. But then, suddenly, against the run of play, Yuvraj got out and the umpires asked for drinks. The scheduled break was more than two minutes away. So, that extra over could not be bowled and Dravid decided to declare at this stage. For carrying on after drinks would have led to another stoppage for the resumption of the Pakistan innings.

There is, of course, another theory that Sourav, the Tour Captain, had advised Rahul, the Stand-in Captain, to address the practicality of the situation and declare as the innings was getting a bit prolonged. Was that true? Sourav, the braveheart, in almost all cricketing matters, refuses to get drawn into this seven-year-old controversy. All he says is, 'I don't wish to speak. This was between two individuals and should stay that way.'

Now it is your turn to guess who he refers to as the 'two individuals'! It could be Dravid and Sachin. Or it could be Rahul and Sourav himself. I was unable to ask Dravid. The day I interviewed him for the book in his Johannesburg hotel room, he was on a drip the whole evening. It was in some way humanly unattainable to abuse that much kindness and rake up old, unpleasant issues, especially with him in that physical state. All we know is that the day after the controversy, Sachin and Dravid had a one-on-one meeting and things were sorted out for the time being. That the scar had not entirely disappeared was not known to me till I interviewed Tendulkar for this book.

About Sachin's detractors, Harbhajan Singh puts it so expressively in the words of an old film song. Bhajji says,

'His detractors! Arrey, kuch to log kahenge.
 Logon ka kam hai kahena.
Choro bekar ki baton mein kahin beet na jaye raina.'

'Oh, people will always have something to say!
That is what they always do.
Let's not waste the night
On such meaningless talk!'

||||||| Harbhajan has been his most loyal supporter

And people did say quite a bit about his captaincy and ability to win matches for India. The statistics in the book clearly show that 38 Test Matches till date have been won by India where Tendulkar has scored 50 plus. What it does not record is at least 20 more matches were either drawn or lost as the rest couldn't take advantage of his batting brilliance. It was a clear case of a genius being blamed for the mediocrity shown by others. A glaring example would be the Chennai test match against Wasim Akram's Pakistan where the remaining batsmen failed to take advantage of a superlative second innings hundred by Sachin. Javagal Srinath, for one, gets angry when someone puts forward criticism of Tendulkar not winning that many matches for India.

Srinath says, 'I find this talk completely rubbish. It was also up to the other ten players in the team to take full advantage of the opportunities that he created. Ask

|||||| A study in concentration

them to put their hands on their heart and only then some may tell you, yes, we let him down.' Ravi Shastri is calmer and more philosophical when he says, 'Before criticising someone like Sachin, just think, you don't have too many champions like him in this country. Is he deserving of your criticism?'

Another big controversy in Tendulkar's life was the Mike Denness incident which, in retrospect, he may have welcomed. For it showed his real standing in Indian society and the integrity and credibility that he represents in the minds of a billion people. As Tendulkar said to this writer recently, 'They said, every time I went out to bat, I took India with me. Here there was no cricket bat, yet they believed and backed me blindly. I was so touched that I didn't know how to repay this love.'

This happened in the Second Test of India's 2001 tour of South Africa.

Match Referee Mike Denness fined four Indian players for excessive appealing as well as the Indian Captain Sourav Ganguly for not controlling his team. In a decision that stunned the cricketing world, Tendulkar was given a one-test match suspension on alleged charges of ball tampering. There was such a hue and cry over the incident that Denness was banned from entering the venue of the Third Test Match. The repurcussions escalated to include allegations of racism and the issue was even raised in the Indian Parliament. After a thorough investigation, the ICC revoked the official status of the match and the ban on Tendulkar was also lifted. The backlash from the Indian public was so massive that to cricket enthusiasts, it was a reminder of the days of the Bodyline crisis!

Ajit Wadekar, who led India in the utterly forgettable three test match series against Mike Denness's England in 1974, said that from personal experience he was not at all surprised that it was his counterpart who happened to be the 'foul' guy. 'Denness was always this stiff upper-lipped Pom who made no bones about his superiority complex. He definitely had a bias against us. His manners were so deplorable that in comparison, a Geoffrey Boycott looked like a friendly chap,' Wadekar signs off breaking into a grin. Sourav, the team captain, who was also fined, emphasizes that even today he can't understand where Denness was coming from. 'I mean, can you tamper with a brand new ball? Absurd. Sachin was completely innocent.' T N Seshan, former Chief Election Commissioner, is a cricket buff and a straight talker. He terms the entire episode in one simple sentence: White man's prejudice!

Jagmohan Dalmiya led Sachin's case strongly with the International Cricket Council. He was successful too as the ban was not only lifted but the test was declared an unofficial one. Here is Dalmiya's recollection of this most bizzare event:

> **'When I was told that the Match referee has held Sachin responsible for ball tampering, I immediately knew this could never have been true. We fought tooth and nail. The**

South African Board Chief, Gerald Majola, was very supportive. With his help, we jointly took it to the ICC. There we demanded that Denness' role should be examined and we should be allowed to interrogate him. Around this time, Denness suddenly got admitted into a hospital. The huge public pressure and the backlash may have had something to do with it. But he stayed there for more than a month. Then the ICC Chief Ehsan Mani requested us to drop the charges against Denness as under such extreme pressure, his health was showing signs of further deterioration. So we dropped the charges and gave it in writing that we are doing so on compassionate grounds.'

July can't be Tendulkar's favourite month as he has attracted media attention at least three times during this month for all the wrong reasons. Be it a Manjrekar article, the Kambli television interview, or an unwanted Ferrari controversy. The last one was a clear case of completely wrong advice given to an individual without understanding his stature in society. A year earlier, he had equalled Bradman's record of 29 test centuries. To commemorate the occasion, Ferrari invited the Master to its paddock in Silverstone on the eve of the British Grand Prix. He was also gifted a Ferrari 360. Tendulkar subsequently applied for exemption of customs duty from India's then Finance Minister Jaswant Singh. Jaswant wrote back saying that the Government would waive the duty imposed on importing the car in appreciation of his recent feat. But it was in sharp contrast to the existing rules which stated that customs duty can be waived only when receiving an automobile as a prize and not as a gift. So while the Audi that Shastri had won for becoming the Champion of Champions, was allowed a duty-free passage and no one could question it, here the initial reaction was hostile to Tendulkar. There were huge protests against the waiver. There was also a PIL filed in the Delhi High Court which questioned how the duty had been waived. Tendulkar has never ever faced such an outcry in India.

With controversy becoming such a big issue, Tendulkar promptly offered to pay the customs duty. Fiat, the owners of Ferrari, stepped in and agreed to pay the import duty, thereby bringing an end to this most talked about controversy.

|||||||| The car which somehow became controversial

Some close to Tendulkar say that the idea to ask for a waiver on the import duty came from the late BJP minister Pramod Mahajan. Mahajan had kept his word and Sachin was offered an exemption. But he didn't realize Sachin's stature as a role model was such that even the slightest departure from the benchmark that was set against him was viewed with anger and disillusionment. A country that had given its autopilot verdict on the Mike Denness case without knowing the full details looked disappointed here – their hero was asking for something that was not due to him legally.

All through his life, Tendulkar has had to deal with this extra pressure of remaining a perfect role model in the public eye. A Dhoni or a Saif Ali Khan can get away endorsing Royal Stag. But if tomorrow Sachin decides to feature in an alchohol ad, there will be millions of broken hearts. For them, Tendulkar is not just the most valuable cricketer but the biggest Indian icon – a combination of fairy

|||||||| One leg in India, the other in Pakistan

SACH

tale and hardcore reality rolled into one. To his credit, Tendulkar has done justice to this huge Cross. For someone born thirty-six years after Independence, he has strong nationalist feelings and wears a national flag on his helmet. On Independence Day the Tri- colour is still hoisted at the Tendulkar household. It would be fair to say that along with the desire to remain the best of the best, it is also a passion with him to bring glory to the Tri-colour.

While the Indian team was on its last tour to Pakistan, it was taken to the Wagah Border. They were sightseeing in the Pakistan part of the border, when suddenly Tendulkar decided to put his other foot in India. That made a beautiful picture – Tendulkar with one leg in India, the other in Pakistan. And it also showed the man's mindset! In the Ferrari controversy, he could have tried to absolve himself by saying that the idea to appeal for a waiver had been mooted by the Government. He did not initiate it. He could have reiterated that just four months ago, he had played a knock against Pakistan at the World Cup. This was said to have liberated Indian cricket against the might of Pakistan. Couldn't he, therefore, appeal for waiver of an import duty after performing spectacularly for so many years for the country! Yet he didn't say anything. Just bore the pain silently. Possibly realizing that others can get away with departures from their public image. He, Sachin Tendulkar, could not. He preferred not to question this, but respect it the way it was.

The last controversy Tendulkar had got into was perfectly in line with his nationalist thinking. Who does Mumbai belong to? He was asked this question at a crowded press conference. Without batting an eyelid, he replied, 'Mumbai belongs to India. That is how I look at it. I am a Maharashtrian and I am extremely proud of that. But I am an Indian first.'

Akshay Sawai , from a Mumbai-based weekly magazine, had asked him the question. Akshay says he was surprised that Sachin said what he said. He expected the cricket star to play safe and offer a typical 'No Comments' reaction. Despite his belief of not unearthing anything sensational, Akshay still took a chance. The venue of the press conference was the Taj Lands End Hotel in Bandra, only a few kilometres from Balasaheb's house. Word immediately got around and what followed was media hysteria. Akshay was subsequently blamed for stirring up a controversy. But he has no remorse. 'That was the burning topic at that time. Tendulkar had to be asked that question because of his status. He is no longer just an important cricketer and has gone much beyond that,' explains the Mumbai-based journalist.

Kapil Dev, a former colleague sitting in Delhi, approved of Sachin's reaction with admiration. 'For me, till date, this has been Sachin's best statement. I have been impressed with him on the cricketing field for various reasons. Once, in Jamshedpur, we were doing throwing practice from the outfield. Sachin was throwing with his left hand and still throwing so well. I am yet to see so much talent in one individual. But standing up for the country well ahead of any other sentiments was the most impressive act of his.'

The Shiv Sena supremo sitting in his Bandra residence was hardly impressed though. He wrote an angry editorial in *Saamna* some hours later targetting Tendulkar. Right till then, Sachin had been Balasaheb's favourite nephew if not a grandson. And for him to suddenly start a tirade against Sachin shocked the nation. Thackeray wrote,'You said you are proud of being a Marathi. But that you are an Indian first. This has hurt the Marathi people. From the cricket pitch you have entered the political pitch. You also said all Indians have an equal right on Mumbai. What was the need for this? You have been "run out" on the Marathi pitch. People praise you when you hit fours and sixes. But if you speak against the rights of the Marathi people, they will not tolerate it.'

Most cricketers kept quiet in this hour of crisis for Tendulkar. Kapil was the only exception who spoke up in his defence very strongly. Cricketers not coming out in the open was understandable as they feared for their personal safety and didn't want to get drawn into a highly political issue. But surprisingly, the Cricket Board which ought to have issued a statement in support of Sachin, turned a deaf ear. What was even worse was when the Board spokesperson Rajiv Shukla said something in Tendulkar's defence, the Board President quickly issued a statement saying the statements of Mr Shukla were his own and he had made them in his personal capacity. They were not those of the Board. A humiliated, badly let down Sachin could have spoken again. He could have explained the entire issue again in the proper light. He could have lamented: 'I have played for them for so many years, yet at the first sign of a crisis, they have left me in the lurch.' But true to his pain-bearing character, Tendulkar remained silent. However, to the outside world and not just in Kapil Dev's mind, he rose in estimation.

Filmmaker Mahesh Bhatt, who was anyway a great Sachin fan, opined that his respect for Sachin grew after this incident. 'Every child who goes to school is taught that India comes first. He is a Maharashtrian icon. But India is bigger than that. I endorse his sentiments totally and completely.' But Bhatt does not only stop at that. He fires a salvo at those faces that are trying to degrade Sachin. 'Somebody wants to use him as a tool to put across a narrow world view. Wants to piggyback on that sentiment to sell their political ideology.'

The past few months have been free of negativity from either side. There has been no further face off between Sachin and Balasaheb. From the outside it appears that the Shiv Sena is now in a conciliatory mood. After Tendulkar completed his 50th test hundred, the Mumbai Municipality announced a felicitation function for him. That most certainly is an indicator. As it is, the Sena that controls the Mumbai Municipality has obtained feelers that Balasaheb's outbursts against Sachin didn't please the average Maharastrian. Hence, the strategy has been revisited. Apparently some insiders felt that the outburst was a hasty action. Yet others maintain that had Udhav Thackrey been present in Mumbai around that time, the sudden rush of blood would have given away to solid, practical thinking. Udhav was then out of the country. And according to reports, didn't term the move to attack Sachin the best political decision ever made by Sena!

Sanjay Raut, Executive Editor of the *Dainik Saamana*, rubbished the notion that there was ever any controversy with Sachin. In an e-mailed response to the author who had framed certain questions for the Shiv Sena to answer, Raut played down the entire episode. This seems to be the Sena's revised thinking. Raut gave the following reply:

'What controversy are you talking about ? I do not see any controversy. People tried but I would say their plans failed. Sachin is beyond controversy. Mumbai is a hot issue on the political map of India and the world. One hundred and eight hutama's gave their lives for the cause of Mumbai. And this Mumbai is the capital of Maharashtra. Even Sachin knows that. But the media asked irrelevant questions to stir an unnecessary controversy. There was no need of such questions, I think. Whatever Balasaheb said was a fatherly suggestion made to Sachin. He only suggested that since Sachin is a cricketer of great calibre, he should speak on the topic of his expertise "cricket" and not waste time and focus on other topics. I believe Balasaheb has the right to do so.

'Mumbai belongs to India. That is how I look at it. I am a Maharashtrian and I am extremely proud of that. But I am an Indian first.'

Sachin Tendulkar

'The thought of an attack on the icon itself is unacceptable as there was no attack made. Even Amitabh has faced the burnt of chaos created by the media. We have many icons in different fields. Their achievements are Everest-high. We consider Sachin's achievements much beyond that too. A father advising a son cannot be an attack. Why are people making it an issue? Don't elders advise the young ones ?

'What Balasaheb said about Sachin has nothing to do with vote banks or politics. Balasaheb is an artist. He does not equate emotions and relations with political issues. Balasaheb's statement to Sachin was a fatherly gesture. An advice. Vote banks or nothing crude came to his mind when he said anything to Sachin ever. And this is not the first time Balasaheb has advised Sachin about something. Sunil Gavaskar, Sachin, Lata Mangeshkar have all given the country global fame and made India proud. Marathi people love their culture and their heroes. Marathi people may not even remember what you are calling 'controversy' right now.

'Sachin and his family have been close to Balasaheb for decades. He is a neighbour too as he has grown up in Bandra, Kalanagar. Sachin's family has always loved and respected Balasaheb. Balasaheb has also seen Sachin grow. Sachin has visited Balasaheb several times. They are connected telephonically. There has not been any problem between them in spite of people trying to make things difficult for Sachin. Even after all that you call a controversy, there has been a great relation amongst the two. Sachin was and will always receive Balasaheb's blessings. Balasaheb is an ardent fan of cricket. When Sachin is on the wicket, he is glued to the TV. He forgets politics at such times. There is no controversy. Balasaheb loves him and will keep advising him like a father in future ….'

The tone clearly suggests the Sena won't go on to the front foot now. Raj Thackeray, supposedly a close friend of Sachin and the Maharastra Navnirman Sena Chief, maintained a stony silence on this all through. Politically, it made little sense for him to popularize a concept initiated by his political rivals.

At the start of 2011, Raj can now afford a chuckle. A delivery that he left well outside the off stump is now paying him rich dividends.

|||||| He has always been the reliable pilot!

CHAPTER 10

'SACH' IS WHAT SACH DOES

When you speak to people outside the cricketing world about Sachin, interesting and well-rounded perspectives invariably emerge. You then realize the sum total of his achievements. A clear perspective also emerges as to why he is called the greatest ever unifying force in the country. In more ways than one, Tendulkar is the biggest ever love story that India has produced. Not Raj-Nargis. Not Amitabh-Rekha. Not Shah Rukh-Kajol. But Tendulkar alone. Mahesh Bhatt, for one, gets very romantic discussing Sachin and talks about the essence of him in the form of poetry:

Let the Sachin magic be there.
Let us not know why and how it happened
Let us not take him to the laboratory and analyse ...
Let the sparkle remain.
Let us not spoil his charm with our fingerprints.
Let him fly in awe and wonder.
Life is magical and Sachin represents the magic ...

However, the life of an international cricketer, just like any other top-quality professional, is not exactly a bed of roses. There was a line written on Ganguly's cricket-coffin—'If you don't have problems in your job, then it is not a job'.

I know of a business journalist in Kolkata who had hit a rough patch with his boss. This man felt like quitting and saw only darkness all around him. Till he came up with a profile on Ganguly which mentioned this motivational line. His thinking pattern changed miraculously. He started thinking that if Sourav Ganguly could face a problem in his job, then who was he to feel so dejected. His frustration lessened. Years later, Ganguly came to know how, without even knowing someone, a line in his cricket-coffin had changed a certain city-based reporter's thinking. He then smiled and completed the last part of the motivational sentence – which I suspect was his own creation.

'If you don't have problems in your job, you are a clerk.'

So Tendulkar, despite the romance and innocence he exudes, has a huge job pressure. He has been the subject of the most intense questioning by the opposition and the media. Remember, in a life like his, there are no retakes. Everything is out in the open. No favourite cameraperson is available at his workplace to show his best profile. On the contrary, his worst shot is scanned unlike a movie star who has the liberty of the best take being selected. Cynical observers are always on the look out to capture his worst profile. And always in a hurry to declare that his time is up and he is done with cricket.

Of the eighty-odd interviews that I have done for this book, one particular observation was repeated so often by so many interviewees that I lost count. **Sachin is born to bat.** I remember that none, I repeat – none of them said that he was born to captain a cricket team.

If there was an Achilles' heel in Tendulkar's cricket – it lies in his performance as a captain. Bradman led Australia in 24 test matches and won 15 of them. No one has ever said he was an outstanding captain. But the records are such that no one can say his records are not impressive.

Sachin has led India during two different periods. His test record is anything but impressive as a captain. In the 25 Tests that he has led, only 4 wins were recorded against 9 losses. 12 matches were drawn. In ODIs the team lost 43 out of 73 matches under his captaincy. Strangely, people who have played under him didn't think he was a bad captain. They put it down to lack of proper coaching support, poor team strength, lack of spirit within the team and Sachin's own inexperience at that stage.

As Srinath, one of his key bowlers, is willing to share, 'When for the first time he took over as the captain, he was too dreamy-eyed and immature, and had huge expectations of everyone. I found him extra demanding, wanting all the players to match up to his standard.' Much against Sachin's wishes, Ajit Wadekar's selection committee appointed him captain for the second time. Srinath felt that the second time round, he was better but still didn't quite understand that the team he was leading did not comprise world-beaters. 'A good team can handle that logic of "nothing else matters except winning" philosophy of its captain. But a bad team can't. Especially when we toured outside the subcontinent, his expectations were unrealistic.'

'When for the first time he took over as the captain, he was too dreamy-eyed and immature, and had huge expectations of everyone. I found him extra demanding, wanting all the players to match up to his standard.'

Javagal Srinath

Yet Srinath felt that the second time around, Sachin showed signs that he had improved as a captain. He was also maturing as an individual. 'Who knows, if he had someone like a John Wright with him, he may have done better,' Srinath says today. Sachin only had Indian coaches throughout his career as captain – Sandip Patil, Madan Lal, Anshuman Gaekwad and finally Kapil Dev. Perhaps, the most difficult part of his challenge was to put up with a Board Secretary called Jaywant Lele. In those days, Lele was called the 'Johnny Lever of Indian Cricket'. Though likening him to Johnny Lever was hardly appropriate. It was merely his physical build and very special manner of speaking that had prompted such a comparison. But deep inside Lele was a street-smart man who always found method in his madness. From the unique style of his operations

|||||||| With two of his former teammates – Srinath and the legendary Kapil

he gave a clear message that if you thought he was a comedian, you only thought so at your own peril!

While Lele was the secretary, Jagmohan Dalmiya ruled the Indian Board. Apparently an understanding had been reached that any correspondence that was sent in the name of the Board Secretary would be composed at Dalmiya's Secretariat in Kolkata. It would be sent on the Board letterhead and the Secretary would just sign at the bottom. This practice went on for quite some time.

Dalmiya remained elated with the perception that he had the unquestionable loyalty of his team. Then he started getting regular phone calls from the media on certain outrageous comments made by the Secretary in his official correspondence and on certain decisions taken by the Board quoting the same source. Dalmiya and his office were astonished. They knew exactly the script they had prepared for

Lele to sign. Now what the media reports were suggesting was contradictory to what they had prepared for the Secretary. Lele added to the confusion almost on a 70mm frame by saying he had been misquoted and that he would send a strong rejoinder to the concerned agency/newspaper. It is another matter that soon he was nicknamed 'Denial Lele' by the media. By this time, Dalmiya had also realized that the misquotes had a pattern to them. That Lele was, of course, signing the letter composed by the Board supremo's Secretariat in Kolkata, but was adding one original paragraph of his own towards the end. This vital paragraph – often in a tone quite contradictory to the earlier part of the letter, was igniting the fire.

If a seasoned campaigner like Dalmiya was finding it difficult to negotiate the Lele-swing, it was obvious that in negotiating him, Sachin would always be a suspect. Soon there were occasions when, as the captain, he had asked for a replacement 'A' player to be flown in, only to discover that player 'E' had landed. Then there was the infamous incident when despite asking for someone else, the Board Secretary sent Noel David from Hyderabad on a West Indies tour. When the media confronted Sachin as to why he had selected Noel David, his astonished reply was, 'Noel who?'

Jaywant Lele dismisses all the allegations against him. Lele defends his case by saying: 'It was the then coach Kapil Dev who was responsible for the breakdown in the relationship. Kapil, even when he left, did not spare me. Towards the end of his resignation letter, there was a line, " Mr Lele, now you will have to find a new whipping boy!"'

Ten long years have gone by but Lele has not forgotten. He still has problems with Kapil's modus operandi, not so much with his objective.

'He wanted a single room for every player, even overseas. He wanted increased laundry allowance. He wanted a greater say in selection meetings. On some occasions, he called the president of the Board directly to organize things for the team. Little did he know that as per the Board rules, the Secretary was all-powerful,' Lele rests his case.

He claimed that he never had any problems with captain Tendulkar and feels he suffered because of the coach. Lele thinks that even today, Sachin remains a simple, down-to-earth man, who just the other day, greeted the former Board Secretary warmly at a function.

According to Lele, Sachin had resigned as the Captain on the third day of the Mumbai Test Match against South Africa. Lele requested him to reconsider and not resign during the Series. Sachin apparently took back his resignation, changed his letter and only resigned after the Series.

As it was, Sachin remained burdened with a relatively poor bowling attack. Bradman had Miller and Lindwall. Llyod had four fearsome fast bowlers. Gavaskar had a Kapil Dev. Brearely had a Willis and Botham. Steve had a McGrath. Akram had himself and Waqar. Cronje had a Donald.

The man who succeeded Sachin as the Captain and thereby began a golden era in Indian cricket sympathizes with him. 'Sachin did not have a good team. Sehwag, Bhajji, Zaheer, Yubaraj, Dhoni all came later. I felt sorry for him, especially on that Australia tour of 2000. It was sad to see a great cricketer like him feeling helpless on a cricketing field,' says Ganguly.

Sachin's apparent lack of ability to negotiate with the Board bigwigs and ensure a good deal for the team also came in the way. Outside the subcontinent, a captain can get away without having such skills. But in countries like India, Pakistan or Sri Lanka, a captain has to bargain constantly with the Board and its selectors. Ganguly did that remarkably well. He not only had a hot line with Dalmiya but also maintained good links with the selection committee. Kapil Dev while working with Ganguly briefly in his capacity as a Board member, found that this captain could 'speak fluently' to the Board people in their own language.

The leader that Ganguly succeeded lacked the flamboyance to work around the various factions of the Board. 'Sachin, the great batsman that he is, has remained too quiet as a leader and obviously found it difficult to function. A captain has to be street-smart and a leader, even off the field. He has to be communicative. He has to have good media relations. Has to ensure smooth functioning with the Board. Sachin was too quiet and remained in his shell,' observed Kapil.

In comparison, Kapil found another great batsman from his generation, a certain Gavaskar, a lot better. 'Sunil was sharp and knew how to get the best out of everyone. He was a good captain.' Kapil concluded the discussion on the Sachin captaincy by saying, 'He is in the Richard Hadlee mould. The kind that can provide priceless suggestions to the captain but themselves can't lead. It wasn't only his fault. We forced him to become a captain when he wasn't ready.'

A Sachin Tendulkar of 2011 would surely have made a much better Indian captain. Not only has the Indian team strength gone up substantially in recent times, but also his standing within the dressing room has improved to such an extent that today it is almost god-like. In the Mumbai Indians dressing room they call him 'The Master'. The trend of calling him by this name began with foreigners like Dwayne Bravo and Pollard. But the practice has been continued by others. Even the local players. The most important point is that Sachin, the individual, is not the same as he was in the year 2000. Today he is much more relaxed, much more confident about dealing with the outside world. As a natural by-product his leadership instincts were bound to improve. One of the Mumbai Indian players told me after losing the closely fought IPL final, that when half the team was in tears, Sachin gave an inspiring speech. Deep inside the privacy of the dressing room he consoled the crestfallen team by saying he was extremely proud of them to have come such a long distance. He praised all of them for their efforts. And finally egged them on saying, 'Next time, our team will change the script, don't worry, friends.'

In the higher echeleons of Indian cricket, there are many who share a deep sympathy for Captain Sachin. There is a school of thought that, based on a study of various incident, opines that, at times, Sachin didn't get the full support of his team. That there were forces working in his team that were involved in fixing matches. There were some strange matches like the Barbados Test Match in 1997 where, needing 120 to win, India ended up losing the match. Then another One-day at St Vincent raised doubts whether a racket inside the team was working against it! I had covered the same series and kept on hearing strange rumours that in ODI matches, betting began sharp at the time Tendulkar was dismissed.

Not only did the bookies never dare to approach him but he alone in the team had the capability those days to win a match for India single-handedly. So any amount of betting was meaningless till Sachin remained at the wicket.

There was another curious match in Sharjah where Azhar, under the captaincy of Sachin, ran himself out in such a manner that Gavaskar sitting at the commentary box openly expressed his disgust. Sachin could have said a lot. After all, he was the worst sufferer. But he kept quiet.

||||||||| With Azhar: the relationship suffered in early 2000

Even in later years, Sachin never came out openly against such forces. But in private circles he would express hopelessness and disappointment that people were working against the interests of the team. According to Shastri, 'When he saw some of the players indulging in malpractices, he got disillusioned and then completely bitter. Those incidents shook him mentally.' Sachin could also see the Board was clearly not interested in nailing down the concerned players. Manoj Prabhakar did get disciplined for disobeying the team management's instruction and batting strangely in a Kanpur One-dayer in 1994. But that action was only triggered off at the Selection Committee Chairman Viswanath's initiative. That the Indian Board was least bothered about finding out who the culprits were became more apparent when years later they formed a Chandrachud Committee to look into the match-fixing allegations. The eye-wash committee that it was, Justice Chandrachud didn't even call Viswanath to depose. Come to think of it! The man who could have provided the most vital clue was not even called! Viswanath could have told the

||||||| With Shastri: the relationship has always been good and solid

retired Justice how Asif Iqbal had approached him for a designer toss way back in 1979. And how he detected another crime after fifteen long years!

Incidentally, two days later I interviewed the same distraught Prabhakar at his New Delhi residence. Rather than express shock at the disciplinary action taken against him, Prabhakar was most upset that when he went to the ground to collect his cricket coffin, Sachin didn't look at him even once. 'I gave him company at Manchester from the other end when he completed his first ever test hundred. We shared such a long partnership. We were teammates for five years. How could he pronounce me guilty before it was proved?' a shocked Prabhakar went on. But Sachin knew exactly what he was doing. Silently he was narrating an essay to Prabhakar. Subsequently, the Delhi-based medium pacer tried to make amends with Sachin again and didn't succeed. Exasperated, Prabhakar even wrote an open letter addressed to Sachin where he pleaded with him to come out with the facts on match-fixing that he knew about and help clean the game.

A Prabhakar talking about cleaning the game must have been a bit too much for Sachin. It would probably have provoked him to laughter. He didn't even respond to this open letter delivery and gave it its rightful due!

Sachin did go to depose before Chandrachud. But, like many others, he was first asked to pose for pictures, sign autographs and then partake in some chit-chat. Any one could have seen that this committee was unlikely to provide a shot in the arm for honest Indian cricketers. He also appeared before the CBI which finally sentenced the likes of Azhar, Mongia and Jadeja – three players from his team.

It is rumoured that Sachin disclosed the entire truth to the CBI. It is also rumoured that the case against Azhar was so watertight because Sachin provided some vital clues. There is no official confirmation on this and there never will be. But it is certainly not a rumour that it did cast a long shadow on the relationship between these two former Indian captains. When have you last seen Sachin and Azhar in the same frame? Neither in public, nor in private do they meet. I didn't see a single Azhar quote on Sachin when he completed twenty years in international cricket. Nor did I try to call him up for this book!

Compared to the Chandrachud Committee's findings, the King Commission report published in South Africa on Hansie Cronje and match-fixing allegations was a revelation. I asked an ailing Justice King over the phone that the definition of Cronje in South Africa had interestingly bordered on two extremes: that of a cheat and a champion cricketer. Which definition did he think was more appropriate? Pat came the reply, 'A cheat and a champion cricketer.' At the beginning it was Justice King's wife who was relaying my questions to her husband and dictating the answers. Then Justice King came on the line himself. At eighty-plus and with failing health, he struggles to talk. Yet he spoke about this beautiful game and one of its great ambassadors – Tendulkar. If I heard him correctly, all Justice King was trying to say was that he had broken many records with the bat. Attained impossible feats. But history will remember Sachin Tendulkar fondly as a great reformer, not just a batsman if Sachin comes out with all the full facts that he has if he takes the lead against the threatening darkness in cricket. While we were speaking, the Mohammad Amir-spot-fixing controversy was at its worst and King was referring to Sachin only in that context.

||||||| It rains outside, so he practices inside the dressing room

Sachin, however, has not shown any initiative to fight the cricket war as a reformer. Talking to him you would get an idea that he believes a cricket war is best fought on the cricketing field and in a cricketer's uniform. Not before the intelligence agencies or at police stations. As a cricket-yogi his job is to concentrate on the beauty of the game and its upliftment through the bat. He perhaps believes in the school of thought that two masterly hundreds are worth a few spot-fixing allegations. He also possibly questions why a cricketer should lose his focus and run after such damning disclosures! It is the job of the ICC sleuths and law-enforcing agencies to ensure a strict vigil. They get paid for doing so. He gets paid for what he knows best – playing cricket to the best of his potential. If others are prepared

||||||| Yet another triumph!

to create a bad image for cricket through their greed, he can restore sanity and balance in it through his cricketing exploits.

Sachin – the very image in India stands for credibility. For purity. For excellence. As Vinita Kamte, wife of the late Ashok Kamte, the brave police officer who laid down his life following a massive terror attack on 26/11 in Mumbai, says, 'For every terrorist that brings out the bad and the evil, there is a Tendulkar to balance and represent the good.' Sachin not only dedicated the Chennai test match win to the 26/11 victims but also took off time to meet Kamte's son and offered him encouragement. That speaks for his commitment towards social and human causes, which, incidentally, runs so deep in the family that his daughter Sara is already involved in doing charity work.

On the cricket field, however, his fight is much more significant. He is the game's most credible face in the hour of disaster. Of course there are others who have not been bought. A Dravid. A Laxman. A Dhoni. A Kumble. A Ganguly. A Sehwag. A Harbhajan. A Srinath. But in all fairness, Sachin is the vital wicket that separates the doubters from the sincere cricket watchers. Sachin of course has been guarding the cricket fort single-handedly for the last ten to twelve years ever since the match-fixing scandals broke. Here he bats for cricket. Not just for India. And effectively he is the last wicket standing.

Don's average may stand at 99.94. But did he ever play a knock to save the sport itself? Any Indian will be elated and proud with the answer!

And now the
Don comes closer!

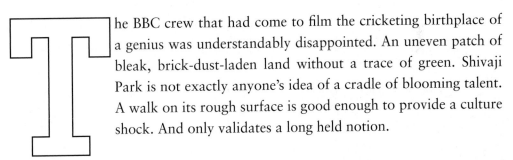

CHAPTER 11

TO BEAT 99.94

he BBC crew that had come to film the cricketing birthplace of a genius was understandably disappointed. An uneven patch of bleak, brick-dust-laden land without a trace of green. Shivaji Park is not exactly anyone's idea of a cradle of blooming talent. A walk on its rough surface is good enough to provide a culture shock. And only validates a long held notion.

God said let there be Tendulkar! And there was Tendulkar!

The state of the ground is such that it couldn't have created him. In fact the moment you step on to this historic ground, there are more questions than answers. Why isn't Shivaji Park preserved for posterity on account of its place in history? Why have none of Sachin's many sponsors never felt the need to have a plaque installed at Shivaji Park, marking the exact spot where the childhood prodigy took his first cricketing lesson? How come the influx of sponsorship money has not made practice facilities on this ground any better? How can the art of fielding be perfected on this rough surface notwithstanding the fact that it has given birth to so many Indian cricket stars?

The dreamy-eyed cricket tourist would also note with wonder the gregarious generosity of a ground that hosts events as varied as football matches, the yearly

Durga Puja celebration of the Bengali Cultural Association, Shiv Sena and Raj Thackeray's meetings and political rallies. In the past the Chowpatty Beach at Marine Drive used to be the main venue for all political gatherings. However, since Balasaheb Thackeray became the most influential man in Mumbai, the scenario has changed. It has obviously not struck any of the political parties that repeated makeshift constructions and the constant invasion by large crowds, peanut and cold drinks sellers, nariyalwallahs (coconut sellers) and the endless setting up of improvised podiums and stages on this patch of land might throw a spanner in the life of an aspiring cricketer.

If you are a cricket writer by profession and have had the opportunity of visiting both Shivaji Park and the ground at Bowral where Don Bradman had served his apprenticeship, you may begin and close any discussions about the comparisons between them within a minute. The floor levels are so very different!

Located only a few hundred kilometres away from plush downtown Sydney, is the middle class suburb of Bowral. If Sydney presents a James Bond style setting, Bowral could be a Shyam Benegal film locale. Yet the cricket ground is gorgeous. A lovely velvet of emerald green.

Bradman's ashes were spread across this ground. It is so picturesque that every cricket tourist gets photographed sitting there. The place is completely pollution free, with hardly any disturbance of noise. There is no hustle bustle. Don's original house is a half minute's walk from the ground. So commuting with the cricket coffin in an overcrowded second class compartment in a suburban train, is something Bradman would have only seen in documentaries made on India.

The small ground at Port of Spain which was eventually regarded as the Brian Lara nursery is smaller. Yet it is as pretty as some of the county cricket grounds. The Nuncargate ground on the outskirts of Nottinghamshire where Harold Larwood is said to have bowled his first ball is even prettier. It is even more verdant than the mustard fields of Punjab. The ground is now named after Larwood and there is a tavern next to it. Although it today flaunts a portrait of Alex Ferguson in a nod to the popularity of another sport, it looks largely like the extension of a cricket museum with relics from a far-off time. Unlike the much-celebrated 221B Baker Street, where overlooking the tube station, two stage actors disguised as Sherlock Holmes and his friend Dr Watson, make regular appearances for visitors.

||||||| The famous Bradman residence at Adelaide

In the Larwood Tavern nothing is make-believe. Everything is for real. You even come across men in their 80s who saw Larwood bowl and were with him when he last visited Nuncargate. The place has an almost magical feel as these septuagenarians are always willing to share their stories. There are pictures of Bill Voce, the fast bowling partner of Larwood for Nottinghamshire and England. There are clippings from the stormy *Bodyline* series so very well preserved. Some 20 kilometres away is Robin Hood's favourite haunt – the Sherwood Forest. There is something about the place. Surrounded by legends and folklore, the mystique and the tranquility combines well to send out a message to the kids in the locality – Go, boys, go ... dream big ... be prepared to fight. Even if you fall, I will hold your hand and the two of us will jump into eternity ....

Every time you stand in such places, you invariably visualize a dust-filled ground with a cacophony of human and mechanical voices and milling crowds. And one Sachin Tendulkar. That a product of such a milieu still dares, even

|||||||| The Larwood statue in his own city

now, to run a marathon! Still chases the ultimate signature tune in cricket – Bradman's 99.94.

I found three cricketing legends who were eagerly awaiting the arrival of a worthy Bradman-challenger in their lifetime. So that the signature tune of ultimate greatness in cricket was passed on. And unbelievable as it may seem, all three of them selected the same nominee – Tendulkar. That too, way back in 1992.

Somehow Tendulkar managed to impress the Aussies so much in his maiden outing in that country that his nationality was forgotten. Before the 1992 World Cup took place, a series of cricket supplements adorned the national dailies, featuring write-ups on famous cricket stars. Wasim Akram wrote one exclusively for *Ananda Bazar*, Kolkata.

Instead of paying him in cash dollars due to prevalent foreign exchange restrictions, the ABP management decided to pay him in kind. Thus a beautiful Kashmiri carpet bought from the local Kashmir Emporium became part of my cabin baggage. Those were the days of a relatively peaceful world. 9/11 had not happened. International travel had not been reduced to appearing for a final exam!

But the Australian Customs has always been as unrelenting as its cricket team. The object smartly wrapped in gift paper invited suspicious looks. And continuous grilling. I did explain the background of the item and who it was meant for. Also showed them my World Cup accreditation pass.

By such time the people at the Immigration had gathered around the customs officers. And one of them asked, 'But what are you carrying for your own man?'

Own man? Who?

'The little boy. Tendulkar.'

I instantly realized by their tone that the wonder boy of nineteen had won over Australia. The ruthless customs guys suddenly became softer. I did suffer a barrage of questions from them subsequently. But nothing on the *mysterious item* that I was carrying. All their questions were focussed on one teenage boy. Did I know him well enough? Had I done any interviews with him? How did India relate to him? And so on ....

I have no shame in admitting today that I did say I was very close to him which I was not. But anyone who has faced Australian Customs would know it is almost like facing McGrath and that there is no harm in resorting to harmless half-truths if they provide you with the password. So Down Under opened up to this visiting Indian journalist with a magic name. Tendulkar. And the password remained with the user, like a fairy tale. Till the day of his departure.

On the final day of the tour I was privileged enough to be granted a long telephonic conversation with William Joseph O'Reilly. Popularly known as Bill O'Reilly. By such time he had almost turned a recluse and was physically immobile. O'Reilly spoke to me from the wheelchair. Towards the end of the predictable question-answer session on whether this era was better than his own, whether Bradman would have been as successful today, he suddenly stopped.

'Can you do me a favour, my Indian friend?' the great O'Reilly, who according to Bradman was the greatest spinner that he had seen, asked.

This interviewer was completely taken aback. For nearly four weeks he had had to run from pillar to post for an appointment with this cricketing legend. And now the same person was asking for a favour.

O'Reilly spelt it out. Could I, on his behalf, pass on a message to one Sachin Tendulkar who, by such time, had left Australia with Azhar's spiritless Indian team that even failed to make the semi-finals of the World Cup.

Of course I would. But what was the message?

'Sachin, you are like my grandson. Please treat this as grandfatherly advice and don't misunderstand me. I have a request to make. Please don't play One-day cricket. This is ladies' cricket and not meant for a man like you. Remember you are as good as the Don. Also remember, Don never played such stuff which would have played havoc with his technique. If you want to beat Don, concentrate only on test cricket.'

The advice was passed on to Sachin several years later as I was not very sure how he would react. I was not sure whether he knew the significance of a Bill O'Reilly. Incidentally, the confident Tendulkar you see today was not the one journalists dealt with early on in the prodigy's career. He was an extreme introvert. He spoke so very little unless he knew someone well enough. And I did not fall in that category.

Keith Miller was another former legend, who had the highest praise for Tendulkar. Miller, you would often read and hear, was a Bradman basher. The questions that I had framed for him were obviously influenced by the background.

'Sachin, you are like my grandson. Please treat this as grandfatherly advice and don't misunderstand me. I have a request to make. Please don't play One-day cricket. This is ladies' cricket and not meant for a man like you. Remember you are as good as the Don.'

William Joseph O'Reilly

A sample: The British press often expresses its apprehension as to whether Bradman would have survived against the four fast bowler-pronged West Indian attack? Mr Miller, what are your views?

I was certainly looking at a potential headline which would read – 'Don was lucky that he got away without having played Llyod's West Indies,' says Miller.

Little did I know that the question would, on the contrary, raise the seventy-five-year-old's blood pressure. Miller, who till such time had behaved like an honourable old man, gently reminiscing his days in Kolkata, suddenly wore the firebrand fast bowler's uniform.

'Who said that? Just repeat.'

I repeated, 'The British press.'

'That is why they are the pits of the world,' Miller started showing possibly the same amount of irritation and anger that he reserved while bowling to Len Hutton. 'Graham Gooch has scored hundreds against them. Robin Smith has. And that chap – what's his name – Allan Lamb … even he has. And you want me to say Don would have struggled against them!'

By such time, Miller, a confirmed heart patient, had raised his voice to such an extent that I got deeply worried. The conversation was quickly brought back to the modern era and Tendulkar. I thought this was the last headline potential I was left with in a dramatically changed circumstance.

It would read like this: I don't care what the rest of Australia says but this fellow is not even a poor man's Don: Miller

The famous all-rounder again flattered to deceive. For someone who seemed to be so very possessive of Bradman, he went to the extent of saying Jack Fingleton was the real Bradman hater for his own selfish reasons. He was not. The same Miller now started equating Tendulkar with Bradman. Miller, incidentally, was not watching World Cup cricket that was being played in his own country. As he felt baseball or Australian Rules Football on telly presented a far more competitive spread. Miller had watched Tendulkar's Perth hundred and based on that, had a quick opinion to offer.

'This little fellow is blessed. He might be a worthy challenger to Don.' It was not an unusual headline but at least you knew Miller would not compare someone so easily with the Don. That at least, at a ripe old age, his opinions would not be clouded by the rivalry that they had apparently shared in their playing days.

Harold Larwood was another unique incident straight from the pages of a fairy tale. Talking to him anyone would have felt: (a) This was1949 and certainly not 1992; (b) the legendary Bradman had just retired last season; (c) Sydney Hall was still in tact with the violent spectators; (d) the world of mobile phones and faxes had not arrived and you still communicated via telegrams and telexes; (e) the Maharaja of Patiala still ruled Indian cricket, and (f) the Nawab of Pataudi whose father was a former cricketing colleague of Larwood, led the Indian cricket team.

Meeting Larwood was like watching Jurrasic Park, to put it mildly. You were transported to an old world. He brought out old cuttings, faded black and white photographs, balls that were used in the 1930s and telegrams. One telegram that he excitedly handed over read, 'Well bowled Harold. Congratulations.'

'See, Archie was gracious enough to send me this. He was a real MAN. Archie never cribbed about Bodyline and all that nonsense.' I actually tried hard to remind myself that this telegram was sent some sixty years ago by a person who died the same year!

Larwood suddenly turned his gaze towards me and declared, 'I am not going to give you an interview. As I have stopped giving interviews long time back.' To say the visitor was shell-shocked would be an understatement! I had made the interview appointment from India a few weeks ago only after speaking to him. How would I know sitting a thousand miles away that the 83-year-old Larwood had now gone senile! He had also turned half blind as he autographed his book *The Bodyline Story* for me with the help of his wife. It was painful watching the great executioner of Bodyline being directed by his wife, 'You have completed the H. Now go down for A and again come right up for R.'

The wife, however, salvaged my interview plans. As she reminded her husband, 'You had told me someone from India was coming over to interview you. And that you would ask him all about that player.'

Larwood's brain for once showed signs of being alive. 'Yes, I remember. Now tell me, all you know about this Tendulu. (That was how he pronounced the name.) You will only get an interview after that.'

I thought it was bizarre: it was almost akin to saying, 'I will treat you to dinner only if you dance at my daughter's wedding'. But interview compulsions were compulsions and after all I was dealing with the chief protagonist of Bodyline.

So I told him all about Sachin's childhood exploits: The World record partnership that he held with Kambli; his 1028 average in school cricket; how the sub-editor at our Kolkata office got confused and changed it to 128. Larwood was beaming and remarked: 'Oh, then he *is* the man!'

There was a slight confusion and it needed to be cleared fast. For someone who was still living in the times of the Second World War, who claimed to have not heard of an Ian Botham, how did he know about the Indian wonder boy?

'I got a phone call from a former cricketer,' Larwood quipped. But he was not in a hurry to disclose the name. Years later after his death, I spoke to Larwood's daughter, Enid. She too had no clue whom he had been referring to. But according to her, in the early 1990s, her dad kept in touch with very few people. And that list included both O'Reilly and Miller. We will never know who it was. As all three of them are dead.

But the message was retrieved. 'Harold, watch this boy. He is as good as Don.'

Problem was that Larwood, having lost his eyesight, could not see anything on TV. Everything looked blurred. So he kept on asking his wife who was only too happy to find an Indian cricket correspondent to step in for her. I didn't know why a simple question which she could have really answered was not asked. Or may be a senile Larwood forgot to ask. Which the visitor had to answer.

'Does he wear that head protection stuff?'

'Yes, Mr Larwood. Sachin does wear a helmet.'

And Larwood seemed to have immediately lost all interest. 'What are you saying? He uses a helmet. Then how can he be compared to Don! Rubbish.'

I tried to restore a bit of romance by saying that the helmet was now commonplace and without exception, everybody used headgear. Larwood would have nothing of it.

Seeing him so dejected I brought up the great Viv Richards story. Viv never wears a helmet. 'Yeah, but I went and watched that fellow. Seeing him bat I was convinced I would always have a 50-50 chance of getting him out. Don gave you no chance.'

Now I had only one card left and placed it gently: Sunil Gavaskar. Gavaskar scored thirteen hundreds against the mighty West Indies without wearing a head protection. But Larwood seemed unimpressed.

|||||||| Sachin with his idol Viv

'I was also told about that chap. But he wore something – I found out.'

'Mr Larwood, that wasn't a helmet. Gavaskar used a skull cap. That too towards the closing stages of his career.'

'It is all the same. Don was so good that he never needed a protector,' Larwood almost scolded me. And he closed the discussion by announcing tragically, 'So Don goes unbeaten then.'

I was starting to have a suspicion and now it grew further. Are the Bodyline bloodstains still intact? Has Larwood, for all these years been harbouring a long-standing secret grievance to launch a final assault against Don? Only through someone who would be better and bring Bradman down from his high pedestal? Is that known in his private circle? That alone can explain whenever a promising batsman makes a big stride, his friends call up Larwood to check the new one out.

Remember Larwood in 1992 remained the only living symbol of Bradman's once-in-a-life time mediocrity. Though in real life, Don was the successful oppressor who marched on gainfully post the Bodyline series. And Larwood, the winner in that series, ultimately became the oppressed. He didn't apologize and as a punishment was never selected to play for England again.

It looked straight out of a film script that someone could harbour such a grudge even after sixty years. But was beginning to sound like reality. And poor Sachin somehow got entangled in this. His only fault was his own genius which merited a comparison with the great Don. The bitter Larwood that I met in 1992 didn't have any personal contact left with Bradman. In those days the Bradman Museum in Bowral didn't seem to acknowledge the presence of Larwood in Bradman's life. Strange as it was, Bradman's life was featured with not even a passing reference to the most talked about series in cricket history. And the museum wall had photographs of famous cricketers all over the world, including Bishan Bedi. But there was no Douglas Jardine. No Larwood. I immediately called Larwood to get his reaction. All I got was uncontrolled laughter and sarcasm, 'Really! What has happened is that Don had made the shipment from his Adelaide home. It has my stuff in it and since it's a ship, it's taking some time to reach Sydney.'

But all this was in 1992. Around 1997 Larwood received an OBE from the British Government. There was renewed interest in him. The bitterness and the frustration held for all these years went away as the British Prime minister described him as a 'Great hero'. The Larwood house received phone calls from all over the world. Strange as it was the caller list included a certain Don Bradman. Two proud men – one, the biggest cricketing hero and the other, an all-time best tragic hero spoke to each other after twenty years. It completely melted the ice.

The Larwood family also received calls from the curator of the Bowral museum to share some of the fast bowler's personal belongings with them. Larwood did that. After his death Bradman called again and enquired about the family. Enid, one of his Brisbane-based daughters, says that though they found Bradman's son, John, difficult to comprehend in the later years, the senior Bradman, over the phone from his Adelaide residence was very sincere and caring.

The great champion and his controversial challenger did patch up before both left this world. But the cricketing debate remained: Does the helmeted Tendulkar get additional unreasonable advantages pitted against the greatest who played in the 1930s?

Riddle Number Two: Would he have survived against Bodyline?

Replying to the first question, Sachin says, 'I think it is only sensible to use protective gear if it is in circulation. Twenty years from now on there will be some protective gear which I can't think of today. Look, in the past such protective equipment didn't exist. You can only use what you have today.' Rahul Dravid is with Sachin in this debate which he finds 'ridiculous'. Dravid for all his life can't understand the argument. 'You can't compare Sachin and Bradman accurately as you can't compare different eras. But if you suggest Sachin should have played without a helmet the next thing you will suggest is try out pad-gloves from the 1930s as Bradman had to play with them.'

David Frith, the former *Wisden* Editor who nurtured a close relationship with Bradman, had picked the great man's mind on this. As per Frith's sensational disclosure, Bradman had told him he would have worn a helmet had they been in vogue all those years ago. He did use additional protection during the Bodyline series which, of course, is a pointer. He did use some stuff to protect his chest which was shown in movies.

Some neutral observers I had spoken to, at random, felt the comparison was a little harsh on Sachin. He only uses what the technology of his times has provided and why should he be made guilty for using the same?

Some journalists felt, 'Would you then not give credit for a super-exclusive story of the current era by saying, "Oh, so and so had the advantage of cellphones and e-mails over his predecessors." Can you devalue a modern-day writer by saying, Oh so and so had the advantage of Google search which the earlier authors did not. As life moves on, you embrace the new technology of your times. And why would you be frowned upon for using the same!'

The second pertinent question: how would Sachin have tackled Bodyline if it was bowled against him? This is mere conjecture. We will never know the answer. The rules have since changed. Playing conditions are not the same. Frith feels, 'Entering the realm of fantasy – if Sachin had been facing Larwood and Voce, helmeted and well padded, he might have averaged 50.' Peter Roebuck, for one, has no doubt that Sachin would have passed the Bodyline test with flying colours. 'I would ask – hasn't he faced enough Bodyline during his playing career? The heavy pounding that Wasim Akram and his fellow bowlers tried giving him on his maiden tour. The bounce, pace and hostility that he faced in Perth as a teenager against Australia in 1992. Sachin, as his career records suggest, remained very alert in finding solutions to problems. For Bodyline too, he would have found a solution.' Scyld Berry, the current *Wisden* Editor and a cricket writer of repute does not get into the debate, but opines, 'It is now fair to call Sachin the modern Bradman after scoring so many tests and ODI hundreds. There is a good case for arguing that the four greatest batsmen have been Grace, Bradman, Viv and Sachin.'

History records that during Bradman's time there were no real fast bowlers except for Larwood. Fredie Trueman may have poised a serious challenge. But he did not play in that era. Bradman did face Alec Bedser. But the great mover that he was, Bedser remained only yards faster than Madan Lal. And that he did not have to face the most fearsome attack in the cricketing history – Lloyd's four fast bowlers.

Lloyd himself had once said during an interview that Don may have been successful against the West Indian quicks. But his so very distinctive average and the rate of scoring would surely have gone down. They would have given him no respite. It is common knowledge that some of his contemporaries felt that Bradman's preparation against Bodyline was inadequate. He apparently hated bouncers. Gubby Allen, one of the softliners on that Bodyline tour, wrote a letter from Australia saying Bradman was terribly afraid of fast bowling. This, incidentally, was kept away from the public gaze till Bradman's death.

There are not many who would dispute the fact that judging purely from that angle, batting conditions were most difficult in the 1980s. Where you had all the fiery fast bowlers and the early days of reverse swing. Bradman may have been the best without having to negotiate the toughest conditions for batting!

It is often said that despite being a great champion, there were aspects in his personality that didn't endear him to people. Bradman was a hugely controversial man and remained one even after his death.

Sachin is not. Despite a 22-year long running career, he has never ever run into problems with the international media. Has rarely, very rarely reacted and never held grudges. Sachin can grace any cricket dressing room in this world and will be greeted with warmth.

Don would be hugely respected and heard. Won't be loved in most cases.

Bradman did patch up with Larwood as he possibly felt at an advancing age, that the Nottinghamshire born fast bowler was only the instrument, not the instrumentalist. In Don's dictionary, Douglas Jardine remained the chief architect and culprit of the 'Evil Bodyline design'.

Jardine was someone Bradman never forgave. Someone changed their seats in such a manner in 1953 at the Headingley Press Box that the two men, covering the Test, sat next to each other. Incredible as it may seem, no words were exchanged. Again, during Bradman's famous last tour of England, they came face to face at a party. Both pretended they had not seen each other. Jardine wrote a book *Ashes and Dust* in which he expressed surprise that Bradman with his peerless ability to hook the ball and keep it down had been a comparative failure against Larwood.

Jardine had invited some of Bradman's invincibles over drinks during the 1948 tour. Sensing trouble they asked the skipper whether they should go and were told, No. Jardine subsequently wrote that in his mind Jack Hobbs was the most complete batsman. Bradman, he pretended, never existed! DRJ met with an untimely death at a clinic in Switzerland at the age of fifty-seven. He was suffering from lung cancer. In a fit of fury Jardine's widow burned his cricket clothes and the famous harlequin cap that he wore during the Bodyline series. Contacted at his Adelaide residence, Bradman refused to give a reaction. In today's era the 24x7 media would have run a story on this alone. But that was 1959 and only cricketing colleagues remembered Bradman's lack of grace.

Sachin had also been humbled by a visiting English captain's defensive strategy. Nasser Hussain's tactics brought him to a standstill in Bengaluru. It immediately prompted a comparison with Bodyline and henceforth got termed as the New Bodyline. Hussain, like Jardine, could really get under someone's skin. With Tendulkar he was successful as his tactic of drying up runs by employing an outside leg stump line was hugely successful. Hussain didn't have a Larwood, but he had a tall left-arm spinner, Ashley Giles. He asked Giles to pitch outside the right hander's leg stump into the footmarks and even beyond so as to leave Tendulkar with one possible scoring shot – the sweep. That too would be risky. Tendulkar averaged high in the series – an honourable 76. But pitted against the strategy, he seemed disturbed.

Nearly 90 per cent of Giles' deliveries landed a foot outside the leg stump and the leg side field remained packed. Even wicket keeper James Foster stood a few inches outside the leg stump. Sachin, bewildered that he was, had to mostly use his pads to keep the balls away. All his scoring shots were cut off , barring one. Before this innovation Sachin was batting well and looked set for a three-figure knock. But now he got thoroughly fed up. Sehwag at the other end effected some attractive shots. Sachin, by now, had decided that he would also go for it by trying to hit Giles. And while attempting to do so, got stumped for the first time in his cricketing career. Sachin's score read 90 of 198 balls. He clearly looked angry with England's negative tactics employed specifically to curb his batsmanship skills.

This had sparked off a huge uproar in the cricketing world. Some felt that Nasser killed the spirit of the game. Some felt it was a brilliant strategy. Apparently the Indian dressing room remained miffed with it for quite some time. Today, however, no such animosity is left. Sachin, in this book, clearly states that Naseer is one of the best captains he has come across. And Naseer in a recent interview, has strongly opined that Sachin is bigger than Bradman. Off the field their relationship thankfully didn't go the Bradman-Jardine way.

If you compare the respective eras, however impossible the task is, the difference in situational reality comes out. Some of them support Sachin's case. Some strongly support Bradman.

ROEBUCK PLAYS DOUGLAS JARDINE

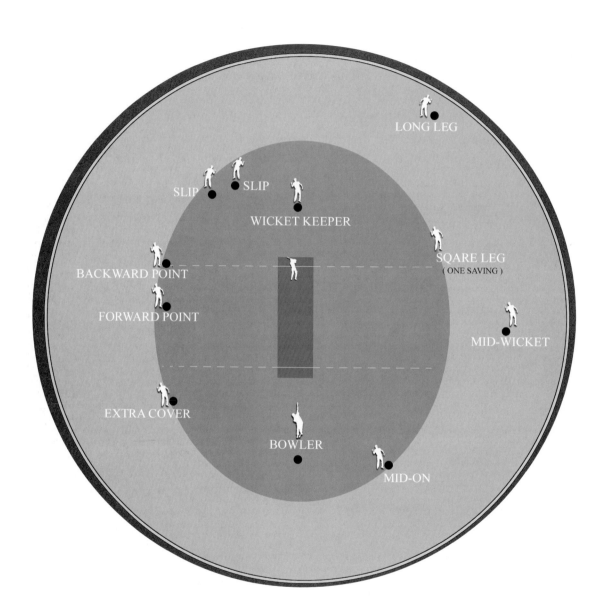

PETER ROEBUCKS'S INNOVATIVE PLAN
My Bowlers will be told to (A) Bowl straight to him. Pace bowler with a relatively new ball is preferable. (B) Try for LBW or bowled – he has thus been dismissed several times in his career. (C) Hope that while driving on the up he makes an adjustment mistake. (D) Finally keep your fingers crossed.

NASSER HUSSAIN'S NEW LEG THEORY TO CONTAIN TENDULKAR

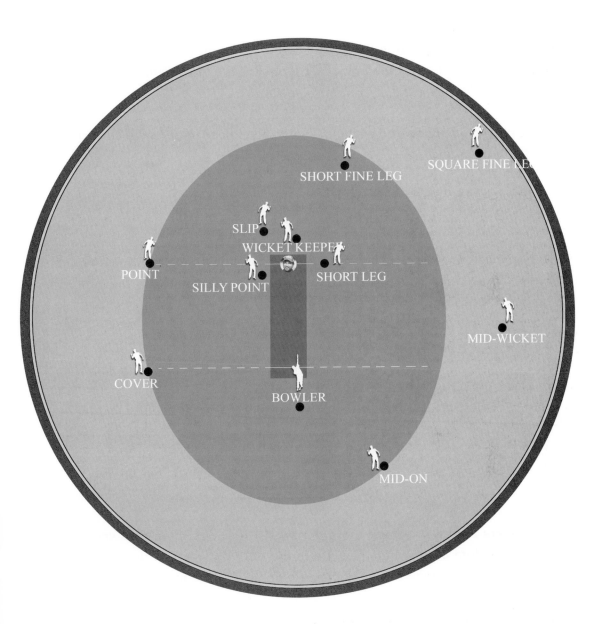

British Press had termed it The New Bodyline. Bowler was Ashley Giles. He had sent down 34 tiring overs. Most of the deliveries were well outside the leg stump. As a result of which Sachin's strike rate came down to 45. How Nasser had set his field for Giles, both Sourav and Sachin till this day remember vividly ...

FOR BRADMAN

1. His 99.94 average. It is the biggest ivory tower in cricket. The next best is sixty something and the holder Graeme Pollock didn't even play twenty-five tests.

2. He played on uncovered wickets. That used to pose many more challenges for the batsmen.

3. He played without a helmet. The helmet has been the batsman's greatest benefactor in the last 30 years.

4. Non-existence of the front foot rule. In Bradman's time the bowler could have dragged his front foot as much as he wanted outside the bowling crease if the other foot was well inside that. Effectively, because of the rule, pace bowlers could sent down a delivery from nineteen yards, making them so much more hostile and difficult to negotiate.

5. Throughout his career, Bradman has scored at a rate much faster than that of Sachin. He has two triple hundreds to Sachin's none. And on another occasion remained not out on 299.

6. Percentagewise, Bradman has won many more matches for Australia than Sachin ever did for India.

7. Bowlers feared Bradman more. He was a real destroyer and scored 29 hundreds from 52 test matches. He is the only batsman to score 100-plus runs in all the three sessions of play. He achieved that six times.

8. He played with inferior equipment. Sachin's bats are so much better. What would Bradman have done with the modern-day bats? We would never know but can imagine!

FOR TENDULKAR

1. Tendulkar has been enormously successful in all forms of the game. Experts feared that One-day cricket would play havoc with his technique. Yet he survived the onslaught quite magnificiently. Don didn't have to sit for this exam. Luckily.

2. He has had to handle the pressure and expectations of a billion people almost single-handedly every time he went out to bat. For a period of twenty–two years, he has had to be at his best to continuously provide the healing touch to an unsure, developing nation. Compared to that, Don's pressure was very little. On a durability quotient, Tendulkar shines and scores much above Bradman.

3. Tendulkar has handled better bowling attacks. He has had a dozen fast bowlers of premier quality in his life. Ambrose, Walsh, Akram, Waqar, Donald, McGrath, Steyn, Brett Lee, Shoaib, Fernando, Imran and Malinga. Forget the Pollocks, the Flintoffs, a Richard Hadlee who were fast medium. Compared to that, Bradman played only one. And was brought down to the level of a good batsman by the same. One Harold Larwood. In an all-time best World XI based on conventional wisdom, most have included three fast bowlers as a routine selection. Akram, Marshall and Lillee. The spinner in the side would be Warne. History records that Bradman batted against none. Sachin did, barring Lillee, and was quite successful. That made Bradman the unquestionable lion king in an era of medium pacers.

4. Tendulkar has faced bowlers armed with better techniques. Reverse swing was non-existent in Don's era. It surely would have tested his genius.

5. Bradman didn't negotiate Murali's Doosra. Nor did he face the chuckers – spinners and pacers alike. A Shoaib bowling at 145 mph and chucking the odd delivery didn't exist in his time. Based on previous records, he would

have moaned and complained. Sachin didn't do any such thing but carried on gently and continued to get hundreds.

6. In his career, Sachin has so far played on 57 cricket grounds. Bradman played on only 11.

7. Sachin has played in an era where fielding standards are much improved. He has faced remarkably brilliant fielders. The likes of Jhonty Rhodes. They turned even quarter chances into catches.

8. Sachin has been analysed much more comprehensibly by coaches all over the world. Coaches and captains with the help of advanced computer analysis, have dissected his game. Every movement of his has been analysed with the help of slow motion replays. At least ten major strategies have been evolved and executed against Tendulkar. And the process carries on. Don faced only one major cricket strategy in his lifetime and the average came down to the fifties. Luckily for him, computer analysis didn't exist in that era. Imagine an Akram or a Woolmer sitting with the computer analyst and plotting Bradman's dismissal. His life surely wouldn't have been happier.

9. Bradman, in his time, enjoyed the advantage of playing with home umpires. Without taking anything away from the undisputed greatness, his comeback after the war wouldn't have been possible without the generosity of the Australian umpire George Borwick. Bradman was clearly out caught. But was given not out. He recovered well to make another big score but to many, the dismissal would have finished his career as Bradman himself was uncertain about his form. In cricket such things do happen. But have you ever heard Bradman given out wrongly? Not even once in his career. Sachin mostly played with neutral umpires. And has been given out wrongly at least a dozen times, if not more.

10. Sachin didn't have a Miller or a Lindwall in his team. Right through he has been playing with fast medium or medium pacers. If he had champion

|||||||| At Imran Khan's cancer hospital in Lahore

bowlers on his side, the match-winning records would surely have glittered more. Half the time his batting opened up opportunities that the pacers or the remaining batsmen seldom capitalized upon. A great example was the Chennai test against Pakistan in 1999.

David Frith, a staunch Don loyalist reckons, 'Looking at Tendulkar in a wider spectrum, there can be little doubt that he is the nearest thing the world has seen to Don since the supreme Australian put his bat away. The opinion is based not only on Sachin's gargantuan set of statistics but on his technique and style, his approach, and his temperament.'

In 1992, I had gate-crashed into Bradman's 2, Holden Street residence at Adelaide despite him making it clear in writing that he was not prepared to grant me an interview at his advanced age of 83. And that he had said NO to all other channels and papers.

Word had it that Don would go to Adelaide Oval to watch Tendulkar play in what was to be India's last World Cup Group League match against South Africa. I had gate-crashed into his house the previous day and was expecting to get a final confirmation – Yes, coming to Adelaide Oval tomorrow to watch Sachin. Bradman sitting at the Adelaide Oval and watching Tendulkar in flesh and blood would have been the story of the summer!

Instead next day's headline in our paper said: **Don not coming to Adelaide as his wife is unwell.** But the brief fifteen-minute meeting that Don had with me and a fellow journalist, who had also gate-crashed, convinced us about his love for Sachin. There was a certain unmistakable glow on his face when he discussed Sachin. Five years later, Sachin was one of the main invitees to that same red-brick bungalow. By such time Don had announced to the world that 'this fellow' batted like him. That is the ultimate certificate in cricket which Tendulkar proudly possesses like a soldier displaying his war medals.

After Bradman's death, Ronald Perry brought out a book claiming it was Bradman's choice of his best all-time eleven. It created a stir as the team left out

'Looking at Tendulkar in a wider spectrum, there can be little doubt that he is the nearest thing the world has seen to Don since the supreme Australian put his bat away. The opinion is based not only on Sachin's gargantuan set of statistics but on his technique and style, his approach, and his temperament.'

David Frith

both Gavaskar and Viv. Both were annoyed. Gavaskar doubted whether it was like Hitler's diary which later on was discovered to have been forged. Viv said, 'God allow him to rest in peace in heaven. But Don is not the Bible of Cricket.'

Yet Tendulkar found a place at Number Four. Somehow Bradman made him the heir apparent of his cricketing tradition. And today's endless comparison may not have angered him. As events suggested, if the challenger was a certain Viv or a Hammond or an Hutton, Bradman was expected to display signs of irritation. As precedence suggested, he may have proved his supremacy through irrefutable cricketing logic. May not be directly. But in a roundabout way. With Sachin there was hardly any need. Bradman viewed him as his loving grandson. For all you know, he may have been proud to see the favourite grandson being compared to him.

The Bradman story is that of an extraordinary man who sold millions, yet led a modest lifestyle. The Wall Street Crash of 1929 had brought the Great Depression to Australia. As it was, so many Australians had died in the First World War. The Depression saw their wages being cut and taxes being increased.

Around this time Bradman started displaying his magic. For Australia, he provided the ultimate healing touch. Bradmania was such that his son was forced to change his surname. He became Bredsen. And completely went underground.

However, in India, the romance surrounding Sachin is so much more. He is not just the man you take home to your mother. He has several other priorities before just influencing another family. He has to think big and think collectively. He has to look after the Great Indian Family. Not just one prospective household. Tendulkar has been India's life-saving device as well as the biggest entertainment moghul whose shows run to packed houses at any given time of the day, depending upon wherever India is playing in the world. In a day of relative gloom, a hundred from him can lift the spirits of people all across the country. If he ever sustains an injury, a detailed story on the mishap will appear anywhere from page one to page twelve in all newspapers. The ailment, in any case, will also become a household name within the next twenty-four hours.

There are pressures and expectations on him all the time. Wasim Akram once led in a festival match where Sachin played for his side. According to reports, Wasim came and told Sachin, 'Win this for us'. And at the very next minute he instantly realized that even in a festival match, he was putting pressure on Sachin.

Don Bradman will always live in his own orbit with 99.94. Many, including Brian Lara feel, that in today's era of non-stop cricket, the dream average would have come down substantially to seventy plus. Even then the Don would have remained supreme. Sachin's average at 56 is way below. But on the durablity count and because of his continued mastery over all forms of game, Sachin is the worthy challenger to the throne.

In India his lifestyle is such that he would not venture to go to a movie hall, either in disguise or otherwise. Once, before a Brian Adams show was to begin in Mumbai, Sachin and his friend were standing near the wings. The organizers didn't dare to expose Sachin openly to the public. The singer's security guards meanwhile were objecting and saying they should go down and sit with the crowd. This is when Sachin's friend interrrupted and said, 'Thank yourself that he has agreed to stand here. For if he went down and showed his face, your show would be the worst sufferer. There would be complete pandemonium.' By such time the local organizers had gathered. They were most embarassed. And the security was quickly brought to their senses!

The Sachin fairy excites reactions from all living Indians – professionals from cross-sections. To them he is not simply a cricketer but an Indian they are extremely proud of. Prakash Padukone, the former badminton legend, is a man of few words and rarely given to hyperboles. Yet Padukone, who is a cricket buff says, 'Sachin is as good as Bradman. If not better.'

Jagjit Singh, the ghazal maestro, is prepared to dedicate his favourite song to Tendulkar:

Yeh daulat bhi le lo.	**Take this wealth of mine.**
Yeh shauharat bhi le lo.	**Take this name and fame.**

Devi Shetty, the famous heart surgeon from Bengaluru, openly admits that he gets inspired by Sachin's heroics. Dr Shetty says, 'His importance is in the realization that an honest and gentle person can attain the pinnacle of glory in the most competitive field. He should not just be an icon of success but an example of a good person for generations to come.'

Sania Mirza and Saina Nehwal, two talented Indian sportspersons do not have much in common except that they come from the same city – Hyderabad. There is only another meeting point. Respect and love for Tendulkar. Saina, India's biggest sporting hope in recent times, is a huge fan of Sachin. She finds this attitude of not showing off very arresting. As for Sania, she still remembers at a sponsors' function, Sachin gifted her a car key. The next day he also called out of courtesy. Sania felt the call was more valuable than the car key. There are so many instances where well-known icons have felt proud to announce their place amongst the Tendulkar captive audience.

The day Sachin completed his 50th hundred, India's greatest cinestar Amitabh Bachchan wrote a blog on the Sachin-Bradman comparison. In an emotionally charged piece he opined, 'Why must there be a debate on whether Sachin is greater than Don Bradman or not? Sachin is greater. Period. By bringing the topic up for debate you are somewhere unsure whether he is really deserving of being great or not. And this is objectionable to me. How much more does one have to do to prove one's credentials!'

Don Bradman will always live in his own orbit with 99.94. Many, including Brian Lara feel, that in today's era of non-stop cricket, the dream average would have come down substantially to seventy plus. Even then the Don would have remained supreme. Sachin's average at 56 is way below. But on the durablity count and because of his continued mastery over all forms of game, Sachin is the worthy challenger to the throne.

And then his possible tally of 100 international hundreds – will be a staggering achievement. It will help Sachin set up his own orbit where 99.94 would require an entry permit. A hundred centuries are a hundred centuries. That record will possibly never be broken. The owner of the orbit has earned it the hard way!

Why would he dish out gate passes just like that?

Who cares, even if you are a Bradman !

||||||| Has also been the dressing room megastar

CHAPTER 12

MESSIAH OF THE DRESSING ROOM

The Berlin Wall had not yet collapsed. Communism was still a reality. India had not opened up her market. Rajiv Gandhi was at the helm of Indian politics. Dilip Vengsarkar was Captain of the Mumbai Cricket team and Vasu Paranjape, the coach.

A promising teenager was to be a new inclusion at the Mumbai nets. However, he didn't show up for the first three days. The captain and the coach were both so annoyed with his absence and felt that this was another case where top-quality talent was unhinged by indiscipline. On the fourth day the boy reported at the camp, the coach summoned him.

Coach: It seems you are not at all focussed on the game.
Youngster: No, Sir, I am.
Coach: Then why didn't you report for the first three days?
Youngster: Sir, I had a drawing exam at school.
Coach (now very angry): Ask your teacher to take your driving exams. Not drawing exams. And for heaven's sake try to remain focussed.

End of conversation.

Quite a historic one – where Sachin Tendulkar for the first and last time in his career got a solid firing for not taking cricket seriously.

The coach didn't buy the convincing argument that Sachin had to give a school exam. Today, this story is part of Mumbai cricketing folklore. The person who gets most embarassed with its repeated mention is not Sachin himself, but the hapless Vasu Paranjape.

Since then, the legend of Tendulkar has only grown. Before he played for India, Tendulkar was part of the Mumbai team that played the Ranji Trophy in the season that followed the drawing exam episode. On his first tour with the state team, Sachin was sharing a room with the team coach Jo Kamath who succedeed Paranjape. One day, well past midnight in a Hyderabad hotel, Kamath woke up suddenly to some familiar sounds. The only difference was that it was a hotel room. His roommate hardly seemed aware of that. He was walking and speaking to his non-existent non-striker at a non-existent batting crease. Urging the partner to run for quick singles. Sometimes he was shouting, 'No ... Don't ... stay back', in the typical running between the wickets lingo. Kamath was stunned and according to reports, couldn't sleep well for the rest of the night. He had shared rooms with cricketers before but had never seen something like this: that someone could sleepwalk cricket.

The next morning, the first thing Coach Kamath did was to break the news at the breakfast table. Naturally, the players were quite amazed to hear this. The same incident took place when the youngster was touring Pakistan with the Indian team. As it was Pakistan, peaceful sleep was not the order of the night for the touring Indians. And then to be confronted by the most unusual sight of a fellow cricketer sleepwalking and discussing cricket was on the face of it, slightly over the top. Yet, in dressing room discussions, the incident was only mentioned in a complimentary tone.

Raman Lamba, who suffered one of the most tragic deaths on a cricket ground, was part of that 1989 team. The late flamboyant Delhi-based opener, as is mentioned elsewhere in the book, had abused a senior journalist for suggesting in his match report that Lamba's crying off before the first test in Karachi had everything to do with the Pakistani fast bowlers. Closer to this incident, Mudar Patherya from *Sportsworld* and yours truly decided to play a little prank on Lamba.

The sort of prank that is unthinkable in today's era. But in those days, pranks were commonplace on a *bilateral* basis!

We somehow composed a short telex message for Lamba. With the help of Karachi's Pearl Continental Hotel Front Desk, we put that inside the pigeon hole of Lamba's room. Remember those were the days of wooden keys and even in a swanky, five-star hotel, you had to come down to the Reception to collect or drop the keys.

So the next morning, along with the key, Lamba was handed over a brief message which read:

'Extremely annoyed with the senior journalist episode. You are hereby served a show-cause notice. Must reply before the Test series ends.'

B N Dutt.

B N Dutt, incidentally, was the then Board President. Players were treated very firmly in that era and a show-cause at any given point of time hardly seemed out of place. The next day, after the nets, Lamba called me aside. Most certainly it had everything to do with the belief that since I came from Kolkata, I might be having an impressionable hold on the Board President.

'Yeh kya chakkar mein phas gaye hum.' ('What have I got myself into?') 'It seems they might ban me for a few matches,' Lamba observed. His tone was very pensive. And then Lamba broke the news. 'Forget me. You know the big news is that the new kid in the team sleepwalks. Kya involvement hai. (What commitment!)' Even in his dreams he is committed towards cricket.' Lamba's anxiety over a show-cause notice looming large had vanished. By then it had given way to genuine elder-brotherly praise.

As history unfolded in the years to come, Tendulkar would always be the central talking point inside the Indian dressing room. Juniors made a routine of observing him closely. Most like Suresh Raina were keen to share with their families how Sachin conducted himself in private and what kind of a person he was. Raina, like so many others in the team, was candid enough to admit that it was his dream to see Sachin from close quarters. 'My first test century was scored with him standing at the other end. Now this was more than a dream. Can't imagine even now that I have regular lunch, dinner, breakfast with the same person,' gushes Raina. The

||||||||||||||||||||||||||||||||||||||||||||||||||||||||||||||||||||||||||||||||||||||||||||||||||||

According to Zaheer, what he does do, at times, is to help himself to an extra bowl of ice-cream. Or order some dessert. Apparently, that has been Sachin's most violent visible reaction of disappointment till date!

young left-hander is so taken up with what he has seen in Sachin that he doesn't hold back his enthusiasm. Some day, say eight or ten years from now, if Raina is made captain of the Senior Indian team, he will request Sachin to speak to his boys. 'You know what? Everyone seems so happy when he is around in the dressing room,' says Raina. 'He hardly looks like a colleague and is more of a supporter.'

Seniors have also watched him at close quarters and tried to emulate him and improve their own cricket. Some, of course, have viewed with interest as to how he has handled the most difficult phases in a top cricketer's life: for instance, getting an atrocious LBW decision on a good batting wicket; playing a suicidal shot to get out after a good start; going through a series of low scores ....

Zaheer Khan, for one, has identified Tendulkar's tell-tale signs of frustration. Unlike some biggies of the past, Sachin doesn't abuse. He has never ever broken the dressing-room glass. He never throws personal equipment around. According to Zaheer, what he does do, at times, is to help himself to an extra bowl of ice-cream. Or order some dessert. Apparently, that has been Sachin's most violent visible reaction of disappointment till date!

Insiders will tell you how cricket stars behave inside the four walls of the dressing room. Dravid supposedly remains as intense as he is in personal life. The most common scenario is of him doing shadow practice either with or without the bat. Or watching the match with rapt attention. Sehwag, in complete contrast, remains immersed in his Ipod or moves around in a relaxed manner. Laxman is a fitness freak who stretches or exercises. He remains relaxed, yet very focussed. Dhoni belts out Kishore Kumar songs. Apparently the Indian captain is a Kishore Kumar devotee and remembers most of his songs in their entirety. In comparison, Sachin is a man for all seasons inside the dressing room. You can sense his mood by just looking at him – you can tell whether a ruthless winter or spring is currently passing through his mind. But irrespective of the mood, the cricketing mind ticks all the time. It is never ever on a pause button.

There is a school of thought and a pretty strong one at that, that to get the optimum out of Tendulkar, happiness around the dressing room is very important. Some of his teammates have shared with me that he requires positive energy around him all the time. In the dressing room he requires an extension of his family peace. Which Gary Kirsten has managed to provide. That possibly explains Sachin's fascination with the South African.

Some teammates, including Harbhajan, observed how Sachin was singing and listening to Ganapati Arati on his way to the double hundred at Bengaluru. And when Sachin scored that match-winning Chennai fourth innings hundred against England, for three sessions, he didn't speak to anyone in the dressing room. He came and spoke to his teammates only when the match was won. Players felt that Tendulkar had transported himself mentally to a world outside the dressing room where only he and the Creator remained. Whenever Sachin is in such a mood, everyone can sense that. Almost dutifully they leave him alone.

What is remarkable is that during such a long career there has never been a single bat-abuse case against him. Ramesh Mane, the team masseur who has been with Tendulkar on so many tours, thinks that Tendulkar could never do that as he worships a bat. Inside his *cricket coffin*, a bat finds its place next to the picture of the deity. To put it in short, the bat is to Tendulkar what the sitar was to Ali Akbar Khan. Or what the harmonium is to Jagjit Singh.

Inside the privacy of the dressing room, Tendulkar is characterized by various factors. If one of them is the deep love for his equipment, then another is his ever-

|||||||| Demonstrates at the coaching clinic

helpful attitude, which begins from the confines of the dressing room and extends to the batting crease.

Sehwag recalls how Sachin guided him at Multan during his first triple hundred. When Sehwag hit a six and was attempting to repeat the stroke, the non-striker Sachin came over and warned him, 'If you try to attempt one more shot like that, I am going to slap you.' Sehwag followed his instructions with rapt attention. When he was batting at 294, he actually walked over to take his idol's permission to try for a six. Sachin approved. Armed with the official license, the next minute a sixer followed.

The scoreboard recorded the first ever Indian getting a triple hundred. What it didn't record was how the man was guided at every step towards this triple hundred by his idol.

Zaheer admits that his remarkable comeback would not have been possible without the advice and encouragement provided by Sachin. 'He had told me as far back as 2001 that my kind of bowling required more and more practice. Based on his advice I played county cricket and it was extremely useful.' Zaheer also admits that while he is bowling, Sachin stationed at mid-off or mid-on is very beneficial, as he guides him constantly. During the last Mohali Test match against Australia, Marcus North was playing the left-handed pacer comfortably. This prompted Sachin to run from the outfield and provide Zaheer with a tip, 'Keep the wrist straight as he is watching your hand.' In the very next delivery, Zaheer did as prescribed. He disguised his hand movement well and had North caught. It is obvious whom he thanked first in the midst of the celebration!

VVS Laxman still thanks Tendulkar profusely for his silent role in that epic match-winning knock at the same Mohali test. 'The moment I stepped out at the crease, he started telling me, "Play your normal game. Don't worry about the situation." ' Then the discussion centred around what kind of shots were advisable on that track. The partnership did not last long as Sachin got out. But on hindsight, Laxman realized why Tendulkar in a manner so unlike him, was talking so much. Most of it had to do with Laxman's back injury. By talking constantly, Tendulkar wanted to divert his partner's attention. So very thoughtful, Laxman was to think later.

Laxman and Tendulkar share a unique relationship. The world of 'haves' and 'have-nots' is how they are presented to the cricketing world. Tendulkar is someone who shines as if he is the cricketing monarch. And Laxman happens to be the classically tormented hero who, despite his many major test-winning knocks, somehow doesn't attract attention. His glorious cricketing life has failed to create the magnetic charisma of a Sachin. But Laxman has no remorse.

To him, Sachin represents the best in the business. Laxman's Tendulkar memory goes back as early as 1992 when he watched his sensational Perth hundred sitting in front of the TV. For him, 'It has been a great honour to play alongside Tendulkar for years. To discover how his cricketing mind comes up with so many creative suggestions while batting.' If you ask Laxman to nominate three of his favourite sportsmen, he would pick Roger Federer, Pete Sampras and Sachin Tendulkar. Not necessarily in that order.

Laxman saw Tendulkar almost moved to tears after the unsuccessful run chase attempt against Akram's Pakistan in Chennai. But leaving aside that stray incident, he has noticed how quickly Tendulkar puts his disappointments behind him. He either sleeps for some time inside the dressing room or goes to the gym to work out. When he returns, he is ready to start preparing for the next innings!

The tales of personal kindness related to Sachin are many. Once, in Durban, when the team bus had just reached the hotel, a disabled old man was trying hard to cross the road. With no help forthcoming from any quarters, out came Tendulkar from the bus. He not only helped the old man cross the road but also spoke to him for sometime. Sitting inside the bus, his opening partner was touched that while the others were all getting down to head for the confines of the hotel room, his hero took the other route. This was Sehwag and he will not forget the incident in a hurry. As for Very Very dependable Laxman, what attracts him in Sachin is the willingness to discuss and share it all – even with the youngest member of the team. He has never ever been the great selfish superstar who is absorbed and immersed only in himself.

For all he has done and given to Indian Cricket, Laxman wishes his long-time colleague a World Cup winners' medal. Dhoni and Sehwag echo the same sentiments. And Raina, who represents the new Indian brigade, hopes that the team will be able to give Sachin a befitting parting gift. 'Without the Cup, his story will remain incomplete. So we have decided to try the hardest and hand over the World Cup to him,' quips Raina.

But the same dressing room also views with great interest the spark of competitiveness this good-hearted man brings along, when confronted with a game situation. His whole take is to better others. To be on top always. Harbhajan records with amusement how Sachin has to be the Number One in a match held inside the dressing room. Or even in a light-hearted banter. Anil Kumble endorses his long-time bowling partner's sentiments to the tee: 'Sachin is extremely competitive.

|||||| They are all anxious inside the dressing room

He doesn't like anyone getting on top of him.' Sachin and Kumble shared a deep personal relationship based on mutual professional respect. Surprisingly, the Anil-Sachin friendship is not very well advertised in the outside world, including the media. But the day Kumble retired at Kotla, Sachin looked almost down and out as if he himself had left the game. During Kumble's playing days, the duo took up respective responsiblities in bowling and batting. One was the unannounced bowling captain. The other took responsibilities of the batting group.

So who would know the famous Sachin mindset better than India's greatest match-winning bowler. 'Sachin has unbelievable discipline. He would always undertake special preparations to win his battles. That attitude armed with

|||||||| With Kumble, arguably his most respected colleague

a God-gifted talent is a winner all the way,' remarks Kumble, standing on the same Centurion cricket ground where Tendulkar had scripted that magic innings against Pakistan. This is where the Mumbai Indians team bus will arrive shortly for practice. And Anil Kumble from the Royal Challengers will be gone.

I asked Harbhajan and Zaheer as to what they thought of Sachin's critics.

ZAHEER: What critics! He has answered them all. They are now jobless.

HARBHAJAN: Will tell them: Friends, please look after yourself.

The very next day, a few thousand miles away, sitting in his Mumbai studio, Atul Kasbekar remarked how Sachin always kept in mind one simple formula:

You are a sportsman. To look good elsewhere first you will have to look good on the sports page. And for that, you must win consistently.

|||||||| Sachin with his faithful army – Zaheer and Harbhajan

Once, during the shooting of an ad commercial, Sachin's manager was playing video games on his phone in which his score showed a certain number of points. This was at ten o'clock in the morning. Sachin challenged him: 'By lunch I will beat your top score. If I do that, will you buy me a new phone and vice versa?' Sachin eventually won and with that, secured a new mobile phone for himself. To quote Kasbekar, 'Moments like those brought out his game face strikingly.'

Yograj Singh, the former Indian pace bowler, has never shared a dressing room with Sachin but has heard the stories from a good first-hand source. You can imagine who! Yograj, the temperamental former pace bowler has three framed photographs on his drawing room wall – one expectedly of Yuvraj, his son; the other two – of Viv and Sachin. Even today, he advises his son to spend as much time with Sachin as possible. Sitting inside his Chandigarh Petrol Pump, Yograj says, 'Mumbai ki dharti ko mera lakho salaam. Jisne Tendulkar ko paida kiya hai.' ('I salute the soil of Mumbai many times over for having given birth to Tendulkar.')

||||||| All part of the preparation

||||||| Pool session

Kasbekar calls him a *Zen monk* — the type who would never fall for outside-cricket distractions. This photographer friend is sick and tired of stories every now and then that Sachin is acting in Vidhu Vinod Chopra's new film and that Kasbekar is the go-between. Once and for all he wants to put an end to the rumours: 'Usually well-known non-actors only do films to add layers to their personality. Sachin doesn't need to add layers. He is a complete man. I do not ever see him acting in movies.' End of story.

But no one can put a definitive end to when Tednulkar will finally walk past the dressing room into the sunset. The likes of Kasbekar believe that Sachin will not overstay his welcome. The day he realizes that he has fallen even slightly short of his own standards and expectations, he will call it a day. Like Adam Gilchrist did. Zaheer, somehow feels, there is still plenty of cricket left in Tendulkar. Bhajji is more forthcoming as always: 'Don't you see how he retrieves the deliveries from the boundary with the same zeal that he did on his first Test match. Why talk about retirement!' Both are close cricket buddies of Sachin and they can't imagine an Indian dressing room without him. They certainly have a point as Sachin, all of 37, proved in South Africa with two fighting hundreds in a three-Test Match series.

Yet whatever their wishes and those of millions of Indians, and his current incredible form, all good things come to an end some day. There is a famous line in cricketing terminology which extends well into the circle of life:

For you must know when to declare.

When will Sachin declare? Historian Ramachandra Guha is a hardliner. He is in line with Zaheer and Harbhajan's thinking. Guha believes that 'God has sent him from upstairs for a definite purpose. To play cricket. So it is only fair that Sachin must play as long as he can. If possible till the age of 45.' Conventional wisdom has it that he will play as long as his body permits. It is universally felt that muscle power will determine Tendulkar's timeline. Not a hostile spell, lack of eyesight, or a run of a few low scores.

Ravi Shastri did the post 50th-hundred interview with him in South Africa. Shastri returned with the feeling that his job as a TV interviewer was hardly over. He just might have to interview the same person again some day. Who knows – may be after the 60th!

What will Tendulkar do once he is finished with cricket? Zaheer, for one, shrugs at the possiblity. 'Really difficult to answer. His whole life has been cricket. More than two-thirds of his life is spent on a cricket field.' Atul Ranade, a childhood friend, doesn't rule out the possibilities of Sachin taking up golf big time. Ranade functioned as the caddy during an afternoon of golf exercise for Tendulkar in London sometime ago. One hit that Sachin effected was so huge and yet so accurate that it left the onlookers convinced he would grasp even this game fast. The rest of his time, Ranade thinks, will be spent in business. 'May be he will start his own restaurant chain,' he hazards a guess.

And what are the Tendulkar memories that people will carry to the next generation? Or to the generation after that? I asked a couple of players what would be the Tendulkar story that they would carry to their grandsons? The answers provide an interesting mix. But the common thread remained the same – his humility.

Dravid: I will tell Sumit (his son) and possibly the generation after, how he conducted himself off the field. How remarkably he retained the middle-class values despite being such an icon.

Kambli: I will talk about how long he played and how much cricket he has played with the same amount of passion. Also that he never played for personal milestones. But always for the team.

Ganguly: Sachin's change of strategy at the Cape Town Test Match in 1997 after going out to bat. The sheer adjustment ability was mind-blowing as he started shuffling from middle to leg stump. He was doing it for the first time and yet walked away with a brilliant hundred. For me, that was genius!

Harbajhan: I will tell my grandchildren that I could play with such a big champion for so many years. Someone who even after achieving so much in life, remained so extraordinarily simple.

Srinath: I will tell them that I was lucky to share the dressing room with him. I saw an exceptional talent flower before my own eyes. But mostly I will talk about the wonderful manner in which he has conducted himself in public life despite coming from a middle-class family.

Zaheer: The enjoyment that he gave. The passion that he showed to remain the very best.

Laxman: Shall tell them that I was lucky to have known him. Forget playing alongside. That he had great family values. That despite the success he retained himself so well.

It is said the quantum of happiness that Tendulkar has brought to the Indian race has no parallel in any sportsperson. Dead, living or contemporary. But the best part of his success is that even fellow players remain devotees. Why blame a supporter who always found him a gloom-reliever!

The day India found herself on the top of the ICC test rankings for the first time quite befittingly in the cricketing city of Mumbai, I made a private trip to the narrow lane next to the Cama Hospital. The idea was to experience the cricketing highest of the high along with the lowest of the low tragedies that had occurred there one and half years ago. It had left unmistakable scars. It took very little time to locate the red letter box and the ATM counter in front of which three bodies lay on that ominous night.

Karkare ... Salaskar ... Kamte.

Life seemingly was absolutely normal. People talking, moving around, chatting. Traffic passing by slowly. Yet somehow the shadow of 26/11 hung like a shroud of despair and gloom all around. Any point of reference in that narrow by-lane leads to the spot where the bodies were found and the red letter box.

That is where Kasab killed them brutally. But the teenager who was practising next door seemed completely single-minded. Bare-chested, he was practising hitting against the moving ball. I noticed a poster behind his back. Who else but Tendulkar! Even in this narrow lane of horrific memories, Tendulkar remained the biggest life-saving drug.

Honestly, what will India do once her biggest ever stock of *Boost* runs out?

When he decides to finally pack his bag and go!

The fairy tale has to end some day. The apprehension is: With that will also end so many different sources of inspiration! Tendulkar minus his instrument is Ravi Shankar without the sitar.

There is a high possiblity in Shantanu Moitra's prediction that once Tendulkar decides to call it a day, players and non-players alike will invariably remember a particular song.

Behti hawa sa tha woh
Udti patang sa tha woh
Kahan gaya use dhoondo ....

He was like a whiff of wind
He was like a flying kite
Where has he gone away? Find him ...

The beauty of Tendulkar is that there will possibly never be another Tendulkar! But who cares. We have seen him in our lifetime!

THE SACHIN MANTRA

1. At the outset: Remember – there is no 'Sure Success Sachin formula'. To quote Salim Khan,'There is nothing called Formula films. Only a Pepsi or Coca Cola has a formula that their bottles would be identical irrespective of wherever they are packed.'

2. Take a chance only if you have passion. Passion is the magical force that will keep you afloat amidst all kinds of calamities. It will provide steadiness of purpose throughout the journey.

3. Choose the subject of your attempt with utmost care. Even passion without proper selection is of no use. Pick what you are naturally good at. If Sachin taught Marathi literature or wrote poems, chances are that he may not have been half as good as his father was. So before you begin, do a brutal self-analysis.Am I really good at it?

4. Be prepared to work extremely hard and forego some of the earthly pleasures of youth. Remember, respect comes with a costly price tag. Even someone as brilliant as Tendulkar pays it on a daily basis. So how can you and me escape that!

5. Work on your body while you are in the teens. Develop strength. Irrespective of what you want to become in life, the body must stand up to handle the likely wear and tear.

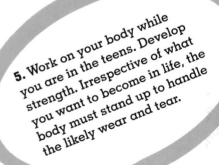

6. In case you face preliminary rejection from the outside world, or even when you have become an established pro, don't pick a quarrel with the world. First look internally within yourself. Try and address the faults internally instead of pointing fingers at others.

7. Don't think about money all the time. If you establish yourself as a top quality professional, sustaining yourself is usually not a problem. At some point of time money will chase you. But obsession about money can take away the vital focus. Just think of the new breed of IPL players. Did money teach them how to play the short ball?

8. If you start achieving a little bit of success, use that to push yourself harder. If you face disappointment, that should be a good enough reason for you to work harder.

9. If you are not humble by nature, try and practice humility. Remember that in Sachin's life, this has been the most vital stroke. Much bigger than his straight drive. Even in a proudest moment of glory, he has acknowledged that he still has not learnt enough.

11. You have to develop an ability to handle extreme pain as you go along. Otherwise you won't be able to run the full distance. This could be an ability that you may not be born with. The ability to handle the most excruciating pain. The ability to handle the most hopeless situation with grace. It could be the deadly tennis elbow threatening to finish your career. The untimely death of your father when you are representing the country. Or negative criticism from your own coach.

10. Take good care of your equipment. If you are a musician, then it has to be your instrument. If you are a footballer, than the pair of boots and the jersey you wear on the field. If you are a journalist, then your laptop or the pen that you use. Equipment is the medium through which your talent is showcased to the outside world. If that is not in prime condition your performance will invariably suffer.

12. Conserve energy. Be it physical or mental. Energy abuse is the biggest roadblock for a performer. Energy armed with talent wins you the most important battle.

P.S. Vinod Kambli and Sairaj Bahutule are childhood friends of Sachin. Both played for India. Both would like to leave a message for the future generation: that if you attempt to become a Sachin, chances are that you will never become one. But if you follow his mantra diligently, even a failure will ensure you have become someone in life!

From the Statistician's
Scoreboard Statistics Updated till the Beginning of the South African One-day Series 2011

CAREER ||||||||||||||||||||||||

SERIES / TOURNAMENTS	PERIOD	MAT	INNS	NO	RUNS	
Tests	1989 - 2011	177	290	32	14692	
ODIs	1989/90 to 2009/10	442	431	41	17598	
T20s	2006/07	1	1	0	10	
Total		620	722	73	32300	
All First-class (all 3+ day matches)	1988/89 to 2010/11	280	442	48	23585	
All Limited overs (all 50-ov matches)	1989/90 to 2009/10	529	516	55	21150	
All Twenty 20 (all 20-ov matches)	2006/07 to 2010/11	44	44	5	1516	
Ranji Trophy (for Mumbai)	1988/89 to 2008/09	33	50	7	3865	
Duleep Trophy (for West Zone)	1990/91 to 2004/05	8	11	0	604	
Irani Trophy (for ROI/Mumbai)	1989/90 to 2003/04	3	5	1	299	
English County Championship (for Yorkshire)	1992	16	25	2	1070	
Deodhar Trophy (for West Zone)	1989/90 to 1993/94	7	6	1	149	
Wills Trophy (for WillsXI/Mumbai/Board President'sXI)	1989/90 to 1995/96	14	14	5	723	
Challenger Trophy (for India Seniors/India A)	1994/95 to 2006/07	20	20	1	1039	
Ranji One-dayers (for Mumbai)	1993/94 to 1998/99	12	11	2	489	
English County limited over tournaments (for Yorkshire)	1992	17	17	2	540	
Indian Premier League (for Mumbai Indians)	2007/08 to 2009/10	35	35	5	1170	
Champions League (for Mumbai Indians)	2010/11	4	4	0	148	

SACH

HS	AVE	100	50	CT	BALLS	RUNS	WKTS	BEST	AVE	R/O	SR	5WI
248*	56.94	51	59	106	4096	2388	45	3\10	53.06	3.49	91.02	0
200*	45.12	46	93	134	8020	6817	154	5\32	44.26	5.10	52.00	2
10	10.00	0	0	1	15	12	1	1\12	12.00	4.80	15.00	0
248*	49.76	97	152	241	12131	9217	200	5\32	46.08	4.55	60.66	2
248*	59.86	78	105	174	7461	4280	70	3\10	61.14	3.44	106.58	0
200*	45.87	57	111	169	10196	8445	201	5\32	42.01	4.96	50.70	2
89*	38.87	0	11	19	93	123	2	1\12	61.50	7.93	46.50	0
233*	89.88	16	17	34	825	449	2	1\8	224.50	3.26	412.50	0
199	54.90	3	1	5	714	366	7	3\60	52.28	3.07	102.00	0
103*	74.75	1	2	2	174	69	1	1\6	69.00	2.37	174.00	0
100	46.52	1	7	10	375	195	4	2\35	48.75	3.12	93.75	0
45*	29.80	0	0	3	168	153	3	2\38	51.00	5.46	56.00	0
121	80.33	3	4	4	504	397	14	3\23	28.35	4.72	36.00	0
139	54.68	3	7	8	564	390	10	2\18	39.00	4.14	56.40	0
120*	54.33	2	3	8	468	330	9	2\17	36.66	4.23	52.00	0
107	36.00	1	1	3	248	167	6	2\21	27.83	4.04	41.33	0
89*	39.00	0	8	15	36	58	0	-	-	9.67	-	0
69	37.00	0	1	2	-	-	-	-	-	-	-	

AGAINST EACH OPPONENT

OPPONENTS	MAT	INNS	NO	RUNS	HS	AVE	SR	100	50
v Australia	67	66	1	3005	175	46.23	85.12	9	14
v Bangladesh	10	9	1	354	82*	44.25	86.97	0	2
v Bermuda	1	1	1	57	57*	-	196.55	0	1
v England	36	36	4	1335	105*	41.71	88.06	1	10
v Ireland	1	1	0	4	4	4.00	133.33	0	0
v Kenya	10	9	3	647	146	107.83	97.00	4	1
v Namibia	1	1	0	152	152	152.00	100.66	1	0
v Netherlands	1	1	0	52	52	52.00	72.22	0	1
v New Zealand	42	41	3	1750	186*	46.05	95.36	5	8
v Pakistan	67	65	4	2389	141	39.16	87.70	5	14
v South Africa	54	54	1	1859	200*	35.07	75.38	4	8
v Sri Lanka	78	74	9	2965	138	45.61	87.64	8	17
v U.A.E.	2	2	0	81	63	40.50	79.41	0	1
v West Indies	38	38	9	1571	141*	54.17	78.08	4	11
v Zimbabwe	34	33	5	1377	146	49.17	91.55	5	5

IN EACH COUNTRY

	MAT	INNS	NO	RUNS	HS	AVE	SR	100	50
Australia	40	39	3	1348	117*	37.44	74.55	1	10
in Bangladesh	12	12	0	627	141	52.25	105.20	1	4
in Canada	12	11	2	313	89*	34.77	67.02	0	3
in England	26	26	2	1051	140*	43.79	88.39	3	4
in India	156	152	15	6522	200*	47.60	88.18	18	36
in Ireland	4	4	0	204	99	51.00	78.46	0	2
in Kenya	4	4	0	171	69	42.75	83.41	0	1
Malaysia	4	4	1	222	141*	74.00	80.14	1	1
New Zealand	22	22	1	821	163*	39.09	97.39	1	5
in Pakistan	13	13	0	480	141	36.92	88.72	2	1
in Singapore	5	5	0	253	100	50.60	88.77	1	1
in South Africa	38	36	0	1422	152	39.50	80.11	4	6
in Sri Lanka	44	41	5	1531	138	42.52	81.87	5	6
in U.A.E.	42	42	5	1778	143	48.05	92.79	7	7
in West Indies	9	9	3	282	65*	47.00	90.38	0	3
in Zimbabwe	11	11	4	573	127*	81.85	86.68	2	3

HOME/AWAY/NEUTRAL

OPPONENTS	MAT	INNS	NO	RUNS	HS	AVE	SR	100	50
home	156	152	15	6522	200*	47.60	88.18	18	36
away	140	139	10	4873	163*	37.77	82.13	11	24
neutral	146	140	16	6203	152	50.02	87.71	17	33

IN EACH CALENDAR YEAR

	MAT	INNS	NO	RUNS	HS	AVE	SR	100	50
year 1989	1	1	0	0	0	0.00	0.00	0	0
year 1990	11	10	0	239	53	23.90	98.76	0	1
year 1991	14	14	2	417	62	34.75	74.46	0	4
year 1992	21	20	2	704	84	39.11	69.08	0	6
year 1993	18	17	4	319	82*	24.53	73.16	0	1
year 1994	25	25	2	1089	115	47.34	88.60	3	9
year 1995	12	12	1	444	112*	40.36	101.36	1	1
year 1996	32	32	2	1611	137	53.70	82.44	6	9
year 1997	39	36	3	1011	117	30.63	84.95	2	5
year 1998	34	33	4	1894	143	65.31	102.15	9	7
year 1999	22	22	2	843	186*	42.15	88.64	3	1
year 2000	34	34	0	1328	146	39.05	81.77	3	6
year 2001	17	16	3	904	146	69.53	91.31	4	3
year 2002	20	19	5	741	113	52.92	87.48	2	3
year 2003	21	21	1	1141	152	57.05	87.36	3	8
year 2004	21	21	1	812	141	40.60	80.07	1	5
year 2005	16	16	1	412	123	27.46	77.29	1	2
year 2006	16	16	2	628	141*	44.85	77.05	2	3
year 2007	33	32	2	1425	100*	47.50	85.58	1	13
year 2008	12	12	1	460	117*	41.81	84.24	1	3
year 2009	21	20	2	972	175	54.00	94.00	3	3
year 2010	2	2	1	204	200*	204.00	134.21	1	0

IN EACH SEASON

	MAT	INNS	NO	RUNS	HS	AVE	SR	100	50
season 1989/90	5	5	0	66	36	13.20	82.50	0	0
season 1990	2	2	0	50	31	25.00	81.96	0	0
season 1990/91	6	5	0	176	53	35.20	101.73	0	2
season 1991/92	26	25	4	885	84	42.14	74.18	0	9
season 1992/93	17	16	2	343	82*	24.50	69.85	0	1
season 1993	3	3	0	61	25	20.33	56.48	0	0

IN EACH SEASON

OPPONENTS	MAT	INNS	NO	RUNS	HS	AVE	SR	100	50
season 1993/94	17	17	3	528	82	37.71	90.72	0	5
season 1994	4	4	1	127	110	42.33	83.00	1	0
season 1994/95	17	17	1	834	115	52.12	88.72	3	4
season 1995/96	19	19	1	988	137	54.88	85.68	4	5
season 1996	11	11	1	331	110	33.10	78.43	1	1
season 1996/97	20	20	1	809	114	42.57	85.97	2	5
season 1997	17	15	1	423	117	30.21	78.18	1	2
season 1997/98	24	23	1	1035	143	47.04	99.71	3	6
season 1998	9	8	1	491	128	70.14	98.39	2	3
season 1998/99	14	14	3	654	141	59.45	104.30	4	0
season 1999	13	13	1	549	140*	45.75	83.68	2	1
season 1999/00	22	22	1	758	186*	36.09	83.29	2	2
season 2000	3	3	0	154	93	51.33	102.66	0	1
season 2000/01	19	19	0	917	146	48.26	90.43	3	4
season 2001	5	5	3	282	122*	141.00	82.45	1	2
season 2001/02	15	14	2	707	146	58.91	86.96	2	3
season 2002	7	7	1	337	113	56.16	93.09	2	0
season 2002/03	19	18	2	714	152	44.62	82.06	1	6
season 2003/04	19	19	1	915	141	50.83	86.48	3	4
season 2004	6	6	1	281	82*	56.20	72.42	0	3
season 2004/05	9	9	0	227	123	25.22	84.38	1	0
season 2005/06	14	14	1	504	100	38.76	81.55	1	3
season 2006	1	1	1	2	2*	-	66.66	0	0
season 2006/07	21	20	3	699	141*	41.11	81.09	2	5
season 2007	11	11	0	578	99	52.54	83.04	0	6
season 2007/08	22	22	1	936	117*	44.57	83.27	1	6
season 2008/09	8	8	1	323	163*	46.14	95.00	1	2
season 2009	3	3	0	211	138	70.33	95.47	1	0
season 2009/10	14	13	2	703	200*	63.90	100.00	2	2

CAPTAINCY

	MAT	INNS	NO	RUNS	HS	AVE	SR	100	50
as captain	73	70	5	2454	186*	37.75	83.49	6	12
not as captain	369	361	36	15144	200*	46.59	86.72	40	81

IN EACH INNINGS

OPPONENTS	MAT	INNS	NO	RUNS	HS	AVE	SR	100	50
1st match innings	213	212	15	9216	200*	46.78	84.28	29	43
2nd match innings	223	219	26	8382	175	43.43	88.53	17	50

RESULTS

in ODIs won	222	219	34	10737	200*	58.03	90.66	33	56
in OdIs lost	193	193	2	6312	175	33.04	79.59	12	35
in tied ODIs	3	3	0	31	24	10.33	93.93	0	0
in NR ODIs	24	16	5	518	105*	47.09	86.91	1	2

BATTING POSITIONS

1st position	47	47	2	1625	120	36.11	82.82	2	9
2nd position	272	272	21	12857	200*	51.22	88.92	40	63
3rd position	10	10	1	92	31	10.22	48.16	0	0
4th position	61	61	8	2059	140*	38.84	77.08	4	15
5th position	36	36	8	797	82*	28.46	81.07	0	5
6th position	4	4	1	148	57*	49.33	134.54	0	1
7th position	1	1	0	20	20	20.00	80.00	0	0
OVERALL	**442**	**431**	**41**	**17598**	**200***	**45.12**	**86.26**	**46**	**93**

||||||||||||||||||||||||||||||||||||||||||||||||

TENDULKAR IN TEST |||||||||||||||||||||

AGAINST EACH OPPONENT

v Australia	31	59	7	3151	241*	60.59	11	13	2
v Bangladesh	7	9	3	820	248*	136.66	5	0	1
v England	24	39	4	2150	193	61.42	7	10	10
v New Zealand	22	36	5	1532	217	49.41	4	8	0
v Pakistan	18	27	2	1057	194*	42.28	2	7	1
v South Africa	25	45	4	1741	169	42.46	7	5	0
v Sri Lanka	25	36	3	1995	203	60.45	9	6	1
v West Indies	16	25	2	1328	179	57.73	3	7	8
v Zimbabwe	9	14	2	918	201*	76.5	3	3	14

IN EACH COUNTRY

OPPONENTS	MAT	INNS	NO	RUNS	HS	AVE	SR	100	50
in Australia	16	30	4	1522	241*	58.53	6	5	10
in Bangladesh	7	9	3	820	248*	136.66	5	0	4
in England	13	22	1	1302	193	62	4	6	3
in India	79	130	15	6547	217	56.93	22	27	4
in New Zealand	11	18	1	842	160	49.52	2	5	36
in Pakistan	10	13	1	483	194*	40.25	1	2	2
in South Africa	15	28	3	1161	169	46.44	5	3	1
in Sri Lanka	12	19	2	1155	203	67.94	5	4	1
in West Indies	10	14	1	620	117	47.69	1	5	5
in Zimbabwe	4	7	1	240	74	40	0	2	1

HOME/AWAY/NEUTRAL

OPPONENTS	MAT	INNS	NO	RUNS	HS	AVE	SR	100	50
in Tests at home	79	130	15	6547	217	56.93	22	27	36
in Tests away	98	160	17	8145	248*	56.95	29	32	24

IN EACH CALENDAR YEAR

	MAT	INNS	NO	RUNS	HS	AVE	SR	100	50
1989	4	6	0	215	59	35.83	0	2	0
1990	7	10	1	373	119*	41.44	1	2	1
1991	2	4	0	78	40	19.5	0	0	4
1992	7	11	1	419	148*	41.9	3	0	6
1993	8	9	2	640	165	91.42	2	5	1
1994	7	11	1	700	179	70	2	3	9
1995	3	4	2	58	52*	29	0	1	1
1996	8	15	0	623	177	41.53	2	2	9
1997	12	17	1	1000	169	62.5	4	3	5
1998	5	9	1	647	177	80.87	3	1	7
1999	10	19	3	1088	217	68	5	4	1
2000	6	10	1	575	201*	63.88	2	1	6
2001	10	18	2	1003	155	62.68	3	6	3
2002	16	26	1	1392	193	55.68	4	5	3
2003	5	9	0	153	55	17	0	1	8
2004	10	15	5	915	248*	91.5	3	2	5

SACH

OPPONENTS	MAT	INNS	NO	RUNS	HS	AVE	SR	100	50
2005	6	10	0	444	109	44.4	1	3	2
2006	8	12	1	267	63	24.27	0	1	3
2007	9	16	2	776	122*	55.42	2	6	13
2008	13	25	3	1063	154*	48.31	4	3	3
2009	6	9	1	541	160	67.62	2	3	3
2010	14	23	3	1562	214	78.1	7	5	0
2011	1	2	1	160	146	160	1	0	0
IN EACH SEASON									
1989/90	7	10	0	332	88	33.2	0	3	0
1990	3	5	1	245	119*	61.25	1	1	0
1990/91	1	1	0	11	11	11	0	0	2
1991/92	5	9	1	368	148*	46	2	0	9
1992/93	9	12	1	566	165	51.45	2	4	1
1993	3	3	1	203	104*	101.5	1	1	0
1993/94	4	5	1	298	142	74.5	1	1	0
1994/95	3	6	0	402	179	67	1	2	0
1995/96	3	4	2	58	52*	29	0	1	2
1996	3	5	0	428	177	85.6	2	1	9
1996/97	12	20	1	706	169	37.15	1	4	1
1997	2	3	0	290	143	96.66	2	0	0
1997/98	6	9	1	645	177	80.62	3	1	0
1998/99	7	13	1	625	136	52.08	3	2	0
1999/00	8	16	2	859	217	61.35	3	3	2
2000/01	6	10	1	684	201*	76	3	2	9
2001	2	4	1	199	74	66.33	0	2	1
2001/02	12	19	1	1085	176	60.27	4	4	0
2002	4	6	0	401	193	66.83	1	2	0
2002/03	5	9	1	406	176	50.75	1	1	0
2003/04	9	15	3	659	241*	54.91	2	2	2
2004/05	9	14	2	664	248*	55.33	1	4	9
2005/06	9	13	1	335	109	27.91	1	0	1
2006/07	3	6	0	199	64	33.16	0	2	0
2007	5	9	1	482	122*	60.25	2	2	0

IN EACH SEASON									
OPPONENTS	MAT	INNS	NO	RUNS	HS	AVE	SR	100	50
2007/08	7	12	2	632	154*	63.2	2	4	2
2008	3	6	0	95	31	15.83	0	0	9
2008/09	9	17	2	896	160	59.73	3	4	1
2009/10	7	10	2	674	143	84.25	5	1	0
2010	3	5	0	390	203	78	1	2	2
2010/11	8	14	3	855	214	77.72	3	3	9
CAPTAINCY									
as captain	25	43	3	2054	217	51.35	7	7	12
not as captain	152	247	29	12638	248*	57.97	44	52	81
IN EACH INNINGS									
1st team innings	176	174	9	10557	248*	63.98	38	41	43
2nd team innings	130	116	23	4135	176	44.46	13	18	50
1st match innings	83	83	6	5397	241*	70.09	20	19	43
2nd match innings	93	91	3	5160	248*	58.63	18	22	50
3rd match innings	67	66	8	2764	176	47.65	10	13	43
4th match innings	63	50	15	1371	136	39.17	3	5	50
RESULTS									
in Tests won	61	97	16	5473	248*	67.56	20	21	56
in Tests lost	46	92	2	3431	177	38.12	11	13	35
in Tests drawn	70	101	14	5788	241*	66.52	20	25	0
BATTING POSITIONS									
2nd position	1	1	0	15	15	15	0	0	9
4th position	154	237	26	12275	248*	58.17	44	49	63
5th position	25	28	3	1540	169	61.6	5	6	0
6th position	14	20	3	745	148*	43.82	2	4	15
7th position	3	4	0	117	41	29.25	0	0	5
OVERALL	177	290	32	14692	248*	56.94	51	59	93

SACH

SACHIN'S PERFORMANCE DURING THE GREG CHAPPELL ERA IIIIIIIIIIIIIIIIIIIIII

(1-5-2005 TO 31-3-2007)

TESTS	12m, 19i, 1no, 534runs, 29.67ave, 100s-1, 50s-2, HS-109
ODIS	36m, 35i, 5no, 1205runs, 40.17ave. 100s-3, 50s-8

AFTER THE GREG CHAPPELL ERA (FROM 1-4-2007)

TESTS	42m, 73i, 10no, 4024runs, 63.87 ave, 100s-16, 50s-16, HS-214
ODIS	58m, 57i, 4no, 2751runs, 51.91ave. 100s-4, 50s-16

IIIIIIIIIIIIIIIIIIIIIIIIIIIIIIIII

MAN OF THE SERIES AWARDS IN ODIs IIIIIIIIIIIIIIIIIIIIII

MAN OF THE SERIES AWARDS	MAT	RUNS	HS	BAT AV	100	WKTS	BEST	BOWL AV	CT
Singer World Series (in Sri Lanka), 1994	4	127	110	42.33	1	0	-	-	0
West Indies in India ODI Series, 1994/95	5	247	105	49.4	1	1	1\39	122	1
Wills World Series (in India), 1994/95	5	285	115	57	1	8	3\36	19.75	3
Silver Jubilee Independence Cup (in Bangl), 1997/98	5	258	95	51.6	0	5	3\45	29.6	6
Coca-Cola Cup (in UAE), 1997/98	5	435	143	87	2	2	1\27	50.5	0
India in Zimbabwe ODI Series, 1998/99	3	158	127*	79	1	0	-	-	1
Coca-Cola Champions Trophy (in UAE), 1998/99	5	274	124*	91.33	2	2	1\14	25.5	1
South Africa in India ODI Series, 1999/00	5	274	122	54.8	1	6	4\56	35.5	1
Coca-Cola Cup (in Zimbabwe), 2001	5	282	122*	141	1	0	-	-	0
England in India ODI Series, 2001/02	6	266	87*	53.2	0	2	1\30	79	3
ICC World Cup 2002/03	11	673	152	61.18	1	2	2\28	38.5	4
TVS Cup (in India) 2003/04	7	466	102	77.66	2	1	1\39	125	0
West Indies in India ODI Series, 2006/07	4	191	100*	63.66	1	3	2\25	37.33	0
Future Cup (v SAf in Ireland), 2007	3	200	99	66.66	0	2	2\10	10	1
Compaq Cup (in Sri Lanka), 2009	3	211	138	70.33	1	-	-	-	0
South Africa in India ODI Series, 2009/10	2	204	200*	204	1	-	-	-	0

BAT	WKTS	CT	OPPOSITION	VENUE	TEST START DATE
53	2\39	2	v Sri Lanka	Pune	05-Dec-90
11*	4\34	0	v West Indies	Sharjah	22-Oct-91
62	1\27	0	v South Africa	Kolkata	10-Nov-91
57*	0\38	0	v West Indies	Melbourne	16-Jan-92
54*	1\37	0	v Pakistan	Sydney	04-Mar-92
81	1\35	0	v Zimbabwe	Hamilton	07-Mar-92
82	-	0	v New Zealand	Auckland	27-Mar-94
110	0\15	0	v Australia	Colombo (RPS)	09-Sep-94
115	0\27	0	v New Zealand	Vadodara	28-Oct-94
62	2\29	0	v New Zealand	Delhi	03-Nov-94
66	1\35	1	v West Indies	Kolkata	05-Nov-94
112*	-	1	v Sri Lanka	Sharjah	09-Apr-95
127*	0\26	0	v Kenya	Cuttack	18-Feb-96
70	-	0	v West Indies	Gwalior	21-Feb-96
118	2\40	0	v Pakistan	Sharjah	15-Apr-96
89*	0\12	1	v Pakistan	Toronto	16-Sep-96
88	1\45	2	v Australia	Bangalore	21-Oct-96
114	-	0	v South Africa	Mumbai (WS)	14-Dec-96
104	0\16	0	v Zimbabwe	Benoni	09-Feb-97
117	0\35	0	v New Zealand	Bangalore	14-May-97
95	3\45	0	v Pakistan	Dhaka	14-Jan-98
8	5\32	1	v Australia	Kochi	01-Apr-98
100	0\19	0	v Australia	Kanpur	07-Apr-98
80	0\21	0	v Australia	Sharjah	19-Apr-98
143	1\27	0	v Australia	Sharjah	22-Apr-98
134	0\12	0	v Australia	Sharjah	24-Apr-98

BAT	WKTS	CT	OPPOSITION	VENUE	TEST START DATE
100*	0\4	0	v Kenya	Kolkata	31-May-98
128	0\13	0	v Sri Lanka	Colombo (RPS)	07-Jul-98
127*	-	1	v Zimbabwe	Bulawayo	26-Sep-98
141	4\38	1	v Australia	Dhaka	28-Oct-98
118*	0\4	0	v Zimbabwe	Sharjah	08-Nov-98
124*	1\16	1	v Zimbabwe	Sharjah	13-Nov-98
140*	0\23	0	v Kenya	Bristol	23-May-99
85	-	0	v Zimbabwe	Singapore	04-Sep-99
186*	-	1	v New Zealand	Hyderabad (LBS)	08-Nov-99
122	0\43	0	v South Africa	Vadodara	17-Mar-00
101	0\22	0	v Sri Lanka	Sharjah	20-Oct-00
139	-	1	v Australia	Indore	31-Mar-01
70*	-	0	v Zimbabwe	Harare	24-Jun-01
81*	0\14	0	v West Indies	Bulawayo	30-Jun-01
122*	0\11	0	v West Indies	Harare	04-Jul-01
146	-	0	v Kenya	Paarl	24-Oct-01
68	0\8	1	v England	Chennai	25-Jan-02
65	1\20	0	v West Indies	Port of Spain	02-Jun-02
113	-	0	v Sri Lanka	Bristol	11-Jul-02
81	-	0	v Zimbabwe	Harare	19-Feb-03
152	-	0	v Namibia	Pietermaritzburg	23-Feb-03
98	-	0	v Pakistan	Centurion	01-Mar-03
100	1\39	0	v Australia	Gwalior	26-Oct-03
141	0\45	0	v Pakistan	Rawalpindi	16-Mar-04
82*	3\35	0	v Bangladesh	Colombo (SSC)	21-Jul-04
141*	-	0	v West Indies	Kuala Lumpur	14-Sep-06
100*	-	0	v West Indies	Vadodara	31-Jan-07

MAN OF THE MATCH AWARDS IN TEST MATCHES ||||||||||||||||||||||

BAT1	BAT2	TOTAL RUNS	WKTS	CT	OPPOSITION	VENUE	TEST START DATE
68	119*	187	-	2	v England	Manchester	9-Aug-90
165	-	165	0\9	2	v England	Chennai	11-Feb-93
52*	-	52	-	-	v New Zealand	Chennai	25-Oct-95
4	155*	159	-	1	v Australia	Chennai	6-Mar-98
0	136	136	3\45	0	v Pakistan	Chennai	28-Jan-99
217	15	232	0\19	0	v New Zealand	Ahmedabad	29-Oct-99
116	52	168	-	0	v Australia	Melbourne	26-Dec-99
97	8	105	3\14	0	v South Africa	Mumbai	24-Feb-00
36	176	212	0\33	0	v West Indies	Kolkata	30-Oct-02
241*	60*	301	0\36	1	v Australia	Sydney	2-Jan-04
153	13	166	0\6	0	v Australia	Adelaide	24-Jan-08
160	DNB	160	-	1	v New Zealand	Hamilton	18-Mar-09
105*	16	121	-	0	v Bangladesh	Chittagong	17-Jan-10
214	53*	267	-	0	v Australia	Bangalore	9-Oct-10

|||||||||||||||||||||||||||||||||||

MAN OF THE SERIES AWARDS IN TEST MATCHES ||||||||||||||||||

MAN OF THE SERIES AWARDS	MAT	RUNS	HS	BAT AV	100	WKTS	BEST	BOWL AV	CT
Border-Gavaskar Trophy (Australia in India), 1997/98	3	446	177	111.5	2	1	1\41	47	2
Border-Gavaskar Trophy (India in Australia), 1999/00	3	278	116	46.33	1	1	1\34	46	0
England in India Test Series, 2001/02	3	307	103	76.75	1	1	1\27	50	4
India in Bangladesh Test Series, 2007	2	254	122*	127	2	3	2\35	19	4
Border-Gavaskar Trophy (Australia in India), 2010/11	2	403	214	134.33	1	0	-	-	0

DEFINING INNINGS IN THE FOURTH INNINGS OF A TEST ||||||||||||||||||

119* (189 BALLS)	v England at Manchester, August 1990 (put on a match saving unbeaten stand of 160 for 7th wicket with Manoj Prabhakar) (he was 17 yrs old!)
49 (126BALLS)	v Australia at Bangalore, Oct 2008

DEFINING INNINGS IN THE THIRD INNINGS OF A TEST ||||||||||||||||||||||

176 (298 BALLS)	v West Indies at Kolkata, Oct 2002
126* (247 BALLS)	v New Zealand at Mohali, Oct 1999
100* (211BALLS)	v Sri Lanka at Ahmedabad, Nov 2009
92 (113 BALLS)	v England at Nottingham, Aug 2002
74 (97 BALLS)	v England at Nottingham, July 1997
57 (134 BALLS)	v Pakistan at Sialkot, Dec 1989 (as a 16 yr old)

|||||||||||||||||||||||||||||||||

HIS MATCH WINNING BOWLING PERFORMANCES |||||||||||||||||||

IN TESTS

3/31 in 11 overs v Australia at Kolkata Test match, March 2001 (got the wickets of Gilchrist 0, Hayden 67 and Warne 0. In a matter of 7 runs Australia lost 3 wickets and with it the match).

IN ODIs

Tendulkar's top five bowling performances brought ODI wins for India e.g. Sydney World Cup March 1992 (claimed 1/37 in 10 overs. Wicket was top scorer Aamer Sohail for 62).

Dec 1991 (B&H World Series) at Perth … claimed the final wicket to tie the game!

Hero Cup, Eden Gardens (Nov 1993) South Africa needed 6 runs to win in the final over. Tendulkar conceded just 3.

|||||||||||||||||||||||||||||||||

SACHIN'S FIELDING STATS |||||||||||||||||||

THE OUTSTANDING CATCHES HE HAS TAKEN

TESTS: 106 catches (best: 3 catches in an innings – 4 times). He has never taken 4 or more catches in a Test Match.

ODIS: 134 catches (best: 4 catches in a match – v Pakistan at Dhaka, 11-1-1998)

TENDULKAR'S SCORES OF 50-PLUS IN TEST MATCHES WON BY INDIA

BAT 1ST INNGS	BAT 2ND INNGS	OPPOSITION	VENUE	TEST START DATE
50	-	v England	Kolkata	29-Jan-93
165	-	v England	Chennai	11-Feb-93
78	-	v England	Mumbai	19-Feb-93
62	-	v Zimbabwe	Delhi	13-Mar-93
-	104	v Sri Lanka	Colombo	27-Jul-93
142	-	v Sri Lanka	Lucknow	18-Jan-94
96	-	v Sri Lanka	Bangalore	26-Jan-94
-	85	v West Indies	Mumbai	18-Nov-94
61	-	v South Africa	Kanpur	08-Dec-96
-	155*	v Australia	Chennai	06-Mar-98
79	-	v Australia	Kolkata	18-Mar-98
122	-	v Zimbabwe	Delhi	18-Nov-00
126	-	v Australia	Chennai	18-Mar-01
74	-	v Zimbabwe	Bulawayo	07-Jun-01
88	-	v England	Mohali	03-Dec-01
176	-	v Zimbabwe	Nagpur	21-Feb-02
117	-	v West Indies	Port of Spain	19-Apr-02
193	-	v England	Leeds	22-Aug-02
194*	-	v Pakistan	Multan	28-Mar-04
-	55	v Australia	Mumbai	03-Nov-04
248*	-	v Bangladesh	Dhaka	10-Dec-04
52	52	v Pakistan	Kolkata	16-Mar-05
109	-	v Sri Lanka	Delhi	10-Dec-05
122*	-	v Bangladesh	Dhaka	25-May-07
91	-	v England	Nottingham	27-Jul-07
-	56*	v Pakistan	Delhi	22-Nov-07
71	-	v Australia	Perth	16-Jan-08
88	-	v Australia	Mohali	17-Oct-08
109	-	v Australia	Nagpur	06-Nov-08
-	103*	v England	Chennai	11-Dec-08
160	-	v New Zealand	Hamilton	18-Mar-09
53	-	v Sri Lanka	Mumbai	02-Dec-09
105*	-	v Bangladesh	Chittagong	17-Jan-10
143	-	v Bangladesh	Dhaka	24-Jan-10
106	-	v South Africa	Kolkata	14-Feb-10
-	54	v Sri Lanka	Colombo	03-Aug-10
98	-	v Australia	Mohali	01-Oct-10
214	53*	v Australia	Bangalore	9-Oct-10
61	-	v New Zealand	Nagpur	20-Nov-10

SACH

HOW HAVE THE OTHER ALL-TIME BATTING GREATS DONE POST 35-A COMPARISON ||||||||||||||||||||||||||

** Graham Gooch has the most Test runs after 35 years – 4563 runs (ave 48.54) in 52 Tests. He and Tendulkar have the most Test 100s – 12.

** Tendulkar is No 7 in the list with 2910 runs (ave 64.66).

** Tendulkar's ave of 66.66 is the second best among batsmen with over 1500 runs after the age of 35 yrs. Only Don Bradman – 1903 runs in 15 Tests has a better average of 105.72.

BATSMAN WITH MOST TEST RUNS AFTER THE AGE OF 35 YEARS

BATSMAN	MAT	INNS	NO	RUNS	HS	AVE	100	50
GA Gooch (Eng)	52	96	2	4563	333	48.54	12	21
G Boycott (Eng)	45	83	9	3535	191	47.77	10	16
AJ Stewart (Eng)	58	101	12	3310	164	37.19	5	18
EH Hendren (Eng)	44	69	9	3189	205*	53.15	7	18
JB Hobbs (Eng)	33	53	1	2945	211	56.63	10	12
CH Lloyd (WI)	45	62	6	2921	161*	52.16	8	17
SR Tendulkar (Ind)	30	52	7	2910	214	64.66	12	10
SR Waugh (Aus)	40	56	8	2554	157*	53.2	10	8
CG Greenidge (WI)	37	68	3	2525	226	38.84	7	7
AR Border (Aus)	41	66	8	2473	200*	42.63	4	15
BC Lara (ICC/WI)	25	45	0	2296	226	51.02	9	5
R Dravid (India)	33	58	5	2268	191	42.79	7	9
BL D'Oliveira (Eng)	40	64	8	2228	158	39.78	5	12
TW Graveney (Eng)	30	46	3	2195	165	51.04	7	8
IVA Richards (WI)	34	53	4	2107	146	43	4	17
L Hutton (Eng)	26	43	4	2105	205	53.97	6	10
DCS Compton (Eng)	29	48	4	2089	278	47.47	3	13
Zaheer Abbas (Pak)	32	44	5	2039	215	52.28	5	9
DG Bradman (Aus)	15	23	5	1903	234	105.72	8	5
AL Hassett (Aus)	24	41	1	1881	167	47.02	7	8
AD Nourse (SA)	20	36	3	1863	208	56.45	6	10

PLAYED IN HOW MANY GROUNDS ||||||||||||||||||||||

Tendulkar has played at more venues (58) than any other player in Test history (note: actually batted in 57 grounds, as he did not get to bat in either innings in the rain affected game at Kandy in 1993).

||||||||||||||||||||||||||||||||||

TENDULKAR'S FAVOURITE TEST GROUNDS (500 OR MORE RUNS) ||||||||||||||||||||

GROUND	M	INS	NO	RUNS	AVE	HS	100/50
Chepauk	9	14	4	876	87.6	165	01-May
Chinnaswamy	9	14	2	825	68.75	214	03-Feb
Eden Gardens	10	17	2	743	49.53	176	05-Feb
Wankhede	8	14	0	734	52.43	148	06-Jan
Mohali	10	16	2	709	50.64	126*	05-Jan
SinhaleseSC	5	9	2	698	99.71	203	01-Apr
Nagpur old	6	9	2	679	97	201*	01-Mar
SCG	4	7	4	664	221.33	241*	01-Mar
Feroz Shah K	8	15	1	643	45.93	122	03-Feb
Motera	8	15	1	629	44.93	217	Mar-00

|||||||||||||||||||||||||||||||

WORLD CUP RECORDS HE HOLDS ||||||||||||||||||||

(INDIVIDUALLY AND COLLECTIVELY)

If he appears in the 2011 World Cup he will equal the record of Pakistani Javed Miandad of most appearances in single World Cup. Miandad has six appearances (in 1975, 1979, 1983, 1987, 1992 and 1996), while Tendulkar now has five (in 1992, 1996, 1999, 2003 and 2007).

His run aggregate of 1796 in five World Cups from 1992 to 2007 - is a record.

Also his 673 runs in the 2003 World Cup is a record for the most runs scored by a batsman in a single World Cup.

He shares the record for the most World Cup hundreds of four each with Australian Mark Waugh and Ricky Ponting and team mate Sourav Ganguly.

However, his 17 scores of 50-plus is the most by any batsman in World Cup history.

TENDULKAR IN THE WORLD CUP ||||||||||||||||||||||

OPPONENTS	MTS	INNS	NO	RUNS	HS	AVE	SR	100	50
v Australia	5	5	0	141	90	28.2	82.45	0	1
v Bangladesh	1	1	0	7	7	7	26.92	0	0
v Bermuda	1	1	1	57	57*	196.55	-	0	1
v England	3	3	0	107	50	35.66	78.67	0	1
v Kenya	4	4	2	355	140*	177.5	100.85	2	1
v Namibia	1	1	0	152	152	152	100.66	1	0
v Netherlands	1	1	0	52	52	52	72.22	0	1
v New Zealand	3	3	0	115	84	38.33	79.31	0	1
v Pakistan	4	4	1	228	98	76	87.35	0	2
v South Africa	2	2	0	42	28	21	70	0	0
v Sri Lanka	6	5	0	301	137	60.2	85.75	1	2
v West Indies	2	2	0	74	70	37	72.54	0	1
v Zimbabwe	3	3	0	165	81	55	91.66	0	2
TOTAL	36	35	4	1796	152	57.94	88.21	4	13

YEAR-WISE

YEAR	MTS	INNS	NO	RUNS	HS	AVE	SR	100	50
1992	8	7	1	283	84	47.16	84.73	0	3
1996	7	7	1	523	137	87.16	85.87	2	3
1999	7	7	1	253	140*	42.16	90.03	1	0
2003	11	11	0	673	152	61.18	89.25	1	6
2007	3	3	1	64	57*	32	110.34	0	1
TOTAL	36	35	4	1796	152	57.94	88.21	4	13

VIKAS® PUBLISHING HOUSE PVT LTD

E-28, Sector-8, **Noida**-201301
Phone: 0120-4078900 • Fax: 0120-4078999
Registered Office: 576, Masjid Road, Jangpura, **New Delhi**-110 014

*E-mail: **helpline@vikaspublishing.com*** • *Website: www.vikaspublishing.com*
- **Bengaluru** : First Floor, N.S. Bhawan, 4th Cross, 4th Main, Gandhi Nagar, Bengaluru-560 009
  • Ph. 080-2220 4639, 2228 1254
- **Chennai** : Damodhar Centre, New No. 62, Old No. 59, Nelson Manickam Road, Aminjikarai,
  Chennai-600 029 • Ph. 044-2374 4547, 2374 6090
- **Kolkata** : P-51/1, CIT Road, Scheme-52, Kolkata-700 014 • Ph. 033-2286 6995, 2286 6996
- **Mumbai** : 67/68, 3rd Floor, Aditya Industrial Estate, Chincholi Bunder, Malad (West),
  Mumbai-400 064 • Ph. 022-2877 2545, 2876 8301

Distributors:

UBS PUBLISHERS' DISTRIBUTORS PVT LTD

5, Ansari Road, **New Delhi**-110 002
- Ph. 011-2327 3601, 2326 6646 • Fax: 2327 6593, 2327 4261
  E-mail:ubspd@ubspd.com   Website: www.gobookshopping.com
- **Ahmedabad** : 1st Floor, Shop No. 133-134, Aust Laxmi, Apparel Park, Outside Dariyapur Gate,
  Ahmedabad-380 016 • Ph. 079-29092241, 29092248, 29092258
- **Bengaluru** : Crescent No. 148, 1st Floor, Mysore Road, Bengaluru-560 026 • Ph. 080-26756377, 26756362
  • Fax: 080-26756462
- **Bhopal** : Z-18, M P Nagar, Zone-1, Bhopal-462 011 • Ph. 0755-4203 183, 4203 193
- **Bhubaneshwar** : Ist Floor 145, Cuttack Road, Bhubaneshwar-751 006 • Ph. 0674-2314 446
- **Chennai** : 60, Nelson Manickam Road, Aminjikarai, Chennai-600 029 • Ph. 044-2374 6222
- **Coimbatore** : 2nd & 3rd Floor, Sri Guru Towers, No. 1-7, Sathy Road, Cross III, Gandhipuram, Coimbatore-641 012
- **Ernakulam** : No. 40/8199A, 1st Floor, Public Library Building, Convent Road, Ernakulam-682 035
  • Ph. 0484-2353901, 2373901, 2363905, 4064706 • Fax: 0484-236551
- **Guwahati** : 1st Floor, House No.4, Kanaklata Path, Lachit Nagar, Bharalupar, Guwahati-781 007
- **Hyderabad** : 3rd Floor, Alekhya Jagadish Chambers, H. No. 4-1-1058, Boggulkunta, Tilak Road,
  Hyderabad-500 001 • Ph. 040-2475 4472 / 73 / 74
- **Kolkata** : 8/1-B, Chowringhee Lane, Kolkata-700 016 • Ph. 033-2252 1821, 2252 2910
- **Lucknow** : 9 Ashok Nagar, Near Pratibha Press, Gautam Buddha Marg, Latush Road, Lucknow-226 001
  • Ph. 0522-2294 134, 3014 010
- **Mumbai** : 2nd Floor, Apeejay Chambers, 5 Wallace Street, Fort, Mumbai-400 001 • Ph. 022-6637 6922-3,
  6610 2069 • Fax: 6637 6921
- **Patna** : GF, Western Side, Annapoorna Complex, Naya Tola, Patna-800 004 • Ph. 0612-2672 856, 2673 973
- **Pune** : 680 Budhwar Peth, 2nd Floor, Appa Balwant Chowk, Pune-411 002 • Ph. 020-2446 1653, 2443 3976

Published 2011

Vikas® is the registered trademark of Vikas Publishing House Pvt Ltd
Copyright © Lahoma Bhattacharya
Printed at Aditi Print-O-Fast New Delhi

Information contained in this book has been published by VIKAS® Publishing House Pvt Ltd and has been obtained by its Author from sources believed to be reliable and are correct to the best of his knowledge. However, the Publisher and its Author shall in no event be liable for any errors, omissions or damages arising out of use of this information and specifically disclaim any implied warranties or merchantability or fitness for any particular use. Disputes if any are subject to Delhi Jurisdiction only.